Savoury Wisdom

Delicious, Healthy Recipes for Two

D0473658

Ellie Topp and Suzanne Hendricks

Prentice
Hall
Canada

A Pearson Company

Toronto

Canadian Cataloguing in Publication Data

Topp, Ellie,

   Savoury wisdom : recipes for simple, healthy eating

Includes index.

ISBN 0-13-040840-9

1. Cookery for one. 2. Cookery for two. 3. Quick and easy cookery. I. Hendricks, Suzanne. II. Title.

TX833.5.T66 2001   641.5'61   C00-932916-1

ISBN 0-13-040840-9

Editorial Director, Trade Division: Andrea Crozier
Acquisitions Editor: Nicole de Montbrun
Copy Editor: Jennifer Glossop
Production Editor: Lori McLellan
Art Direction: Mary Opper
Interior Design: Julia Hall
Cover Design: Julia Hall
Production Manager: Kathrine Pummell
Page Layout: Gail Ferreira Ng-A-Kien

1 2 3 4 5 KR 05 04 03 02 01

Printed and bound in Canada.

ATTENTION: CORPORATIONS

Books are available at quantity discounts with bulk purchase for educational, business, or sales promotional use. For information, please email or write to: Pearson PTR Canada, Special Sales, PTR Division, 26 Prince Andrew Place, Don Mills, Ontario, M3C 2T8. Email ss.corp@pearsoned.com. Please supply: title of book, ISBN, quantity, how the book will be used, date needed.

Visit the Pearson PTR Web site! Send us your comments, browse our catalogues, and more. www.pearsonptr.ca.

Prentice Hall Canada

A Pearson Company

Acknowledgments

Savoury Wisdom is the result of our commitment to a quality of life that is nurtured by healthy eating and to the premise that healthy foods can be both tasty and easily prepared.

We acknowledge the contribution from a wide variety of sources used in our nutrition research, including the *Journal of the American Dietetic Association*, *The American Journal of Clinical Nutrition*, the *Canadian Journal of Dietetic Practice and Research*, the *American Institute of Cancer Research Newsletter*, the *University of California at Berkeley Wellness Newsletter*, *The Johns Hopkins Medical Letter Health After 50*, *Nutrition and the MD*, *Nutrition News Focus*, *The American Dietetic Association's Complete Food & Nutrition Guide* (1998) and *The Wellness Encyclopaedia of Food and Nutrition* (1992).

We would like to offer our special thanks to our editor, Nicole de Montbrun, for her enthusiasm for the book from the very beginning and to copy editor Jennifer Glossop and production editor Lori McLellan for their guidance and expertise in directing this book to completion. The wisdom and expertise of two friends and colleagues, Deborah Reid, PhD, RD, and Jean Armstrong, MS, RD, was much appreciated. They also deserve our very special thanks as do friends and family who tested many of the recipes and provided valuable feedback: Marjorie Harvey, Weldon Burlock, Alicia Wells, Ellen Boynton and Sandra Copeland. And thanks are always in order to our very supportive and much-loved husbands and families who gave willingly of their taste buds and their opinions.

Ellie Topp
Suzanne Hendricks

Contents

Nutrient Analysis of Recipes and Menus   vi

Wisdom for Two   1

Morning Starts   25

Lunch and Supper Fixings   47

Dinner Is Served   65

Meals to Share   115

Shelf Solutions   145

Satisfying Soups   163

Happy Endings   181

Index   205

Nutrient Analysis of Recipes and Menus

The recipe analysis was done with Nutriwatch Nutrient Analysis Program (copyright Elizabeth Warwick, BHSc, 1997) using the 1997 Canadian Nutrient File, supplemented when necessary with data from reliable sources. The analysis was based on imperial measures (except for foods packaged in metric quantities) and with the first ingredient listed where several ingredients are suggested. Unless otherwise stated, recipes were analyzed using canola vegetable oil, 2% milk, 1% to 2% yogurt, large eggs and enriched pasta. Calculations for meat and poultry assumed that only the lean portion without skin was eaten. Folacin values for flour and enriched pasta were based on calculations as no analytical values are available. Salt was included in the analysis only when a specified amount was given. Optional ingredients and garnishes in unspecified amounts were not included.

Analysis is provided for the nutrients that currently present the greatest challenge to a great many Canadians and whose improved intake could have a significant impact on health. Values for calories are rounded to the nearest five, those for protein, fat, carbohydrate, fibre, calcium, folacin and sodium to the nearest one, and those for fatty acids to one decimal point.

The number of servings from the four food groups in Canada's Food Guide to Healthy Eating contributed by one recipe portion was calculated using the serving sizes given in the Guide. These servings are indicated by symbols representing each of the four groups. The Food Guide servings are also given for the complete meal if you follow our suggestions for Rounding Out the Meal. Serving sizes for ingredients not mentioned in the Food Guide were approximated in accordance with the serving size and nutrient contribution of other foods in the same food group. The numbers of servings for the various food groups were rounded to half servings, and their nutrient contribution to the recipe was considered in the process.

Key to Canada's Food Guide Servings

Grain Products

Milk Products

Vegetables & Fruit

Meat & Alternatives

Grain Products
Choose whole grain and enriched products more often.

Vegetables & Fruit
Choose dark green and orange vegetables and orange fruit more often.

Milk Products
Choose lower-fat milk products more often.

Meat & Alternatives
Choose leaner meats, poultry and fish, as well as dried peas, beans and lentils more often.

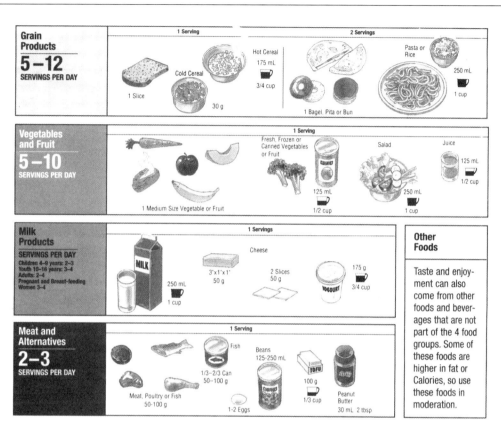

Grain Products

5–12
SERVINGS PER DAY

1 Serving

1 Slice

Cold Cereal
30 g

Hot Cereal
175 mL
3/4 cup

2 Servings

1 Bagel, Pita or Bun

Pasta or Rice
250 mL
1 cup

Vegetables and Fruit

5–10
SERVINGS PER DAY

1 Serving

1 Medium Size Vegetable or Fruit

Fresh, Frozen or Canned Vegetables or Fruit
125 mL
1/2 cup

Salad
250 mL
1 cup

Juice
125 mL
1/2 cup

Milk Products

SERVINGS PER DAY
Children 4–9 years: 2–3
Youth 10–16 years: 3–4
Adults: 2–4
Pregnant and Breast-feeding Women 3–4

1 Servings

MILK
250 mL
1 cup

Cheese
3"x1"x1"
50 g

2 Slices
50 g

175 g
YOGOURT
3/4 cup

Other Foods

Taste and enjoyment can also come from other foods and beverages that are not part of the 4 food groups. Some of these foods are higher in fat or Calories, so use these foods in moderation.

Meat and Alternatives

2–3
SERVINGS PER DAY

1 Serving

Meat, Poultry or Fish
50–100 g

Fish
1/3–2/3 Can
50–100 g

1–2 Eggs

Beans
125–250 mL

TOFU
100 g
1/3 cup

Peanut Butter
30 mL 2 tbsp

Different People Need Different Amounts of Food

The amount of food you need every day from the 4 food groups and other foods depends on your age, body size, activity level, whether you are male or female and if you are pregnant or breast-feeding. That's why the Food Guide gives a lower and higher number of servings for each food group. For example, young children can choose the lower number of servings, while male teenagers can go to the higher number. Most other people can choose servings somewhere in between.

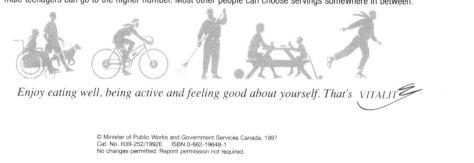

Enjoy eating well, being active and feeling good about yourself. That's VITALITÉ

Wisdom for Two

Quality of life is made of quality moments. Sharing good food is one of them. Not only do good foods make for pleasurable moments in every day, they also hold the promise of a healthier and better life in the future.

With only two of you at the table, whether you are thirty or fifty, upgrading or downsizing, meal preparation presents special challenges. Meeting these challenges is what *Savoury Wisdom* is all about: cooking for two to better enjoy life now and later.

Old wisdom with a new twist

In the new millennium, eating with quality of life in mind continues to be a question of variety, moderation and balance. This conventional wisdom is very much illustrated in Canada's Food Guide to Healthy Eating (page viii and ix), a most reliable guide to food selection.

What we put in our shopping basket and what ends up on our plate determines the quality of our diet. The recipes in this book were designed as simple, delicious, small-scale solutions to healthy eating for everyday living. This is where our wisdom lies. The new twists are that science is now giving us even more reasons to eat well; the market offers us a myriad of flavourful and healthful choices to meet our needs, and all sorts of convenient products and tools now make cooking more enticing than ever.

From the flavour of the month to the phytochemical of the week, food is definitely centre stage in the public's consciousness. Not surprisingly, these new ideas can get rather tangled. Here, a bit of wisdom can come to the rescue. And it is here that we would like to fit in, helping you make the right choices. On the next few pages you'll find our attempt to come to grips with the bottom line of nutrition.

The bottom line of nutrition

Food is a life investment, a source of health and satisfaction, and a powerful link to our environment. There are many ways of eating well, as expressed through various cultural traditions, but for the best return on your investment, nothing beats the time-proven rules of variety, balance and moderation, unless, of course, dictated otherwise by special medical conditions.

In the quest for health, it remains wise to resist any seductive or threatening appeal that promises fantastic returns while drastically narrowing choices. Otherwise, you risk compromising the health benefits you might be seeking. For example, the fat hunt that has swept North America in the last twenty years, driven by a legitimate desire to curb the consequences of cardiovascular diseases, has sometimes yielded strange results. Let's settle this account first.

Fat Is Not a Dirty Word

Essential to good health and body function, fat is vital to the structure of our cells and hormones. It carries essential fatty acids as well as the vitamins A, D, E and K, all of which are soluble in fat. Closely associated with taste, fats lend creaminess to soups and sauces and tenderness to meats. The enticing aromas and flavours of Mediterranean cuisine are largely embodied in the olive, a food with its fair share of fat.

You would think all of this would speak in favour of moderation, balance and variety. Unfortunately not. As the link between fat, blood cholesterol and heart disease started to unfold, sorting out the differences first between saturated and polyunsaturated fats and later taking into account monounsaturated fats, trans-fatty acids and omega-3s was no easy task. All had links to cholesterol and heart disease, and the jargon proved to be overwhelming. In search of a simple approach, "avoid fat at all cost" replaced the golden rule of moderation. For many, "fat-free" became the ultimate product attribute. What to avoid rather than what to eat became the prime concern. As a result, although many people avoided saturated animal fats at all cost, the alternatives they selected were often hydrogenated oils, whose health effects were just as or more negative.

Ironically, the fat-free wave has been accompanied by an increase in obesity. Obviously there is some confusion. To restore a bit of wisdom on the fat scene, let us straighten a few facts.

The heart of the fat concern

Both the amount and the kind of fat we eat have an influence on our risk of cardiovascular disease. How much is too much, however, is still being debated. Even though an average of 30% of calories from fat is still generally advocated, there is mounting evidence that this amount could be somewhat increased without adverse effects, providing the emphasis is on the right kind of fat without excess calories. This is far from saying that no food or no single meal should contain more than 30% of its calories from fat. The 30%-or-so goal is for a total diet, or more or less what your weekly score card should look like.

For women, the 30% goal represents an average of 55 to 65 grams of fat per day and for men, 60 to 90 grams. As calorie needs diminish with age, so should the fat intake. Our recipes invest this fat allowance in flavourful and healthful dishes. They all fit into a pattern that includes variety, balance and moderation.

The new twist to the old concern about fat is that the type of fat we eat is likely of greater importance to our health than the amount. A healthful fat mix will include a balanced variety of fats from animal, vegetable and fish sources, leaving plenty of room for an array of flavourful combinations.

Animal fat: a case for moderation

Keeping the lid on saturated fats is still sound advice. These fats should not make up more than 10% of your total calories. Saturated fats are found mostly in animal foods, so selecting lower fat dairy products as well as leaner meats and poultry will do the trick. But don't let this general guideline prevent you from enjoying higher fat cheeses, sausages and pâtés as occasional treats.

An interesting newcomer on the animal-fat scene is conjugated linoleic acid, or CLA. This fatty acid has been shown to have remarkable effects in experimental animals. In fact, it appears to inhibit atherosclerosis and cancer, although it is not clear how this happens. The interesting point is that CLA is found in meat and dairy fat, with only traces in vegetable oils, making a strong case for the inclusion of some animal fat in the diet. As it unfolds, this is a story to follow.

Vegetable fats: be more selective

Vegetable fats and oils are not all the same since they contain different fatty acids. While most fats from vegetable sources are high in unsaturated fats, the proportion of monounsaturated and polyunsaturated fats in each is different. In recent years, research has more clearly pointed out the positive and the negative elements.

On the positive side, monounsaturated fats appear to best regulate blood cholesterol. What's more, they lower the so-called "bad cholesterol," or LDL, without affecting HDL, the "good cholesterol." At least one-third of our fat intake should come from these monounsaturated fats. Olive oil and canola oil are the best sources, followed by peanut oil. For cooking and flavouring salads, these are the fats to choose. Avocados and nuts are also interesting and savoury sources of monounsaturated fat and bring along a bundle of other nutrients.

A minor but important component of vegetable oils is alpha-linolenic acid, which has been credited with several heart-health benefits. It is a polyunsaturated fatty acid and part of the group of fats known as omega-3s. Soybeans, canola, flaxseed and walnuts are all good sources of alpha-linolenic acid. As well, chickens fed flaxseed are now giving us omega-3 enriched eggs.

In addition, vegetable oils rate first as our source of vitamin E, followed by nuts, seeds and wheat germ. Without vegetable oils, it becomes very difficult to get sufficient alpha-linolenic acid and vitamin E. Consequently, an oil-based vinaigrette makes a more nutritious partner for a salad than does a fat-free dressing.

On the negative side lurk hydrogenated oils and trans-fatty acids. Processing vegetable oils in the presence of hydrogen transforms them into spreadable fats such as margarine and improves their baking and frying quality. In the process, the fatty acids become saturated, and trans-fatty acids are formed due to changes occurring in the structure of the fat. As a result, the vegetable oils lose many of their original health benefits. In fact, the effect of these hydrogenated fats on blood vessels is believed to be more damaging than that of saturated fats.

Margarines and shortening containing hydrogenated oils and trans-fatty acids are used extensively in commercially baked goods and snack foods. Read food labels carefully to detect their presence. Some margarines use a small amount of a naturally occurring saturated fat such as palm or coconut oil to make the margarine solid. This avoids the hydrogenation process and the resulting creation of trans-fatty acids. The softer the margarine, the less trans-fatty acid and saturated fat it contains.

Fish: a double fat winner

It is hard to lose when you feature fish on the menu. Go for a lean fish such as sole or haddock, and you get hardly any fat except that which you introduce in cooking.

Turn to a fattier fish such as salmon, trout or sardines, and things are even better: you reap the benefits of their unique omega-3 fatty acids. Omega-3s are good news indeed, especially when they come from fish. They have been shown to slow down the progression of cardiovascular disease and reduce blood clotting. They may also diminish the inflammation that accompanies arthritis and asthma.

The bottom line: eat fish once or twice a week. Pick fresh fish for unparalleled flavour, and frozen or canned for ultimate convenience. Easy to prepare and to digest, amiable to a variety of food combinations, fish is a perfect choice for two. It suits all ages, all seasons and all occasions.

The fat/calorie/weight connection

Fat provides more than twice as many calories as carbohydrate or protein with 9 calories per gram of fat compared to 4 calories per gram for carbohydrate or protein. Consequently, one teaspoon of butter, margarine or oil contains about twice as many calories as a teaspoon of jam or honey. Replacing one pat of butter on your toast with one teaspoon of jam is both a fat- and calorie-saving step.

The problem is that most people like to get their calorie kick by bundling fat and carbohydrate in irresistible mixtures. Two mouth-watering chocolate chip cookies, for instance, typically contain 75 calories from fat and 75 calories from carbohydrate, with a minor 10 calories from protein. Should these little marvels be made fat-free, they would certainly not become calorie-free as well, especially if the fat is replaced by more carbohydrate.

To satisfy the fat-free frenzy, products with very little fat and sometimes little nutritional value but containing a sizeable number of calories have inundated the market. Moreover, the temptation is always great to eat yet another fat-free cookie! On the other hand, fat-free or lower fat products such as cheese or yogurt have been welcome additions, allowing us to reap their nutritional benefits along with a fat and calorie saving.

While it is true that calories from fat are more easily converted to body fat than calories from carbohydrates, the body will store any kind of excess calories in fat deposits. Whether you are on an "avoid at all cost" approach to fat or eating mostly low-fat foods, overeating will still result in excess weight. Even in lower fat products, invest your calories wisely. Go for good taste and good nutrition: this is savoury wisdom.

Putting the lid on both calories and fat and increasing physical activity is the key to successful weight management. Be especially vigilant as the years add up and calorie needs diminish. For women over fifty, 1800 calories and 60 grams of fat are reasonable goals. For men in that age bracket, 2300 calories and 75 grams of fat will generally suffice. Attaining these goals means savouring smaller portions, using fat sparingly and making a clear distinction between everyday fare such as fresh fruits and special treats like fruit crumbles.

An Apple a Day: Just the Beginning

The strongest and most consistently demonstrated link between the food we eat and lowering the risk of certain diseases is the intake of fruits and vegetables. However, an apple a day plus a few lettuce leaves won't quite do it.

The five-a-day-plus magic

According to the American Institute of Cancer Research, if the only change people made to their diet was to eat five servings of fruit and vegetables each day, cancer incidence rates could drop by 20%. This is powerful advice and worth posting on your refrigerator, just beside Canada's Food Guide with its five-to-ten-servings-a-day recommendation.

But the five-a-day minimum guidance is not only cancer related. The vegetable-fruit food group delivers many other health-related benefits:

- Vitamins C and A, pillar nutrients in fruits and vegetables, play a key role in boosting immunity.
- Magnesium, potassium and vitamin K, all well distributed in fruits and vegetables, have been associated with greater bone density.
- Folic acid, one of the B vitamins present in fruits and vegetables, is emerging as an important element in heart health. Also heart friendly is soluble fibre, known for its cholesterol-lowering ability, and potassium for its controlling effect on blood pressure.

And all these benefits come with very little fat and a minimum of calories. It is not surprising, therefore, that the risk of heart disease diminishes when there are plenty of fruits and vegetables on the menu.

Cancer-fighting compounds

The powerful cancer-protective effect of fruits and vegetables comes from a combination of various substances. Some, like vitamin C, which is abundant in citrus fruits, or beta carotene, which is found in deep yellow vegetables and fruits, have been known for a long time to give nutritional benefits. Others, newer on the scene, include lycopene, the red pigment in tomatoes, and indoles, compounds present in the cabbage family, whose members include broccoli and Brussels sprouts. Lycopene and indoles are examples of non-nutritive substances called phytochemicals, which plants produce naturally as protective agents. Transferred to us, these helpful compounds cleverly take on several beneficial health roles.

The antioxidant effect

A good portion of the value of phytochemicals is their ability to function as antioxidants or free radical scavengers.

Oxidation occurs constantly in our body when cells use the oxygen we breathe in the production of energy. As a result of that cellular combustion, by-products called free radicals are formed. These substances can damage arteries and foster cancer development.

Antioxidants act as cleansers by trapping free radicals and converting them to harmless waste products. Each antioxidant, whether the familiar vitamin C or a more exotic phytochemical like sulforaphane, appears to protect different parts of the body.

Nevertheless, all antioxidants work as a team, complementing each other; therefore, an excess or deficiency of one may inhibit the benefit of another.

Every vegetable and each fruit has its own mix of health promoters and cancer fighters. The more limited your selection, the more likely it is that you will miss out on some great deals.

The bottom line on fruit and vegetables: go for at least five a day plus juice, and choose several different kinds each week. Definitely have some at every meal as well as in between.

Five easy ways to make it to five

- Increase your portion size of fruit and vegetables, fill the salad bowl to the rim and cook two extra carrots.
- Start the day with one or more choices besides a juice.
- When eating out, go for soup or salad, or both.
- Keep ready-to-eat fruits and vegetables at hand and in sight. Crispy vegetables waiting in the fridge to be grabbed when you open the door, attractive fruits sitting in a bowl.
- Dress them up; try some of our savoury suggestions:
  - Carrots Provençales (p. 73)
  - Spinach with Orzo (p. 79)
  - Orange-Glazed Brussels Sprouts (p. 81)
  - Peas with Mint and Lemon (p. 89)
  - Butternut and Greens (p. 95)
  - Oriental Beans (p. 99)

Folate: a nutrient to watch

If folate, which is also known as folacin or folic acid, has not yet caught your attention, there are several good reasons that it should. Folate, an anti-anemic factor, is one of the B vitamins. It plays an important role in the formation of red blood cells and is involved in the production of DNA and new body cells.

A few years ago, folate emerged as a women's health issue when it was shown to reduce the risk of certain birth defects. To offer such protection, folate must be present at the time of conception and shortly thereafter. Consequently, when planning a pregnancy, all women are advised to take a daily supplement of folic acid.

Folate has now crossed the gender barrier with its link to heart disease. On the heart front, a lack of folic acid is thought to lead to the build-up of homocysteine in the blood. Homocysteine, a product of protein breakdown, is the villain that increases the risk of cardiovascular disease and stroke. It may very well be that blood homocysteine levels could become as routinely tested as blood cholesterol.

In addition to folate, vitamins B_6 and B_{12} may also play a role in this process. As homocysteine levels tend to increase with age, appropriate intakes of folate, B_6 and B_{12} are especially critical for those who have reached the age-fifty mark.

The latest twists in the folate saga are the potential relationships between folic acid and such diverse conditions as Alzheimer's disease, hearing ability and certain forms of cancer. These reports all come from preliminary studies and need to be confirmed. Obviously these possibilities add to the interest generated by folic acid.

The folate challenge

The most recent recommendations suggest an intake of 400 mcg of folate per day, nearly double the previous amount. Meeting this recommendation is a dietary challenge since most foods contain some folate, but very few are good or excellent sources.

To meet that challenge, white flour, enriched pasta and enriched cornmeal are now fortified with folic acid. It is expected that this addition could contribute between 50 to 150 mcg to the diet. To reach the folate goal, think plant foods first. Eating plenty of grains, fruits and vegetables every day and, for a real bonus, serving legumes at least once a week should do it. Here are our some of our folate winner recipes:

Orange and Sweet Onion Salad (p. 125)

Shrimp with Pasta and Greens (p. 154)

Hummus-Stuffed Pita (p. 55)

Soybeans with Snow Peas and Pineapple (p. 106)

Pasta Layers with Spinach and Ricotta (p. 102)

Barley Lentil Bake (p. 110)

Asparagus with Orange Butter (p. 133)

Mexican Cauliflower Ensalada (p. 137)

Curried Pasta Salad with Wild Rice and Lentils (p. 121)

Chili with Beans and Squash (p. 178)

Grains: The Other Five a Day

From bread to tortillas and from pasta to rice, grains have served through the years as the ultimate sustenance foods and the inseparable companions of the great flavours of the world.

The main source of energy in the diet, grain products also provide a sizeable amount of protein, vitamins and minerals, including valuable folate and iron. But the element that gives grains a special health dimension is fibre. This is where the superiority of whole grains lies.

Looked upon for years as a background food and somewhat taken for granted, grains are making a powerful comeback in the culinary world as well as on the health agenda. Grains crown Canada's Food Guide rainbow with five to twelve servings a day being promoted. Make sure a good portion of those are whole grains.

The regulating power of fibre

The fibre content of grains and, to a lesser extent, the digestibility of their starch can help regulate not only the gastrointestinal function, but also appetite and blood levels of cholesterol, sugar and insulin. Keeping these factors in check can reduce the risk of heart disease and the onset of diabetes.

Insoluble vs. soluble fibre

Different grains present a different mix of insoluble and soluble fibre. Insoluble fibre is most effective in preventing constipation, haemorrhoids and diverticular disease by speeding up intestinal transit time. The reputation of wheat bran as an intestinal regulator is well founded and is built on its high content of insoluble fibre. The bran from corn and rye fall into this same category.

Soluble fibre is heart friendly due to its role in lowering blood cholesterol. It is the main form of fibre found in oat and barley as well as in fruits and vegetables. Total fibre intake, including both insoluble and soluble fibre, has been shown to reduce the risk of coronary heart disease.

Fibre and weight control

Because dietary fibre gives a feeling of fullness and slows the rate of digestion, foods high in fibre will satisfy the appetite at a reasonable calorie cost. Not surprisingly then, a diet with a generous fibre content has been associated with a lower weight gain than one contributing a lesser amount. As an added bonus, it would appear that boosting your fibre intake takes a slice off the calories you absorb from fat and protein. This small but welcome calorie-saving is, however, no license to dip that whole wheat roll into more than a taste of olive oil.

Selecting foods with fibre in mind

The daily target for fibre is 25 to 30 grams. Many Canadians achieve barely half of that. This is not surprising, as most of us seldom read labels carefully to identify whole grain breads or fibre-rich cereals. Nor do we meet the five-a-day goal for fruits and vegetables or serve legumes very frequently.

There are times when only a white crusty French loaf or traditional bagel will do. And hot biscuits or English muffins are wonderful for a special breakfast or to serve with tea. Let's enjoy those moments. In between, it's worth discovering the savoury world of whole grain breads.

Buying whole grain bread can be tricky. Look for "whole wheat" as the first ingredient on the label. The name of a bread and its appearance can be deceiving, since molasses or other substances are sometimes added to give a darker colour. And be wary of multigrain and especially of oatmeal breads. They often feature white flour as the first ingredient on the list. Read those labels carefully and choose accordingly.

In selecting breakfast cereals, seek those advertised as either a "very high" or "high" source of fibre. These claims are regulated and are usually prominently displayed on the front of the package. A very high source of fibre must contain at least 6 grams per serving, and a high source of fibre has at least 4 grams.

Whole wheat flour, oatmeal, brown rice and quinoa are all whole grain products that can be featured in a variety of dishes. Give a try to some new ones like Bulgur for Two (page 109) or Warm Quinoa Vegetable Salad (page 59).

Once you have sorted out the grains, toss a variety of fruits and vegetables in your shopping basket. And make a habit of eating apples, pears or potatoes with their skin. Crunchiness, however, is not necessarily a fibre indicator. For instance, lettuce, celery and corn contain very little fibre, while bananas and avocados are good sources.

Also keep legumes in mind. If you have been avoiding these nutritious seeds, you are missing out on one of the top sources of fibre. More on that in our next section.

Finally, go gently. If your fibre intake has been on the low side, increase it gradually to avoid intestinal discomfort. Drink plenty of water and other fluids to allow the fibre to do its job. Remember, fibre works by holding water and, in tandem with exercise, by keeping waste moving along. Here are some of our winner recipes on the fibre front:

Caribbean Beans and Rice (p. 104)	Chicken Fajitas (p. 68)
Apricot Oat Bran Pancakes (p. 37)	Orange-Glazed Brussels Sprouts (p. 81)
Lentils and Rice Egyptian-Style (p. 161)	Barley Lentil Bake (p. 110)
Scotch Barley Soup (p. 180)	Wild Rice and Barley Salad (p. 60)
Mexican Lasagne (p. 136)	Australian Bulgur Salad (p. 127)

The bottom line on grains

Invest in grains first when planning your menus, and diversify from there. Grains lend themselves to all kinds of nutritious combinations. They are the "little black dress" of the kitchen, a winner for the heart and flattering to the waistline. Dress them up as in our Premier Paella (page 139) or dress them down as in our Caribbean Beans and Rice (page 104). Either way, they will live up to the occasion.

Legumes: Plant Wisdom at Its Best

Are you looking for a nutrition bargain, some kind of a hidden treasure, still available at a good price, that could almost guarantee a rise in the quality of your diet? Chances are legumes are the answer.

Nutrition plus

Take a look at peas, beans and lentils. These small beads of energy are amazing. Not only do they contain a sufficient amount of protein to be considered meat alternatives, they also come loaded with vitamins, minerals, phytochemicals, fibre and very little fat. Legumes combine the goodness of both grains and meat – delivering the full sandwich! And they are just as quick to assemble for perfect luncheon salads.

Legumes are the best source of folate, with many of them providing over 25% of the daily requirement in only half a cup. Their iron content is also remarkable. Serving them with vitamin C rich foods such as tomatoes, red and green pepper or broccoli will enhance the iron absorption. Caribbean Beans and Rice (page 104) or Barley Lentil Bake served with Broccoli with Peppers (page 110–111) are two good examples of the wise use of complementary ingredients.

Legumes rate next to bran cereals as a source of fibre. Not only is their fibre plentiful, it is a good mix of both the insoluble and soluble kind, providing the gamut of fibre-health benefits. And because they are digested slowly, legumes bring about only a gentle rise in blood sugar, thereby reducing the need for insulin, a definite plus for those with diabetes.

The protein in legumes is abundant but it is incomplete, meaning that some of the essential amino acids are lacking. Serving legumes with grains, nuts or a small amount of meat or dairy will solve the problem as these foods provide the amino acids that are missing.

The soy difference

Soybeans contain more protein and more calcium than most other legumes as well as more fat and thus more calories. Among legumes, the protein in soy stands apart as being complete. This means that soy, taken in sufficient quantities, can provide all the amino acids our bodies need. It also explains why soy protein concentrates are often used to boost the protein content of vegetarian entrees or as the base for beverages designed as milk replacements. The proteins in soy have also been found to exercise some protective effect on the heart. Studies have shown that as part of a low-fat diet, soybeans have the ability to lower blood cholesterol.

The fat in soybeans is mostly unsaturated, but soybeans are not a low-fat choice. In fact, nearly half of the calories in soy come from fat, compared to no more than 1% in other legumes.

Because they may reduce the symptoms of menopause such as hot flashes, soybeans have been hailed by some as women's designer food. These effects are attributed to isoflavones, or estrogen-like compounds, that are present in soybeans. Isoflavones, it is claimed, may also offer protection against cancer for some women. When examined closely, all these effects appear to be small and remain to be clearly established.

Moreover, there is a double edge to the story: large doses of isoflavones may also be harmful to women with breast cancer or at high risk for breast cancer. The soy difference is of interest, but the final verdict is not yet out. Consequently, isoflavone supplements are not recommended since their efficacy and safety have not been proven. However, these considerations do not preclude in any way the use of soybeans in a variety of culinary preparations.

Banking on soy to modulate the hormone balance might be asking too much until we have a better understanding of its effects, but there are many good reasons, including that of heart health, to feature soybeans at the table. Soybeans with Snow Peas and Pineapple (page 106) is a good place to start.

Overcoming digestive discomfort

It is not uncommon for people to report flatulence after eating legumes. It occurs because many of us are unable to digest the raffinose sugars found in beans, peas and lentils.

The secret to overcoming this problem is to get rid of the raffinose. When preparing dried legumes, do not cook them in the water used for soaking. Instead, drain, rinse and add fresh water before cooking. This eliminates the raffinose that leaches out during soaking. If you are using canned legumes, drain them and rinse them as well, thereby removing much of the offending compound.

Build your legume tolerance slowly. Start with small amounts and do not serve them with other foods that can give you similar discomfort, such as cabbage.

The bottom line: don't miss out on the legume bargain! Feature them as hearty soups and salads, accompaniments to meat and poultry or main dishes and keep Soy Nuts (page 107) on hand for snacking. There is a whole world out there to be discovered. Think variety, be adventurous.

Riding the Milky Way

From the humblest pitcher of milk to the fanciest cheese tray, dairy products have been adorning Canadian tables since 1608, when Champlain brought the first cow to New France. To this day, milk has been a tremendous asset to the Canadian diet, but an asset that remains under-exploited.

The calcium gap

Dairy products supply 60% of the calcium in the Canadian diet and rate as the number-one source of five other key nutrients: phosphorus, magnesium, potassium, vitamin D and riboflavin. Yet, calcium is the nutrient that Canadians, especially women, most frequently lack. Why? Because few of us heed the Canada's Food Guide advice to enjoy at least two servings of milk products a day. In fact, the average daily intake for adult women is about 1.5 servings, an amount that generally decreases with age.

This is cause for concern. Remember that the need for calcium and vitamin D doesn't remain constant, but increases past age fifty. Baby boomers, especially women prone to osteoporosis, face a major calcium gap as measured against the new recommended intake of 1200 mg per day for those fifty plus. After menopause, as the rate of bone loss speeds up, the threat of brittle bones is a real one. The current prediction is that one woman in four will have an osteoporosis-related fracture in her lifetime. This pattern could be altered by changes in lifestyle, including regular weight-bearing exercise such as walking or dancing, accompanied by avoidance of smoking and excess alcohol and with a healthy helping of milk products.

While the bone-building capacity of calcium constitutes its major benefit, the protection calcium may offer from high blood pressure, heart disease and colon cancer is also valuable.

Nutrition wisdom includes a focus on milk products. Keeping in mind that milk in all its forms is a major source of saturated fats, part of that wisdom is to use lower fat milk, yogurt and cheeses and to enjoy their creamier companions sparingly.

A word on vitamin D

The fate of calcium in the body is very much in the hands of vitamin D, a hormone-like substance that controls calcium absorption and its deposition at the bone level.

Sunshine is our main source of vitamin D, followed by fluid milk and margarine, both of which must be enriched with this bone-building vitamin. A small amount of regular sun exposure on our hands and face should normally suffice for the skin to produce all the vitamin D we need. Unfortunately, access to sunlight is limited for a good part of the year in northern latitudes such as Canada. Moreover, exposure to sunrays can be further curtailed by air pollution, sunscreens and especially lifestyle for those who are homebound or confined to an office through the sunshine hours. Hence, the high value of fluid milk with its calcium/vitamin D team, supported by vitamin A, magnesium, phosphorus and protein, all present in milk and all essential to good bones.

With age, absorption and production of vitamin D by the skin and absorption from food become less efficient. By age seventy, our ability to manufacture vitamin D from sun exposure is about 30% of what it was at twenty-five. Not surprisingly, recommended intakes increase with age, going from 200 IU before age fifty to 400 IU between fifty and seventy and 600 IU thereafter. When sun exposure and milk intake are limited and for those over seventy, supplements are recommended. Under these circumstances, a multi-vitamin supplement with 400 IU of vitamin D is often the best solution.

Coping with lactose, if need be

Lactose, the natural sugar present in milk, is sometimes a cause of discomfort when taken in large quantity. This discomfort occurs in individuals who, after childhood, produce a limited amount of lactase, the enzyme responsible for the digestion of lactose.

Lactose intolerance is common among aboriginal people and those of Asian, African and Middle Eastern descent. Most individuals of western and northern European origin do not experience similar difficulties.

To cope with this problem, it is important to know one's tolerance to lactose. It is not an all-or-nothing situation, but very much a question of degree. Many lactose-intolerant people can support one cup of milk at a time — plenty to enjoy a delicious café au lait or most any recipe in *Savoury Wisdom*.

Most cheeses contain only traces of lactose and are well tolerated. Follow our lead: be generous with Parmesan and other grated cheeses. Yogurt is better tolerated than milk since it contains anywhere from 25% to 80% less lactose than milk. And capitalize on the yogurt advantage with its lower fat options.

For those most sensitive to lactose, lactose-reduced and lactose-free milk are widely available for worry-less milk drinking. Soy beverages that are enriched with calcium constitute another lactose-free milk alternative.

The yogurt advantage

The benefits of yogurt may extend beyond its low-lactose content, excellent nutritional profile and distinctive taste. Yogurt containing adequate numbers of live bacteria can also potentially improve the balance between friendly and undesirable bacteria in the intestine. Products with this ability, including other fermented milk products as well as yogurt, are called probiotics. Their use can help manage intestinal disorders and possibly influence the immune system. Fermented dairy products are generating a lot of interest and await further research to confirm their long-hailed health benefits. Food technologists are also busy developing other tasty products that will contain a sufficient amount of live bacteria to produce a probiotic effect. However, few yogurts on the market meet this criteria.

In the meantime, savour yogurt as a blessing to lower fat cooking and healthy eating on the run. From vinaigrettes to marinades and fruity desserts, great ways for using yogurt are provided throughout this book—be tempted! Once you develop a taste for the tangy flavour of yogurt, it can become addictive. It is never too late to become a yogurt fan.

Having your own way with milk

To close the calcium gap,

- Get your blender working. Try different dairy drinks. Seek inspiration from our Breakfast Blends (page 30).
- Cater to your mood. Feel young with chocolate milk or soothe your soul with a comforting mug of hot milk and honey.
- Add milk to your soups, yogurt to your desserts and cheese to your salads and sandwiches.
- If you are milk shy, how about getting more calcium per glass of milk? Switch to milk beverages with added calcium or use creamy lower fat evaporated milk in cooking.

- Finally, select your favourite *Savoury Wisdom* recipes from among our best calcium performers.
  - Kipper Potato Bake (p. 159)
  - All-in-One Sun-Dried Tomato Quiche (p. 160)
  - Two-Cheese Pizza with Broccoli and Sun-Dried Tomatoes (p. 134)
  - Maritime Fish and Vegetable Chowder (p. 176)
  - Salmon Bake (p. 148)
  - Ham and Broccoli Pasta Sauce (p. 113)
  - Tofu Vegetable Stir-Fry (p. 108)
  - Seafood with Fennel in a Vermouth Sauce (p. 132)
  - Broccoli and Cauliflower Gratin (p. 122)
  - Corn Tomato Chowder (p. 177)

Of Meat Wisdom

Meat is highly valued, so treat it with respect and go for quality not quantity. To partake of the goodness and aroma of meat and poultry with full peace of mind, choose wisely, selecting the leaner members of the meat group. No need to give up those perfect barbecues for two, just watch the portion size.

Moderation: still plenty of nutrition

Meat is more than a protein powerhouse. A little meat goes a long way in providing nutritional benefits. Just consider that 100 grams of beef contains about half the zinc we need plus one-third of the B_6 and iron, as well as a full complement of B_{12}. Without the regular appearance of meat on the menu, it is easy to experience a shortage of these nutrients – a not uncommon scenario among young and not-so-young women.

The call for moderation in meat consumption stems from its high saturated fat content. Lean is the motto, and fortunately lean meats retain all of their nutritional attributes.

Lean meat is in

A fair bit of wisdom has been injected in the meat counter in recent years. Farmers are producing leaner animals; processors and butchers are giving their cuts a closer trim; and lean or extra lean ground meat is prevalent. Buy leaner cuts such as beef sirloin or round, pork or beef tenderloin, chicken and turkey breast and veal in all its forms.

Before eating, trim off the fat from pork and lamb chops and remove the skin from that beautiful roast chicken after you have enjoyed its appearance. Fat and skin can be removed after cooking as well as before to eliminate much of the fat.

Select only lean or extra lean minced beef. Keep in mind that ground chicken or turkey do not necessarily offer a fat-saving alternative to lean ground beef as they are often made from untrimmed dark meat. Be prudent in your intake of luncheon meats and sausages and try the lower fat versions.

Stick to nonstick

Buying lean is one thing, cooking lean is another. For low-fat cooking, nonstick pots and frying pans are a must. Get them in the sizes and shapes you need. They make excellent gifts.

Marinate with little fat. It's the wine, juices and yogurt in a marinade, not oil, that provide the acid needed to assure tenderness and flavour.

Safety reminders

Meat, poultry and fish are highly perishable commodities, always carrying some naturally occurring bacteria ready to multiply to an unruly number when given the slightest chance.

Start on the safe side and check the best-before date before buying. Refrigeration slows bacteria growth, so refrigerate meats and other fresh high-protein foods as soon as possible after leaving the store. Always use ground meat within 24 hours of buying and be sure to cook it until it is no longer pink.

During storage, meat and poultry juices can easily leak from their wrapping and contaminate fresh produce or other foods. To avoid such incidents, store meat, poultry and fish in the meat keeper compartment or on the bottom shelf of the refrigerator in a bowl or pan.

Leftovers should never be left on the counter for more than two hours. Look for other safety tips along with the recipes.

Playing the meat card

Welcome meat without allowing it to overtake your plate. One serving should be approximately the size of a pack of cards.

In their food group, meat and poultry share the limelight with such alternatives as fish, eggs, legumes and nuts. Variety within that group will ensure maximum payoff. For most of us, two servings a day, for a total of about 150 to 200 grams, will do the trick.

With fish twice a week and more legumes on the menu, there is still plenty of room to complete the picture with our savoury meat and poultry dishes. Most of them have been designed to highlight meat in a generous surrounding of vegetables and grains. And remember: buy and cook lean.

The Versatile Egg

The omelette is a strong contender for the title of "the perfect food for two," and we mean a health-conscious two! French or Spanish in style, it welcomes all kinds of vegetables, blends perfectly with almost any bread you can think of, takes but a few minutes to assemble, requires no pre-planning and does not leave any leftovers. What more can we ask?

What about the cholesterol?

There is often misunderstanding about cholesterol. High blood cholesterol is definitely a risk factor for heart disease, and one goal of healthy eating is to keep blood cholesterol in check. A diet with plenty of vegetables, fruits and grains and a moderate amount of fat is key to that effect. On the fat front, it is both the kind of fat we eat and the amount that have the main influence on our blood cholesterol. Dietary cholesterol, which is not the same as fat, plays a much less significant role.

For the majority of people, the cholesterol they eat in eggs or other foods has limited influence on blood cholesterol. In fact, the fat in eggs is quite well balanced, with most of it being the most desirable monounsaturated kind and less than one-third being saturated.

It is also possible to find eggs on the market with extra omega-3 fatty acids as well as additional vitamin E, all good news for the heart. Nevertheless, some individuals are more sensitive to dietary cholesterol and will have to be careful about their cholesterol and egg intake.

Nutrition galore

The egg is known for its very high quality protein but seldom is it recognized for the bundle of nutrients it carries under that shell. With the exception of vitamin C, beta carotene and calcium, eggs contain the full gamut of the essential vitamins and minerals we need for good health. Most of these are present in the egg yolk, while the protein is located largely in the egg white. Systematically discarding egg yolks in cooking could be a bad calculation, unless dictated by the needs of the recipe or special concern about cholesterol. Using the yolk makes much nutrition sense. The egg bottom line? For the two of you, three dozen eggs a month is probably a good average, except of course for the Christmas baking season. But if one of you has a heart condition, you may be advised to cut that back.

With or Without a Grain of Salt?

Salt is the common name for sodium chloride, and sodium is the element that has given salt its bad name. Sodium has been charged with contributing to hypertension (high blood pressure) and salt has been severely condemned over the years. However, this verdict has been appealed and, overall, judged too severe following review, even though some dissension remains.

It appears that some individuals are more salt sensitive and respond to high sodium, but many of us do not. In fact, the best evidence fails to show that sodium restriction has a significant beneficial impact on blood pressure.

The bottom line: have your grain of salt. Unless a medical condition dictates severe restriction, salt is a case for moderation. Don't be too heavy handed with the salt shaker but don't lock it away. It is not the worst sodium offender either. To stay on the moderate side of the fence, pay more attention to the foods you buy. Almost 75% of the sodium in the Canadian diet comes from processed and pre-packaged foods, such as soups, snacks and frozen dinners. Check the labels and compare brands to select wisely.

When our recipes call for salt-containing ingredients such as broth, we often indicate "salt to taste," recognizing that saltiness will vary according to brands. Likewise in many of our vegetable dishes we mention "salt to taste," leaving it to your good judgement. Within these limitations, the sodium value for our meals or recipes is provided for the benefit of those who must follow a sodium-restricted diet. These values do not take into account any salt added "to taste."

A Last Word of Wisdom

Savoury wisdom does not reside in one food or in one meal, nor in mathematics. Throughout these pages we highlight a number of specific facts and figures simply to illustrate that wise food selection, as portrayed in Canada's Food Guide, really works. Once the principles of healthy eating are understood, there is no need to count calories, grams of fat or milligrams of any vitamin or mineral. This wisdom is encompassed in the enjoyment of a variety of good foods, chosen for their complementary flavours and nutritive attributes.

Savoury wisdom is an open-minded attitude that allows for a never-ending discovery of the world of food and flavour in harmony with our body and soul. We invite you to embrace it.

Savoury Wisdom

Delicious, Healthy Recipes for Two

Morning Starts

$\mathcal{S}$tarting the day on the right foot is what breakfast is all about. For many people, a breakfast ritual saves time and energizes the body for the day's activities.

You can make a breakfast routine work for you, too. With sufficient energy and a good share of nutrients, you will have a running start on a productive day. A good breakfast, however, consists of more than a cup of coffee or a glass of juice. The traditional combination of grains, fruit and dairy products is a perfect bet. Juice plus a bowl of fibre-rich cereal with milk and fruit is an excellent standby. Introduce variety with different juices and cereals. Or try one of our Breakfast Blends. If you go for toast, make it with whole grain bread and add a nutritious complement such as peanut butter, lower fat cheese with preserves or a quick Salsa Egg Bake. Or try one of our more adventurous Toast Toppings.

Planning ahead is a time saver in the morning. Prepare some stewed fruits or make a batch of muffins on the weekend. They both go nicely with yogurt.

And for those special mornings when you have the time to sip your café au lait and read the paper, make a breakfast with a difference. Try our Apricot Oat Bran Pancakes or the Zucchini Frittata, two different worlds, two great ways to start the day.

Double-Oat Hot Cereal Mix with Flax   28

Microwave Granola   29

Breakfast Blends   30

Molasses Prune Muffins   33

Blueberry Wheat Germ Muffins   34

Lemon Flax Muffins   35

Breakfast Sandwich French-Style   36

Apricot Oat Bran Pancakes with Cranberry Syrup   37

French Toast with Apples and Molasses Syrup   38

Easy Eggs   39

Savoury Microwave Omelette   42

Toast and Toppings   43

Double-Oat Hot Cereal Mix with Flax

PER SERVING

Calories 110
Protein 4 g
Total Fat 3 g
  saturated 0.4 g
  monounsaturated 0.8 g
  polyunsaturated 1.6 g
Carbohydrate 18 g
  fibre 3 g
Calcium 23 mg
Folacin 16 mcg
Sodium 3 mg

FOOD GUIDE SERVINGS

1 🍞

Ground or Whole Flax

To obtain the full health benefits flax has to offer, rely on ground flaxseeds. If they remain uncracked, whole seeds may pass undigested through the body. Ground flaxseeds are oxidized easily and should be stored in the refrigerator in an airtight and opaque container for up to 30 days.

Plain old-fashioned oatmeal is still one of the healthiest foods around. Add a bit of oat bran and flax for some extra heart-health benefits and you have a great food to start the day. If the mix is made ahead, preparing hot cereal in the microwave is almost as easy as pouring from a box. For a chewy texture, use large-flake oats; for a smoother cereal, choose the quick-cooking kind. Adding a few raisins eliminates the need for sugar as well as providing extra fibre.

4 cups	**rolled oats**	1 L
1 cup	**oat bran**	250 mL
1/2 cup	**ground flaxseed**	125 mL

In large bowl, combine oats, oat bran and flax seed. Store in the refrigerator in a tightly covered container for up to 1 month.

Makes 5 cups (1.25 L) or 20 servings.

For a Single Serving **Microwave:**

1. In a large microwave-safe serving bowl, place 1/4 cup (50 mL) cereal mix.

2. Add 3/4 cup (175 mL) water. Stir in a pinch of salt and a few raisins, chopped dried apricots or dates, if desired.

3. Microwave on 100% power for 1 1/2 minutes and 30% power for 1 1/2 minutes for a single serving. (Times may vary depending on the microwave oven.)

For Two Servings **Stovetop:**

1. In a small saucepan, combine 1/2 cup (125 mL) cereal mix and 1 1/2 cup (375 mL) water. Add a pinch of salt and a few raisins or other dried fruit as desired.

2. Bring to a boil over medium heat, stirring constantly. Reduce heat; simmer for 1 minute.

Microwave Granola

Granola has become a popular morning dish, but commercial versions can be very high in calories and quite expensive. The microwave makes a toasted, low-fat cereal in very short order.

4 cups	**large-flake rolled oats**	1 L
1/3 cup	**slivered almonds**	75 mL
1/3 cup	**wheat germ**	75 mL
1/4 tsp	**salt**	1 mL
1/3 cup	**liquid honey**	75 mL
3 tbsp	**vegetable oil**	45 mL

1. In large microwave-safe bowl, combine oats, almonds, wheat germ and salt.

2. In small measuring cup or bowl, whisk together honey and oil until well blended. Stir into oatmeal mixture.

3. Microwave on 100% power for 3 minutes; stir and microwave for 2 minutes longer. Stir well and continue to microwave until mixture becomes slightly browned, stirring after each minute. Let stand until cool, stirring several times. Mixture will continue to brown while standing. Store in a tightly covered container for up to 1 month.

Makes 10 servings, 1/2 cup (125 mL) each.

Granola Breakfast Trifle

Spoon granola into the bottom of a clear glass serving bowl. Top with vanilla yogurt and a few dried cranberries or blueberries. Add another layer of granola followed by more yogurt. Cover and refrigerate up to 12 hours. At serving time, top with sliced fresh fruit, such as strawberries, raspberries, peaches, mango, kiwifruit or cubed fresh pineapple.

PER SERVING

Calories 270
Protein 8 g
Total Fat 10 g
  saturated 1.1 g
  monounsaturated 4.9 g
  polyunsaturated 3.0 g
Carbohydrate 41 g
  fibre 5 g
Calcium 33 mg
Folacin 10 mcg
Sodium 58 mg

FOOD GUIDE SERVINGS

1 1/2

Breakfast Blends

Use your blender or food processor to whiz together these nutritious starters to the day. Bran and oat cereals add pleasing body as well as a good source of fibre. Serve Breakfast Blends with toast or any of our delicious muffins since they are not a stand-alone breakfast. And there is no reason they can't be equally enjoyed at lunch or for a light snack. Frozen berries or peaches may replace fresh for use year-round.

PER SERVING
(1 1/4 CUP/300 mL)

Calories 220
Protein 8 g
Total Fat 5 g
  saturated 2.8 g
  monounsaturated 1.4 g
  polyunsaturated 0.5 g
Carbohydrate 41 g
  fibre 3 g
Calcium 186 mg
Folacin 53 mcg
Sodium 78 mg

FOOD GUIDE SERVINGS

 1/2 1 1/2

Frosted Fruit Whiz

1	**medium banana, cut in pieces**	1
1/2 cup	**blueberries, peaches or other fruit**	125 mL
3 tbsp	**oat bran**	45 mL
2 tbsp	**orange juice concentrate**	25 mL
1/4 cup	**ice cream or frozen yogurt**	50 mL
1 cup	**milk or plain yogurt**	250 mL

1. If you use a blender, combine all ingredients; process until smooth.

2. If you use a food processor, process banana, fruit, bran, orange juice concentrate and ice cream until smooth. Pour into 2 large glasses; stir half the milk into each.

Makes 2 1/2 cups (625 mL).

PER SERVING
(ABOUT 1 CUP/250 mL)

Calories 160
Protein 6 g
Total Fat 3 g
  saturated 1.6 g
  monounsaturated 0.9 g
  polyunsaturated 0.5 g
Carbohydrate 31 g
  fibre 3 g
Calcium 170 mg
Folacin 23 mcg
Sodium 64 mg

FOOD GUIDE SERVINGS

 1/2 1 1/2 1/2

Apple Berry Shake

3/4 cup	**raspberries, strawberries or diced pineapple**	175 mL
3 tbsp	**oat bran**	45 mL
1 tsp	**honey or more to taste**	5 mL
1 cup	**milk or plain yogurt**	250 mL
3/4 cup	**apple juice**	175 mL

1. If you use a blender, combine all ingredients; process until smooth.

2. If you use a food processor, process fruit, oat bran and honey until smooth. Pour into 2 glasses; stir half the apple juice and milk into each.

Makes 2 1/4 cups (550 mL).

Tropical Sipper

1 1/2 cups	**cantaloupe pieces, about 1/4 cantaloupe**	375 mL
1/2 cup	**crushed canned pineapple, undrained**	125 mL
1/3 cup	**high-fibre bran cereal**	75 mL
1 tsp	**honey or more to taste**	5 mL
1 cup	**milk or plain yogurt**	250 mL

1. If you use a blender, combine all ingredients; process until smooth.

2. If you use a food processor, process cantaloupe, pineapple, cereal and honey until smooth. Pour into 2 glasses; stir half the milk into each.

Makes 2 1/2 cups (625 mL).

PER SERVING
(1 1/4 CUP/300 mL)

Calories 180
Protein 7 g
Total Fat 3 g
  saturated 1.5 g
  monounsaturated 0.7 g
  polyunsaturated 0.1 g
Carbohydrate 37 g
  fibre 5 g
Calcium 180 mg
Folacin 40 mcg
Sodium 172 mg

FOOD GUIDE SERVINGS

1/2  1 1/2 1/2

Golden Smoothie

1 1/2 cups	**cantaloupe pieces, about 1/4 cantaloupe**	375 mL
3/4 cup	**plain yogurt**	175 mL
3 tbsp	**oat bran**	45 mL
3/4 cup	**orange juice**	175 mL

1. If you use a blender, combine all ingredients; process until smooth.

2. If you use a food processor, process cantaloupe, yogurt and bran until smooth. Pour into 2 large glasses; stir half the orange juice into each.

Makes 2 1/2 cups (625 mL).

PER SERVING
(1 1/4 CUP/300 mL)

Calories 165
Protein 8 g
Total Fat 2 g
  saturated 1.1 g
  monounsaturated 0.6 g
  polyunsaturated 0.3 g
Carbohydrate 32 g
  fibre 2 g
Calcium 195 mg
Folacin 77 mcg
Sodium 76 mg

FOOD GUIDE SERVINGS

1/2  1 1/2 1/2

Double-Berry Smoothie

3/4 cup	**strawberries or raspberries**	175 mL
1	**large banana, cut in pieces**	1
1/3 cup	**high-fibre bran cereal**	75 mL
2 tbsp	**strawberry or raspberry jam**	25 mL
1 1/2 cup	**milk**	375 mL

1. If you use a blender, combine all ingredients; process until smooth.

2. If you use a food processor, process berries, banana, cereal and jam until smooth. Pour into 2 large glasses; stir half the milk into each.

Makes 2 1/4 cups (550 mL).

Molasses Prune Muffins

These tasty, understated muffins have molasses as their only sweetener. They are wonderful with plain yogurt and have become a favourite in our families. You can also use raisins instead of prunes.

2 cups	**whole wheat flour**	500 mL
1 tbsp	**baking powder**	15 mL
1/2 tsp	**salt**	2 mL
1	**egg, beaten**	1
1/2 cup	**molasses**	125 mL
1/4 cup	**vegetable oil**	50 mL
1 cup	**milk**	250 mL
3/4 cup	**chopped pitted prunes**	175 mL

1. In large bowl, combine flour, baking powder and salt.

2. In medium bowl, combine egg, molasses, oil, milk and prunes. Add to flour mixture; stir until moistened, being careful not to overmix.

3. Spoon into 12 nonstick or paper-lined muffin cups. Bake in 400°F (200°C) oven for 18 to 20 minutes or until tops are lightly browned and firm to the touch.

Makes 12 muffins.

Muffins on Hand

For readily available muffins, store them in resealable bags in your freezer. To defrost, heat a single muffin for 1 minute on the defrost program of your microwave. It will be nicely defrosted and slightly warm.

PER SERVING
(1 MUFFIN)

Calories 190
Protein 4 g
Total Fat 6 g
    saturated 0.8 g
    monounsaturated 3.0 g
    polyunsaturated 1.6 g
Carbohydrate 32 g
    fibre 3 g
Calcium 145 mg
Folacin 9 mcg
Sodium 200 mg

FOOD GUIDE SERVINGS

1

Two Ways with Prunes

Prunes lend great taste and texture to baked goods, bringing along much sought-after fibre as well as iron and B vitamins. Get most of the same nutritional benefits by using prune juice. Mixed half and half with milk, prune juice is a delicious drink anytime of day.

Blueberry Wheat Germ Muffins

Wheat Germ

Wheat germ is one of our few good sources of vitamin E and also contains iron and some B vitamins. It can become rancid quite rapidly because of its high content of polyunsaturated fat and must be stored in the refrigerator. Enjoy its nutty flavour by adding it to baked goods and meat loaves and sprinkling it on cereal and yogurt.

These light muffins are brimming with blueberries and a hint of lemon. Serve them with a piece of cheese for breakfast or with a cup of tea later in the day.

1 1/3 cups	**all-purpose flour**	325 mL
2/3 cup	**wheat germ**	150 mL
1/3 cup	**granulated sugar**	75 mL
1 tsp	**baking powder**	5 mL
1/2 tsp	**baking soda**	2 mL
1/4 tsp	**salt**	1 mL
1	**egg**	1
1 cup	**milk**	250 mL
3 tbsp	**vegetable oil**	45 mL
1 tbsp	**lemon juice**	15 mL
	Grated rind of 1 lemon	
1 cup	**fresh or frozen blueberries**	250 mL

1. In large bowl, combine flour, wheat germ, sugar, baking powder, baking soda and salt.

2. In small bowl, beat egg lightly. Stir in milk, oil, lemon juice and lemon rind. Add to dry ingredients; stir several times. Add blueberries and stir just until moistened, being careful not to overmix.

3. Spoon into 12 nonstick or paper-lined muffin cups. Bake in 400°F (200°C) oven for 15 minutes or until tops are lightly browned and firm to the touch.

Makes 12 muffins.

Lemon Flax Muffins

These nutritious muffins with a hint of lemon are filled with whole flax seeds, adding both a nutty taste and heart-friendly omega-3 fatty acids. They are made from ingredients generally kept on hand and make a perfect partner for one of the Breakfast Blends (page 30).

1 3/4 cups	**whole wheat flour**	425 mL
2/3 cup	**granulated sugar**	150 mL
1/4 cup	**whole flaxseeds**	50 mL
1 1/2 tsp	**baking soda**	7 mL
1/2 tsp	**baking powder**	2 mL
1/4 tsp	**salt**	1 mL
1	**egg**	1
3/4 cup	**milk**	175 mL
1/4 cup	**vegetable oil**	50 mL
	Grated rind and juice from 1 lemon	

1. In large bowl, combine flour, sugar, flax seeds, baking soda, baking powder and salt.

2. In medium bowl, lightly beat egg. Stir in milk, oil, lemon rind and juice (you should have about 3 tbsp/45 mL lemon juice). Add to flour mixture and stir just until moistened, being careful not to overmix.

3. Spoon into 12 nonstick or paper-lined muffin cups. Bake in 375°F (190°C) oven for 18 to 20 minutes or until tops are lightly browned and firm to the touch.

Makes 12 muffins.

PER SERVING
(1 MUFFIN)

Calories 175
Protein 4 g
Total Fat 7 g
   saturated 0.8 g
   monounsaturated 3.2 g
   polyunsaturated 2.5 g
Carbohydrate 27 g
   fibre 3 g
Calcium 53 mg
Folacin 16 mcg
Sodium 225 mg

FOOD GUIDE SERVINGS

1

The Lignan Connection

Flax seeds are rich in lignans, a phytoestrogen that could possibly play a role in maintaining bone density, lowering blood cholesterol and protecting against cancer.

Breakfast Sandwich French-Style

PER SERVING

Calories 315
Protein 19 g
Total Fat 15 g
 saturated 6.8 g
 monounsaturated 5.1 g
 polyunsaturated 1.4 g
Carbohydrate 29 g
 fibre 5 g
Calcium 228 mg
Folacin 49 mcg
Sodium 854 mg

FOOD GUIDE SERVINGS

2 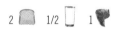 1/2 1

French toast with a savoury filling of ham and spinach with cheese melting between is an elegant entrée for brunch or a special breakfast celebration. Use any kind of melting cheese such as Monterey Jack, Swiss or Cheddar. And keep them in mind to serve as a lunch fixing.

4	**slices whole grain or white bread**	4
2	**thin slices Black Forest-type ham**	2
2	**thin slices part-skim mozzarella cheese, about 1 1/2 oz (40 g)**	2
2-4	**fresh spinach leaves**	2-4
1	**egg**	1
3 tbsp	**milk**	45 mL
pinch	**salt**	pinch
pinch	**ground black pepper**	pinch
2 tsp	**butter or margarine**	10 mL

1. On each of 2 bread slices, place 1 slice ham, 1 slice cheese and half the spinach. Top with remaining bread slices.

2. In shallow bowl, whisk egg, milk, salt and pepper until well blended. Dip each sandwich into egg mixture. Using a spatula, carefully turn to coat both sides.

3. In nonstick skillet, heat butter over medium heat. Cook sandwiches for 5 minutes or until lightly browned on both sides and cheese is slightly melted.

Makes 2 sandwiches.

Ham Lore

All hams begin as a hog's hind leg, but after that, all hams are not the same. Different curing methods produce hams with very different flavours and textures. Speciality cured hams such as prosciutto from Italy have an intense flavour and solid texture and are generally sold in paper-thin slices. Black Forest is a popular smoked ham with a more dynamic flavour than the common sweet-cured hams.

Apricot Oat Bran Pancakes with Cranberry Syrup

These easy-to-make pancakes are a favourite Sunday morning breakfast. Try different dried fruits, such as cranberries, blueberries or chopped apple, to give a variety of flavours. And, of course, they are equally rewarding served with pure maple syrup.

Syrup

1 tbsp	**granulated sugar**	15 mL
2 tsp	**cornstarch**	10 mL
2/3 cup	**cranberry juice or cocktail**	150 mL

Pancakes

1/2 cup	**oat bran**	125 mL
1/2 cup	**whole wheat flour**	125 mL
2 tsp	**baking powder**	10 mL
2 tsp	**granulated sugar**	10 mL
1/8 tsp	**salt**	0.5 mL
1	**egg**	1
2/3 cup	**milk**	150 mL
2 tsp	**vegetable oil**	10 mL
1/3 cup	**finely chopped dried apricots or other dried fruit**	75 mL

Syrup

1. In 2-cup (500 mL) glass measuring cup, combine sugar, cornstarch and juice. Microwave at 100% power, stirring several times, for 1 1/2 to 2 minutes or until mixture comes to a boil.

Pancakes

1. In large bowl, stir together bran, flour, baking powder, sugar and salt.

2. In small bowl, combine egg, milk and oil. Add to dry ingredients. Fold in apricots.

3. Heat large nonstick skillet over medium heat until hot. Drop batter by small spoonfuls onto skillet; cook over medium-high heat until bubbles form on surface and underside is golden brown. Turn pancakes and cook until second side is lightly browned.

4. Serve with syrup.

Makes 2 servings of 5 pancakes with 1/3 cup (75 mL) syrup each.

PER SERVING

Calories 430
Protein 15 g
Total Fat 11 g
 saturated 2.5 g
 monounsaturated 4.7 g
 polyunsaturated 2.6 g
Carbohydrate 81 g
 fibre 8 g
Calcium 462 mg
Folacin 33 mcg
Sodium 557 mg

FOOD GUIDE SERVINGS

2 1/2 1 1/2

Speaking to Your Heart

Oat bran is rich in beta glucan, a soluble fibre also present in barley, which seems not only to play a role in lowering blood cholesterol, but may also help control blood sugar. Oat bran is present in all forms of rolled oats, but as a separate ingredient it offers a greater fibre boost.

French Toast with Apples and Molasses Syrup

PER SERVING

Calories 375
Protein 9 g
Total Fat 11 g
  saturated 5.3 g
  monounsaturated 3.7 g
  polyunsaturated 1.0 g
Carbohydrate 61 g
  fibre 1 g
Calcium 176 mg
Folacin 47 mcg
Sodium 375 mg

FOOD GUIDE SERVINGS

2  1/2 ✿ 1/2 ▨

Molasses gives great flavour to an old breakfast favourite. Served with apples poached in a simple syrup, this dish makes an easy yet elegant breakfast treat.

1/3 cup	**water**	75 mL
1 tsp	**cornstarch**	5 mL
1 tsp	**granulated sugar**	5 mL
1	**apple, peeled and cut in wedges**	1
3 tbsp	**molasses, divided**	45 mL
1	**large egg**	1
1/3 cup	**milk**	75 mL
2 tsp	**butter**	10 mL
4	**slices white bread**	4

1. In 2-cup (500 mL) glass measuring cup, mix water, cornstarch and sugar. Microwave on 100% power for 1 minute or until thickened and bubbly, stirring once. Add 2 tbsp (30 mL) molasses and apple; microwave for 90 seconds or until apple is barely tender. Set aside.

2. In shallow dish, whisk egg, 1 tbsp (15 mL) molasses and milk until blended.

3. In large nonstick skillet, melt butter over medium-high heat. Dip bread into egg mixture and cook in skillet until browned, turning once.

4. To serve, spoon apples onto cooked toast and serve with remaining syrup.

Makes 2 servings.

Molasses

A by-product from the refining of granulated sugar, molasses has long been used in comfort foods such as gingerbread and spice cookies. Light molasses, often sold as fancy grade, is used in most kitchens. Dark molasses is less sweet. The flavour of molasses is unique but it offers no significant nutritive value. Blackstrap molasses, from the very last boiling of the raw sugar, is more commonly used as animal food.

Easy Eggs

Eggs make a nutritious start to the day, and these recipes require only very short cooking times. Eggs are rich in protein, vitamins and minerals. If you have been advised to limit your egg consumption, substitute two egg whites or 1/4 cup (50 mL) thawed egg substitute for each whole egg in these recipes.

Zucchini Frittata

A frittata is an open-faced version of an omelette and is a cinch to cook. Simply pour the egg mixture over a few sautéed veggies, cover and cook until set. Another time, replace the zucchini with mushrooms.

1 tbsp	**vegetable oil**	15 mL
2	**green onions, thinly sliced**	2
1	**medium zucchini, thinly sliced**	1
1/2 tsp	**dried basil**	2 mL
3	**eggs**	3
2 tbsp	**grated Parmesan cheese**	25 mL
	Salt and pepper	

1. In small nonstick skillet, heat oil over medium heat. Add onions and zucchini; cook until soft, about 5 minutes. Sprinkle with basil.

2. In small bowl, beat eggs and stir in Parmesan cheese. Pour over vegetables. Cover and cook over medium heat for 6 minutes or until set. Season with salt and pepper to taste.

Makes 2 servings.

PER SERVING
Calories 215
Protein 13 g
Total Fat 17 g
  saturated 4.1 g
  monounsaturated 7.6 g
  polyunsaturated 3.2 g
Carbohydrate 4 g
  fibre 1 g
Calcium 141 mg
Folacin 41 mcg
Sodium 208 mg

FOOD GUIDE SERVINGS

1/2   1

Maple Poached Eggs on Waffles

Topping waffles with an egg and maple syrup provides an extra energy boost to start the day.

3 tbsp	**maple syrup**	45 mL
2	**eggs**	2
2	**ready-to-eat frozen waffles**	2

1. In small nonstick skillet, heat maple syrup over medium heat.

2. Break eggs into syrup, cover and cook until eggs are set.

3. Meanwhile, toast waffles. Place a waffle on each of two plates, slide an egg onto each; pour maple syrup over top.

Makes 2 servings.

PER SERVING

Calories 250
Protein 9 g
Total Fat 8 g
  saturated 2.1 g
  monounsaturated 3.1 g
  polyunsaturated 1.7 g
Carbohydrate 36 g
  fibre 1 g
Calcium 124 mg
Folacin 53 mcg
Sodium 340 mg

FOOD GUIDE SERVINGS

1   1

Breakfast in a Cup

A microwave cooks a scrambled egg in less time than it takes to make your coffee. Cook it in your favourite mug and eliminate a serving dish. Add a bit of grated cheese after cooking for added flavour.

2	**eggs**	2
2 tbsp	**milk**	25 mL
pinch	**seasoned salt or pepper**	pinch

In microwave-safe cup, whisk together eggs, milk and seasoning. Microwave on 70% power for 1 minute; stir. Cook for another 30 seconds if desired. Let stand for 1 minute before serving.

Makes 1 serving.

PER SERVING

Calories 165
Protein 14 g
Total Fat 11 g
  saturated 3.5 g
  monounsaturated 4.0 g
  polyunsaturated 1.4 g
Carbohydrate 3 g
  fibre 0 g
Calcium 82 mg
Folacin 36 mcg
Sodium 271 mg

FOOD GUIDE SERVINGS

1

Salsa Egg Bake

Commercial salsa and a microwave oven make fast work of this traditional Mexican dish. Serve it with the Tropical Sipper (page 31) for real Down South ambience.

2 tbsp	**salsa**	25 mL
1	**egg**	1
1	**slice toast**	1

1. Place salsa in a microwave-safe cup; with a spoon make a depression in the middle. Break egg into the depression; pierce yolk membrane with sharp knife. Cover dish with plastic wrap, leaving a small vent hole.

2. Microwave on 70% power for 1 to 1 1/2 minutes or until egg is set. Let stand for 1 minute. Serve with toast.

Makes 1 serving.

PER SERVING

Calories 150
Protein 9 g
Total Fat 6 g
 saturated 1.8 g
 monounsaturated 2.3 g
 polyunsaturated 0.9 g
Carbohydrate 15 g
 fibre 1 g
Calcium 63 mg
Folacin 39 mcg
Sodium 269 mg

FOOD GUIDE SERVINGS

1 1

Savoury Microwave Omelette

PER SERVING

Calories 205
Protein 15 g
Total Fat 14 g
  saturated 5.7 g
  monounsaturated 5.0 g
  polyunsaturated 1.4 g
Carbohydrate 5 g
  fibre 1 g
Calcium 106 mg
Folacin 36 mcg
Sodium 361 mg

FOOD GUIDE SERVINGS

1

If you don't have a stovetop omelette pan, use your microwave to make a fast version of this classic dish.

1 tsp	**butter**	5 mL
3	**mushrooms, sliced**	3
2 tbsp	**chopped onion**	25 mL
2 tbsp	**chopped green pepper**	25 mL
2 tbsp	**chopped ham**	25 mL
3	**eggs**	3
2 tbsp	**milk**	25 mL
2 tbsp	**shredded Cheddar or other cheese**	25 mL

1. Place butter in a 6-inch (15 cm) microwave-safe ramekin-type dish. Microwave on 100% power for 10 seconds or until melted. Add mushrooms, onion, green pepper and ham; microwave on 100% power for 1 to 2 minutes or until vegetables are soft.

2. In small bowl, lightly beat eggs and milk. Pour egg mixture over vegetables and microwave on 70% power for 2 to 4 minutes. Stir three times during the cooking time, moving cooked egg from the edges towards the centre of the dish. Remove from oven when top of omelette is still moist and not completely set. Sprinkle with cheese, cover with plastic wrap and let stand for 1 1/2 minutes. Fold over and lift from dish.

Makes 2 servings.

Toast and Toppings

When you crave an easy meal to start the day, a couple of slices of toast with a flavourful topping may be just what you need. Here are our suggestions; you may think of others. If you have a bread machine, make Two-Oat Bread (page 44) and cut into thin slices. Serve with a piece of fresh fruit or fruit juice.

Toast Toppings

Toast a piece of your favourite bread and serve with one of the following toppings:

- A tasty jam such as Fast Apricot Pineapple Jam. Serve with a tall glass of milk.
- A bit of dijonnaise (a mustard-mayonnaise spread, available in the mustard section of most supermarkets) and slices of hard-cooked egg.
- A slice or two of cold smoked turkey and a dollop of cranberry sauce or light mayonnaise.
- Peanut butter and slices of banana.
- Your favourite cheese or cheese spread. Place under the broiler or in a toaster oven for a few minutes to melt the cheese.
- Cottage cheese and a sprinkle of sliced green onion, poppy seeds or canned pineapple tidbits.
- Several pieces of kippered herring.

Watch that Label

Read the label to be sure you are buying 100% fruit juice. Drinks labelled "cocktail" or "drink" have water and sugar added.

Kippers

Kippered herring, also known as kippers, are herring that have been split and then cured by salting, drying and cold-smoking.

Bread Machine Two-Oat Bread

Rolled oats and oat bran combine to make a deliciously flavoured, fine-textured bread in machines baking either one- or one-and-a-half-pound loaves. This wholesome loaf cuts beautifully into thin slices which are perfect for toasting. Serve it with honey or your favourite jam or choose one of the Toast Toppings on page 43.

1 cup	**water**	250 mL
1/3 cup	**quick-cooking rolled oats**	75 mL
2 tbsp	**granulated sugar**	25 mL
2 tbsp	**instant skim milk powder**	25 mL
1 tbsp	**vegetable oil**	15 mL
3/4 tsp	**salt**	3 mL
1/4 cup	**oat bran**	50 mL
2 1/4 cups	**all-purpose flour**	550 mL
1 tsp	**instant yeast**	5 mL

1. Select 1- or 1 1/2-pound loaf size recommended by manufacturer of your machine.

2. Add water, oatmeal, sugar, milk powder, oil, salt, oat bran, flour and yeast to bread pan in that order. Start machine.

Makes 1 1/4 lb (625 g) loaf or 10 servings, 2 slices each.

Homemade Advantage

Commercial oatmeal bread, oatmeal cookies or nutri-bars often contain only a small amount of oats. For this reason, "oats" often appears way down on the package's list of ingredients. However, when you cook with rolled oats, you get whole grains with the full nutritional benefits of the germ and the bran.

Fast Apricot Pineapple Jam

Don't disregard canned fruits when it comes to jam. This combination of canned fruits makes one of the tastiest jams you'll come across, and it couldn't be easier. With the sorting, washing and peeling of the fruit already done, you can have a fresh-tasting batch of jam in less than a half hour.

1	**can (14 oz/398 mL) apricot halves in light syrup**	1
1	**can (14 oz/398 mL) pineapple pieces in own juice**	1
3 1/2 cups	**granulated sugar** 875 mL	
4 tsp	**lemon juice** 20 mL	
1	**pouch (3 oz/85 mL) liquid fruit pectin**	1

1. Drain apricots and pineapple, reserving juice if desired for another purpose. Chop fruit finely in a food processor or by hand.

2. In a large stainless steel or enamel saucepan, combine fruit, sugar and lemon juice. Bring to a full boil over high heat; boil hard for 2 minutes. Remove from heat; stir in pectin.

3. Ladle into sterilized jars. Store in the refrigerator for up to 4 weeks. (Or use jars with sealable lids, following manufacturer's directions. Process in boiling water for 5 minutes.)

Makes 4 cups (1 L).

Sweeten Up

Use the liquid drained from the fruit to sweeten beverages such as tea or lemonade, or combine with plain gelatin for a simple dessert.

PER SERVING
(1 tbsp/15 mL)

Calories 50
Protein 0 g
Total Fat 0 g
  saturated 0 g
  monounsaturated 0 g
  polyunsaturated 0 g
Carbohydrate 13 g
  fibre 0 g
Calcium 1 mg
Folacin 0 mcg
Sodium 2 mg

FOOD GUIDE SERVINGS
None

Lunch and Supper Fixings

*N*owhere is the midday pause so well honoured as around the Mediterranean. It should therefore come as no surprise that we have drawn inspiration from this region for our lunch or light supper suggestions. Tomatoes, olives, feta and fresh herbs enhance our versions of tabbouleh, bruschetta and polenta, all designed to be assembled with very little effort or time. New World sandwich favourites such as tuna and the western have also been revived, along with some interesting fixings for potatoes.

Our aim for lunch or supper is to ensure an input from at least three food groups, as well as an adequate energy intake. These recipes provide the core of the meal but are not meant to stand alone. To complete the plate, a few ideas for "Rounding Out the Meal" are presented. Several carrot sticks and broccoli florets, a glass of milk and a fresh fruit can add much to a traditional sandwich. Give a lift to your sandwich with some wholesome bread, complement the filling with crispy greens, and be prudent with the mayonnaise.

Nutrition shortcomings are common at lunch, a moment often neglected in our hurried world. Absence of variety, a lack of substance and fast food excesses are the main pitfalls. The little salad or the instant soup coupled with a cup of tea and a few cookies is bound to leave you wanting for energy in mid-afternoon and will do little to provide you with health-promoting nutrients. So be inspired by these fixings; then savour your lunch listening to your favourite music, enjoying the sun in your garden or simply relaxing with a friend before resuming the afternoon activities. At home, at the office or on the road, a good lunch is well within your reach.

Polenta with Peppers and Feta   50

Ham and Leek Topped Potatoes   52

Presto Pizzas   53

Quesadillas   54

Hummus-Stuffed Pita   55

Tuna Melt   56

Western Wrap   57

Egg-Topped Bruschetta Bagel   58

Warm Quinoa Vegetable Salad   59

Wild Rice and Barley Salad   60

Tabbouleh Salad with Feta Cheese   61

Mediterranean Chicken Salad   62

Potato Salad with Smoked Oysters   63

Warm Steak Salad with Fruit   64

Polenta with Peppers and Feta

A staple of northern Italy, polenta is a snap to make in the microwave where there is no problem with it sticking. In this recipe polenta makes a base for a lively melange of peppers accented with the tangy flavour of feta.

PER SERVING

Calories 245
Protein 10 g
Total Fat 9 g
 saturated 4.6 g
 monounsaturated 3.4 g
 polyunsaturated 0.8 g
Carbohydrate 31 g
 fibre 3 g
Calcium 151 mg
Folacin 67 mcg
Sodium 911 mg

FOOD GUIDE SERVINGS

1  1/2

Polenta

1 1/3 cups	**chicken broth**	325 mL
1/8 tsp	**salt**	0.5 mL
1/3 cup	**cornmeal**	75 mL

Peppers

1 tsp	**olive oil**	5 mL
1	**small onion, thinly sliced**	1
1	**small clove garlic, minced**	1
1 tsp	**granulated sugar**	5 mL
1/2	**sweet red pepper, sliced**	1/2
1/2	**sweet green pepper, sliced**	1/2
2 tsp	**balsamic vinegar**	10 mL
2 tbsp	**chopped fresh basil**	25 mL
1/3 cup	**crumbled feta cheese**	75 mL

1. Polenta: In 2-cup (500 mL) glass measuring cup, microwave chicken broth and salt on 100% power for 3 minutes or until boiling. Slowly add cornmeal, stirring constantly. Microwave on 50% power, stirring once, for 2 minutes or until mixture is very thick. Let stand 1 minute. Spoon polenta onto greased foil or parchment paper, forming two circles approximately 4 inches (10 cm) in diameter. Let stand for 20 minutes or until firm.

2. Peppers: In small nonstick skillet, heat oil over medium heat. Cook onion and garlic for 5 minutes or until soft. Sprinkle with sugar and cook for 2 minutes or until golden, stirring frequently. Add peppers; cook for 10 minutes or until soft. Stir in vinegar and basil.

3. Place each circle of polenta on a microwave-safe serving plate; top with pepper mixture and sprinkle with feta. Microwave on 70% power for 30 seconds each or until heated through.

Makes 2 servings.

Supercharged Peppers

Colourful and delicious, peppers are supercharged with vitamin C. They fill this polenta dish with your full daily requirement of this vitamin and an array of phytochemicals.

Rounding Out the Meal

Mixed greens with Favourite Vinaigrette (page 81)

glass of milk

fresh fruit

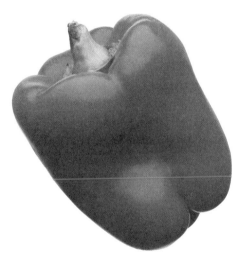

Ham and Leek Topped Potatoes

PER SERVING

Calories 335
Protein 21 g
Total Fat 11 g
  saturated 4.4 g
  monounsaturated 4.2 g
  polyunsaturated 1.2 g
Carbohydrate 40 g
  fibre 3 g
Calcium 204 mg
Folacin 38 mcg
Sodium 975 mg

FOOD GUIDE SERVINGS

1 1/2   1/2   1

Rounding Out the Meal

Spinach Sprout Salad
(page 97)

crisp apple

'P' Benefits

Think 'P' for 'P'otatoes
and for 'P'otassium: one
of the key benefits associated with vegetables and
fruit is their potassium
content. Potatoes are
among the best sources
of potassium and, as
such, may play a protec-
tive role against high
blood pressure.

Dress up potatoes with a variety of toppings. Just a few minutes in the microwave and they are ready for a tasty lunch.

2	**large baking potatoes, about 6 oz (180 g) each**	2
	Vegetable oil for rubbing	
1 tsp	**butter** 5 mL	
1	**small leek, chopped, or 1/3 cup (75 mL) chopped onion**	1
1/2 cup	**chopped ham** 125 mL	
3/4 cup	**plain yogurt** 175 mL	
2 tsp	**Dijon mustard** 10 mL	
2 tsp	**prepared horseradish** 10 mL	
	Ground black pepper	

1. Wash potatoes and dry with a paper towel. Using your hands, rub a thin coating of oil over potatoes. Microwave on 100% power for 6 minutes or until soft. Let stand for 2 minutes.

2. Meanwhile, in small nonstick skillet, heat butter over medium heat. Add leek; cook for 3 minutes or until soft. Stir in ham, yogurt, mustard, horseradish and pepper to taste. Heat through but do not boil.

3. Split potatoes in half and place on serving plate. With a fork, fluff the potato slightly. Spoon half the ham mixture onto each potato.

Makes 2 servings.

Variations:

Broccoli Topped Potatoes

Replace ham with 3/4 cup (175 mL) blanched broccoli. Sprinkle with shredded Cheddar cheese.

Potatoes Topped with Tuna and Red Pepper

Replace leek with 1/4 cup (50 mL) chopped sweet red pepper and replace ham with 1/2 can flaked tuna.

Presto Pizzas

Pita bread or flour tortillas make a convenient base for a quick pizza. Try provolone, mozzarella or Monterey Jack cheese for delicious variations, and use other herbs you may have on hand such as oregano or thyme.

2	large (9 in/23 cm) flour tortillas or pita breads	2
1/2 tsp	olive oil	2 mL
1/4 cup	tomato sauce	50 mL
1/3 cup	diced sweet red or green pepper	75 mL
1 tbsp	chopped fresh basil, or 1 tsp (5 mL) dried	15 mL
1/2 cup	crumbled feta or other cheese	125 mL

1. Place pita on baking sheet; brush with oil.

2. Spread tomato sauce over top; sprinkle with pepper, basil and cheese.

3. Bake in 425ºF (220ºC) oven for 10 minutes or until cheese has softened. Cut into 4 pieces.

Makes 2 servings.

Variation:
Pesto Presto Pizza

Replace the tomato sauce with pesto, and replace the sweet peppers with roasted red peppers. Use mozzarella cheese.

Pizza Ways

Pizza as we have come to know it most likely evolved from the flat breads used throughout the ancient Mediterranean world. The Italian version was brought to North America by soldiers at the end of World War II and has since become one of our most popular foods. Most people prefer pizza made with a thin-rolled yeast dough, but pre-cooked flat breads make very acceptable and time-saving alternatives. For small pizzas, flour tortillas, pita breads or split English muffins are the most convenient; for a larger pizza, use a commercial flat bread such as focaccia. The traditional pizza base is a tomato sauce; but a quick brushing of oil over the crust and a topping of leftover meat or poultry and assorted veggies, all covered with your choice of cheese, makes an ambrosial pizza.

PER SERVING

Calories 280
Protein 10 g
Total Fat 13 g
  saturated 6.6 g
  monounsaturated 4.0 g
  polyunsaturated 1.7 g
Carbohydrate 31 g
  fibre 2 g
Calcium 209 mg
Folacin 57 mcg
Sodium 802 mg

FOOD GUIDE SERVINGS

1   1/2   1/2

Rounding Out the Meal

fresh veggies and pickles

sliced oranges and chopped dates drizzled with a little honey

Quesadillas

PER SERVING

Calories 475
Protein 19 g
Total Fat 20 g
  saturated 9.1 g
  monounsaturated 6.3 g
  polyunsaturated 3.0 g
Carbohydrate 55 g
  fibre 5 g
Calcium 377 mg
Folacin 94 mcg
Sodium 864 mg

FOOD GUIDE SERVINGS

2 ▧   1 ▯

**Rounding Out
the Meal**

Fresh Tomato Soup
(page 175)

fresh fruit

The Mexican equivalent of a sandwich, quesadillas can have a simple cheese filling or include other ingredients, such as refried beans or sautéed onions and peppers. Cook quesadillas in a dry frying pan, under the broiler or on the barbecue. Serve them whole with a salsa garnish for a light meal. Cut in small wedges, they also make tasty appetizers, popular with both adults and children. However you enjoy them, they bring a terrific calcium boost.

6	**small (about 6 in/15 cm) flour tortillas**	6
3 oz	**Monterey Jack cheese, sliced**	90 g
2 tbsp	**chopped pickled jalapeño (optional)**	25 mL
3/4 cup	**salsa**	175 mL

1. Cover one half of each tortilla with cheese and jalapeños. Fold the other half over.

2. Heat a large skillet or grill. Cook quesadillas in a single layer until lightly browned. Turn to brown other side. Serve with a dollop of salsa.

Makes 2 servings.

Cheese Challenge

In the world of cheese, all things are not equal. For instance, cottage cheese and cream cheese fail to deliver the full nutritional benefits associated with dairy products. Even though well endowed in protein and low in fat, 1/2 cup (125 mL) of cottage cheese has only 61 mg of calcium, compared to 224 mg in the same amount of yogurt or 204 mg in 1 oz (30 g) of Cheddar cheese. Cream cheese is not only a poor source of calcium, containing just 24 mg per oz (30 g), but it has very little protein and a fair share of saturated fat, as do most cheeses. So savour a small amount of your favourite higher fat cheeses for their peerless flavour and nutritional bonus, but look to lower fat dairy products as your main calcium source.

Hummus-Stuffed Pita

Hummus is so good we had to include a recipe. Stuff it in pita breads to make a savoury sandwich, or serve it as a dip with tortilla dippers (page 119) or fresh veggies. Fibre-rich and low in fat, hummus is perfect to keep on hand for quick snacks.

1	**can (19 oz/ 540 mL) chick-peas or white kidney beans, drained and rinsed**	1
2	**cloves garlic, minced**	2
3 tbsp	**toasted sesame seeds (instructions below)**	45 mL
2 tbsp	**fresh lemon juice**	25 mL
1 tbsp	**water**	15 mL
1/2 tsp	**ground cumin**	2 mL
1/4 tsp	**salt**	1 mL
1/4 tsp	**hot pepper sauce (optional)**	1 mL
2 tbsp	**chopped fresh parsley**	25 mL
2	**pita bread (about 6 inch/15 cm)**	2
2	**leaves lettuce**	2

1. In food processor or blender, process chick-peas, garlic, sesame seeds, lemon juice, water, cumin, salt and pepper sauce (if using) until very smooth. Add a bit more water if needed to give a smooth consistency. Add parsley and process until mixed.

2. Cut pitas in half. Using a knife, separate each half to form a pocket. Spoon about 1/4 cup (50 mL) hummus into each half and tuck a lettuce leaf on top. Store any remaining hummus in covered container in refrigerator for up to one week.

Makes 2 servings with pita, and 1 cup (250 mL) hummus left for another use.

To Toast Sesame Seeds

Place sesame seeds in a small microwave-safe dish; microwave on 100% power for 3 minutes or until lightly browned, stirring frequently.

PER SERVING

Calories 365
Protein 15 g
Total Fat 7 g
  saturated 0.8 g
  monounsaturated 1.9 g
  polyunsaturated 2.9 g
Carbohydrate 62 g
  fibre 6 g
Calcium 178 mg
Folacin 270 mcg
Sodium 694 mg

FOOD GUIDE SERVINGS

2 1

Rounding Out the Meal

Quick Coleslaw (page 99)
fresh mango slices

Attention All Women

Folate and iron, two nutrients that are often in short supply in women's diets, are plentiful in this hummus pita, with over 40% of the desirable daily intake.

Tuna Melt

PER SERVING

Calories 380
Protein 26 g
Total Fat 12 g
  saturated 4.8 g
  monounsaturated 4.1 g
  polyunsaturated 1.6 g
Carbohydrate 43 g
  fibre 2 g
Calcium 189 mg
Folacin 46 mcg
Sodium 745 mg

FOOD GUIDE SERVINGS

2  1/2   1/2   1

This old favourite is worth remembering when you need a fast meal. Use any type of bread or buns, and if you don't have an apple on hand, just add a bit of celery. To make lunch for special guests, use slices of baguette or crusty rolls as the base.

1	**can (6 oz/170 g) water-packed tuna, drained**	1
1	**small unpeeled apple, cut into small cubes**	1
1/3 cup	**shredded Cheddar cheese** 75 mL	
2 tbsp	**finely chopped onion** 25 mL	
1 tbsp	**light mayonnaise** 15 mL	
1/2 tsp	**lemon juice** 2 mL	
	Salt and pepper	
4	**slices rye or other whole-grain bread** 4	
	Chopped parsley (optional)	

Rounding Out the Meal

raw veggies and assorted pickles

melon slices with lemon

1. In bowl, combine tuna, apple, cheese, onion, mayonnaise and lemon juice. Season with salt and pepper to taste.

2. Lightly toast bread on both sides. Spread tuna mixture evenly over slices. Place under broiler for 2 to 3 minutes or until cheese is slightly melted. Sprinkle with a bit of parsley (if using) before serving.

Makes 2 servings.

Keep It Fresh

If one lemon gives more juice than you need, place 1 tablespoon (15 mL) amounts of juice in individual ice cube containers and pop in the freezer. When frozen, remove the frozen cubes and store them in a plastic bag. The flavour of fresh juice is far superior to the bottled kind.

Western Wrap

A tortilla wrap gives a new twist to this favourite sandwich. Experiment with other additions such as sausage, red onion, chopped jalapeños or a sprinkling of Cheddar or feta cheese.

2	**eggs**	2
1 tbsp	**water**	15 mL
1 tsp	**butter or margarine**	5 mL
2 tbsp	**chopped cooked ham or crumbled bacon**	25 mL
1 tbsp	**chopped sweet green pepper**	15 mL
1 tbsp	**chopped green or cooking onion**	15 mL
	Salt and pepper	
2 tbsp	**salsa**	25 mL
1	**large (about 9 inch/23 cm) flour tortilla**	1

1. In small bowl, gently whisk eggs and water. Set aside.

2. Melt butter in a small nonstick skillet over medium heat. Add ham, green pepper and onion; cook for 30 seconds or until onion is slightly softened.

3. Pour in egg mixture; let cook until almost set, lifting edges to allow uncooked mixture to run underneath. Carefully turn egg and cook other side. Season with salt and pepper to taste.

4. Spread salsa on warmed tortilla, slide western on top and roll up.

Makes 1 sandwich.

Variation:
Classic Western Sandwich
Place western between two slices of toasted whole wheat or other whole grain bread.

PER SERVING

Calories 450
Protein 24 g
Total Fat 22 g
  saturated 7.3 g
  monounsaturated 8.3 g
  polyunsaturated 3.6 g
Carbohydrate 39 g
  fibre 3 g
Calcium 91 mg
Folacin 97 mcg
Sodium 922 mg

FOOD GUIDE SERVINGS

2   1/2   1

Rounding Out the Meal

large glass of tomato juice

fresh pear

Egg-Topped Bruschetta Bagel

PER SERVING

Calories 400
Protein 18 g
Total Fat 13 g
  saturated 3.3 g
  monounsaturated 5.8 g
  polyunsaturated 1.8 g
Carbohydrate 53 g
  fibre 1 g
Calcium 112 mg
Folacin 96 mcg
Sodium 666 mg

FOOD GUIDE SERVINGS

3  1/2   1

**Rounding Out
the Meal**

carrot and celery sticks
fruit topped with yogurt

A bagel grilled with olive oil in the Italian tradition and topped with tomatoes and scrambled egg makes a savoury open-faced sandwich.

1	**ripe tomato, seeded and chopped**	1
1	**clove garlic, crushed**	1
1 tbsp	**chopped fresh parsley**	15 mL
1 tbsp	**chopped fresh basil, or 1 tsp (5 mL) dried**	15 mL
pinch	**salt and pepper**	pinch
2	**eggs**	2
1 tbsp	**milk**	15 mL
2	**plain bagels**	2
2 tsp	**olive oil**	10 mL
4 tsp	**grated Parmesan cheese**	20 mL

1. In small bowl, combine tomato, garlic, parsley, basil, salt and pepper; set aside.

2. In small microwave-safe bowl or 2-cup (500 mL) glass measuring cup, beat together eggs and milk. Microwave on 70% power for 1 1/2 minutes or until almost set, stirring several times during the last half of cooking. Let stand for 1 minute. Do not overcook, as egg will continue to set during the standing time.

3. Meanwhile, cut bagel in half and brush each half with oil. Place under broiler until lightly toasted. Divide tomato mixture among bagel halves; top each with 1 tsp (5 mL) cheese. Broil just until heated. Top each half bagel with a portion of egg.

Makes 2 servings.

Eggs for Mature Palates

The high quality of an egg's protein, its great digestibility and excellent mix of vitamins and minerals make it one of the best food sources for older adults. In addition, egg yolks contain lutein and zeaxanthin, two compounds associated with less macular degeneration in the eye. This condition of the retina is the leading cause of blindness among the aged.

Warm Quinoa Vegetable Salad

Quinoa, a small grain from South America, was a staple of the ancient Incas, who called it the mother grain, having probably recognized the plant's high nutritional value. The initial toasting greatly improves its nut-like flavour. Like rice, it expands to about four times its volume and cooks together with the vegetables for an excellent lunch.

1/2 cup	**quinoa, rinsed and drained**	125 mL
1/2 cup	**water**	125 mL
1/2 cup	**frozen cut green beans**	125 mL
1/2 cup	**frozen corn**	125 mL
1/2 cup	**thinly sliced carrot**	125 mL
2 tsp	**soy sauce**	10 mL
1/2 cup	**frozen peas**	125 mL
4	**lettuce leaves**	4
2 tbsp	**chopped cashew or pistachio nuts**	25 mL
1	**tomato, sliced in wedges**	1

1. In small nonstick skillet over medium-high heat, cook quinoa, stirring frequently, for 10 minutes or until the grains begin to snap and are slightly toasted.

2. Add water, beans, corn, carrot and soy sauce. Bring to a boil; reduce heat, cover and simmer for 12 minutes or until quinoa and vegetables are tender.

3. Rinse peas in hot water to defrost and add to mixture.

4. Place 2 lettuce leaves on each plate; mound quinoa in centre. Sprinkle with nuts and garnish with tomato wedges.

Makes 2 servings.

Starring Quinoa

A star among grains, quinoa is often considered a supergrain due in part to its generous content of iron and magnesium and the high quality of its protein. Quinoa grains are protected by a bitter saponin coating, usually removed during processing. Rinsing the grain before cooking will get rid of any powdery residue.

PER SERVING

Calories 315
Protein 12 g
Total Fat 7 g
  saturated 1.2 g
  monounsaturated 3.1 g
  polyunsaturated 2.0 g
Carbohydrate 55 g
  fibre 8 g
Calcium 65 mg
Folacin 84 mcg
Sodium 329 mg

FOOD GUIDE SERVINGS

1 1/2   2 1/2

Rounding Out the Meal

vanilla yogurt or banana milkshake

Wild Rice and Barley Salad

PER SERVING

Calories 295
Protein 9 g
Total Fat 9 g
  saturated 1.2 g
  monounsaturated 5.4 g
  polyunsaturated 1.3 g
Carbohydrate 51 g
  fibre 9 g
Calcium 36 mg
Folacin 72 mcg
Sodium 572 mg

FOOD GUIDE SERVINGS

2   2

Rounding Out the Meal

cheese-topped toast

fresh fruit

Savouring the Olive

Pressing tree-ripened olives extracts a healthful, mostly monounsaturated oil that can vary widely in flavour and fragrance. Extra virgin and virgin olive oil are cold pressed and have the fruitiest flavour. Oil labelled simply "olive oil" is generally a combination of refined and virgin oil.

The recipe transforms barley into a tasty cold salad. Wild rice adds a pleasing gourmet touch, although it can be omitted. This salad will keep for several days in the refrigerator.

2 tbsp	**wild rice**	25 mL
1/3 cup	**pearl barley**	75 mL
3/4 cup	**frozen corn kernels**	175 mL
1/2	**sweet red pepper, diced**	1/2
3 tbsp	**finely chopped red or sweet onion**	45 mL
1 tbsp	**olive or vegetable oil**	15 mL
1 tbsp	**white wine vinegar**	15 mL
1/2 tsp	**Dijon mustard**	2 mL
1/4 tsp	**salt**	1 mL
1/4 tsp	**granulated sugar**	1 mL
2 tbsp	**finely chopped parsley**	25 mL
2	**leaves romaine or other lettuce**	2
1	**tomato, cut in wedges**	1

1. Bring a medium saucepan of salted water to a boil. Add wild rice; reduce heat, cover and simmer for 10 minutes. Add barley; return to a boil; cover and simmer for 30 minutes or until barley is tender. Remove from heat and drain. Return hot grains to saucepan. Add corn, stirring until defrosted. Stir in pepper and onion.

2. In small bowl or jar with tight-fitting lid, whisk or shake together oil, vinegar, mustard, salt and sugar. Pour over barley and mix thoroughly. Stir in parsley. Transfer to a covered container and chill for several hours in refrigerator.

3. Place lettuce leaves on plates and mound salad over top. Garnish with tomato wedges.

Makes 2 servings.

Tabbouleh Salad with Feta Cheese

It's not traditional, but feta cheese and a bit of balsamic vinegar add superior flavour to this popular salad from the Middle East. Be sure to use fresh lemon juice. And if you have it available, sprinkle the finished salad with a bit of chopped fresh mint.

1/2 cup	**bulgur**	125 mL
pinch	**salt**	pinch
3/4 cup	**boiling water**	175 mL
1	**small clove garlic, minced**	1
1 tbsp	**olive oil**	15 mL
1 tbsp	**fresh lemon juice**	15 mL
1 tsp	**balsamic vinegar**	5 mL
1 cup	**quartered cherry tomatoes, or 1 large tomato, diced**	250 mL
1	**green onion, chopped**	1
1/2 cup	**chopped fresh parsley**	125 mL
1/3 cup	**crumbled feta cheese**	75 mL

1. In bowl, place bulgur and salt; cover with boiling water. Let stand for 12 minutes. Fluff with a fork.

2. In small bowl or jar with tight-fitting lid, whisk or shake together garlic, oil, lemon juice and vinegar. Toss with bulgur.

3. Mix in tomatoes, onion, parsley and feta. Serve at room temperature or chill until serving time.

Makes 2 servings.

The Many Faces of Wheat

Bulgur is the name given to whole grain wheat kernels that have been cooked, dried and cracked. Bulgur carries the goodness of whole wheat, including fibre, and has a pleasant nutty flavour. Cracked wheat is similar to bulgur but is not cooked. Couscous also has a granular appearance, but the pellets are made from wheat flour, then steamed and dried.

PER SERVING

Calories 280
Protein 9 g
Total Fat 14 g
  saturated 5.0 g
  monounsaturated 6.5 g
  polyunsaturated 1.1 g
Carbohydrate 34 g
  fibre 5 g
Calcium 173 mg
Folacin 59 mcg
Sodium 461 mg

FOOD GUIDE SERVINGS

1   1 1/2   1/2

Rounding Out the Meal

pita bread triangles

Maple Bananas (page 188)

Mediterranean Chicken Salad

This salad is so good you may want to cook extra chicken the next time you are grilling to use in this lively luncheon entrée enhanced by Mediterranean flavours. If you get slices of smoked turkey from the deli, ask that they be cut slightly thicker than usual.

PER SERVING

Calories 475
Protein 32 g
Total Fat 17 g
  saturated 5.9 g
  monounsaturated 8.1 g
  polyunsaturated 2.0 g
Carbohydrate 47 g
  fibre 4 g
Calcium 177 mg
Folacin 145 mcg
Sodium 564 mg

FOOD GUIDE SERVINGS

1   1 1/2   1/2   1

Rounding Out the Meal

slices of crusty bread
Warm Peach Gratin
(page 186)

1 cup	medium pasta such as penne or fusilli, about 3 1/2 oz (100 g)	250 mL
1	small clove garlic, minced	1
1/8 tsp	salt	0.5 mL
1 tbsp	red wine vinegar	15 mL
1 tbsp	olive oil	15 mL
1/8 tsp	granulated sugar	0.5 mL
	Ground black pepper	
1/2 cup	cooked chicken or turkey, cut in strips	125 mL
1	ripe tomato, cut into wedges	1
1	small zucchini, sliced	1
1/2	sweet red pepper, cut in thin strips	1/2
1/3 cup	crumbled feta cheese	75 mL
2 tbsp	chopped black olives	25 mL
2 tbsp	fresh basil leaves, or 1/2 tsp (2 mL) dried	25 mL

1. In large pot of boiling salted water, cook pasta for 8 minutes or until tender but firm; drain.

2. Meanwhile, in a small bowl, mash garlic and salt to form a paste. Add vinegar, oil, sugar and black pepper to taste. Whisk until well blended.

3. In salad bowl, place pasta, chicken, tomato, zucchini, sweet pepper, feta, olives and basil. Toss with dressing and refrigerate until serving time.

Makes 2 servings.

Potato Salad with Smoked Oysters

Cook extra potatoes to have ready for this epicurean salad. Another time replace the smoked oysters with smoked salmon, sliced prosciutto or hard-cooked egg.

8	small red potatoes, about 1 lb (500 g)	8
1	stalk celery, thinly sliced	1
1/4 cup	thinly sliced red onion	50 mL
1 tbsp	olive oil	15 mL
1 tbsp	fresh lemon juice	15 mL
1	can (3 oz/85 g) smoked oysters, drained	1
2 tbsp	chopped fresh parsley	25 mL
	Salt and ground black pepper	
4	leaves Bibb or Boston lettuce	4

1. In pot of salted water, cook potatoes for 12 minutes or just until tender. Drain and let cool. Cut into quarters. Place in bowl; add celery and onion.

2. In small bowl or jar with tight-fitting lid, whisk or shake together oil and lemon juice. Pour over potatoes; mix well. Mix in oysters and parsley. Add salt and pepper to taste.

3. Arrange lettuce leaves on 2 serving plates; mound salad over top.

Makes 2 servings.

One Potato, Two Potato

All potatoes are not created equal. Don't worry about varietal names, since it is the shape of white-fleshed potatoes that is an indication of their culinary characteristics. Round whites and round reds are the ones to use for boiling and in salads. Their relatively high moisture and lower starch gives them a waxy texture which holds its shape when cooked. Long potatoes, with less moisture and more starch, cook to a dry, fluffy texture and are a much better choice for baking, mashing and french-frying. Prized for its creamy yellow flesh, Yukon Gold is one of the few all-purpose potatoes. For full nutritional benefits, cook potatoes in their skins. Adding salt to the cooking water (about 1 tsp /5 mL to 4 cups/1L water) helps prevent cut potatoes from crumbling during cooking.

PER SERVING

Calories 275
Protein 9 g
Total Fat 8 g
  saturated 1.3 g
  monounsaturated 5.3 g
  polyunsaturated 1.1 g
Carbohydrate 44 g
  fibre 5 g
Calcium 72 mg
Folacin 64 mcg
Sodium 697 mg

FOOD GUIDE SERVINGS

 3 🍓   1/2 🥬

Rounding Out the Meal

Sherried Cream of Broccoli Soup (page 173)

fresh fruit

Warm Steak Salad with Fruit

PER SERVING

Calories 280
Protein 18 g
Total Fat 16 g
  saturated 3.8 g
  monounsaturated 7.6 g
  polyunsaturated 2.6 g
Carbohydrate 19 g
  fibre 4 g
Calcium 76 mg
Folacin 59 mcg
Sodium 111 mg

FOOD GUIDE SERVINGS

2   1

**Rounding Out
the Meal**

Curried Carrot Parsnip
Soup (page 172) with rye
crackers

frozen yogurt

Steaks for a barbecue are often more than enough to serve one person. If you set aside the extra, you can make this warm salad for lunch the next day. It is also delicious with grilled chicken.

3 cups	**mixed greens (leaf lettuces and spinach)**	750 mL
1	**fresh pear or peach, diced, or 1/2 cup (125 mL) sliced strawberries or canned mandarin oranges**	1
2	**slices Spanish or red onion, separated into rings**	2
4 oz	**cooked steak or roast, cut into thin slivers**	125 g
2 tbsp	**orange juice**	25 mL
1 tbsp	**red wine vinegar**	15 mL
1 tbsp	**vegetable oil**	15 mL
pinch	**salt**	pinch
pinch	**ground black pepper**	pinch

1. In salad bowl, place greens; top with fruit, onion and meat.

2. In small microwave-safe container, whisk together orange juice, vinegar, oil, sugar, salt and pepper. Microwave on 100% power for 20 seconds or until dressing comes to a boil. Pour over salad and toss lightly.

Makes 2 servings.

Dinner Is Served

As a moment to pause and reflect on the day's accomplishments or set aside its frustrations, dinner-time brings an expectation of satisfaction and reward. For answers to the age-old question, "What's for Dinner?" we searched for delicious, nutritious and innovative solutions that require a minimum of preparation. Here, you will find a traditional European favourite, such as schnitzel, adorned with a New World flavour of salsa, red lentils blended into a delicious and healthy pasta topping, and more than half a dozen ways to dress up fish fillets.

Our dinners are served with suggestions for vegetable and starch accompaniments, accented with a variety of savoury flavourings to tempt the most capricious palate. These suggestions bring a remarkable payoff, often delivering a full complement of vitamins A and C and a good third of fibre and folate needs. A basic nutritional analysis for both the main dish and the total dinner is provided. As well, the symbols tell at a glance both the food groups and the number of Canada's Food Guide servings provided by one serving of each satisfying dinner. But one meal can't do it all, no matter how balanced; a good dinner is but a complement to a wise breakfast and lunch. If dinner is served with a crusty roll, a glass of wine or a dessert, select these elements wisely to enhance the quality of the meal and the balance of the day's food choices. This is Savoury Wisdom.

Naturally we invite you to mix and match the suggestions for "Rounding Out the Meals" to accommodate your taste and what you have on hand, or to complement our Shelf Solutions. Be a bit adventurous and try some less familiar grains and vegetables such as bulgur, fennel or Swiss chard; we guarantee a pleasant surprise.

Chicken Fajitas   68

Chicken in Cider   70

Sesame Baked Chicken   72

Roasted Chicken and Vegetables   74

Ground Turkey with Vegetables and Rice   76

Turkey Stuffed Peppers   78

Schnitzel with Salsa   80

Pork Chops with Pears and Ginger   82

Orange Beef Stir-Fry   84

Two-Pepper Beef Stew with Farfalle   86

Steak with Mushroom Wine Sauce   88

Hot Taco Beef with Rice   90

Wine-Poached Salmon with Capers   92

Halibut Steak with Roasted Red Peppers   94

Fish Baked with Vegetables *En Papillote*   96

Citrus Shrimp with Asian Noodles   98

Quick Ways with Fillets   100

Pasta Layers with Spinach and Ricotta   102

Caribbean Beans and Rice   104

Soybeans with Snow Peas and Pineapple   106

Tofu Vegetable Stir-Fry   108

Barley Lentil Bake   110

Pasta Toppings   112

Chicken Fajitas

PER SERVING
OF MAIN DISH

Calories 605
Protein 35 g
Total Fat 19 g
  saturated 3.4 g
  monounsaturated 9.6 g
  polyunsaturated 4.7 g
Carbohydrate 74 g
  fibre 8 g
Calcium 193 mg
Folacin 167 mcg
Sodium 778 mg

FOOD GUIDE SERVINGS

3   2   1

Bursting with bold flavours, fajitas are one of the most popular Tex-Mex dishes. Originally made with beef flank or skirt steak, fajitas now contain all kinds of meat as well as tofu and chick-peas. This nicely seasoned chicken version is brimming with colourful vegetables for a casual supper.

1	**boneless chicken breast, about 6 oz (180 g)**	1
1/2 tsp	**ground cumin**	2 mL
1/2 tsp	**chili powder**	2 mL
1 tsp	**vegetable oil**	5 mL
1	**small zucchini, cut in thin wedges 2 in (5 cm) long**	1
1/2	**sweet red pepper, cut in strips**	1/2
1/2	**sweet green pepper, cut in strips**	1/2
1/2	**red onion, cut in thin wedges**	1/2
6	**small (about 6 inch /15 cm) flour tortillas**	6
1/2 cup	**Guacamole (recipe below)**	125 mL
1/2 cup	**plain yogurt**	125 mL

1. Cut chicken into thin strips. Sprinkle with cumin and chili powder.

2. In large nonstick skillet, heat oil over high heat. Add chicken; cook for 1 minute. Turn chicken. Add zucchini, peppers and onion. Cook quickly, stirring constantly, for 4 minutes or until vegetables are tender-crisp.

3. Microwave tortillas on 100% power for 30 seconds or until warm. Spoon chicken mixture down centre of each tortilla; roll up. Garnish with guacamole and yogurt.

Makes 2 servings.

Guacamole

Combine 1/2 peeled and mashed avocado, 1 small chopped tomato, 1 minced clove garlic, 1 tsp (5 mL) fresh lemon juice, 1 tsp (5 mL) finely chopped red onion, a pinch ground cumin and a pinch salt.

Makes about 1/2 cup (125 mL).

Rounding Out the Meal

Fajitas make a complete meal, but a side dish of sliced cucumbers with a splash of flavoured vinegar or a raw veggie plate are pleasing condiments.

Avocados

Avocados, with their smooth buttery texture and unique flavour, are a hallmark of Mexican cuisine. A tropical fruit, the avocado is unique among fruits for its high fat content. However, most of the fat is monounsaturated, the same heart-healthy type found in olive and canola oil. Avocados are usually sold underripe so allow 2 to 3 days before using. A ripe avocado should yield slightly when pressed. Once cut, avocado flesh darkens quickly with exposure to air. The browning has no effect on the flavour, but the appearance is not appealing. Leave the pit in the unused half and rub the cut surface with lemon juice. Then cover with a piece of plastic wrap and keep in the fridge no longer than two days.

Chicken in Cider

PER SERVING
OF MAIN DISH

Calories 275
Protein 35 g
Total Fat 5 g
    saturated 0.8 g
    monounsaturated 2.1 g
    polyunsaturated 1.2 g
Carbohydrate 23 g
    fibre 2 g
Calcium 28 mg
Folacin 11 mcg
Sodium 213 mg

At the turn of the century, cooks in rural Ontario searched for ways to give flavour to an old boiling fowl. Cooking in apple cider was a popular choice, which makes a satisfying sauce for a rice pilaf.

1 tsp	**vegetable oil**	5 mL
2	**boneless chicken breasts, about 5 oz (150 g) each**	2
1	**small onion, chopped**	1
1/2 cup	**apple cider or juice**	125 mL
1/4 tsp	**dried marjoram**	1 mL
1/4 tsp	**dried savory**	1 mL
1/8 tsp	**salt**	0.5 mL
1/8 tsp	**ground black pepper**	0.5 mL
1	**tart apple, unpeeled and cut in wedges**	1

1. In small nonstick skillet, heat oil over medium-high heat. Add chicken and onion; cook chicken for 3 minutes per side.

2. Add cider, marjoram, savory, salt and pepper. Place apple on top of chicken. Bring liquid to a boil; reduce heat, cover and simmer for 10 minutes or until chicken is no longer pink and liquid is slightly reduced. Remove chicken and apples. Boil liquid several minutes to reduce, if desired. Serve with Rice Pilaf (recipe below).

Makes 2 servings.

Rounding Out the Meal
Rice Pilaf

A sprinkling of currants and nuts adds flavour and texture to pilaf.

In small saucepan, bring 1 cup (250 mL) chicken broth to a boil. Add 1/2 cup (125 mL) rice and 1 tbsp (15 mL) currants. Reduce heat, cover and simmer for 20 minutes or until liquid is absorbed. Stir in 1 tbsp (15 mL) toasted chopped pecans or walnuts and salt and pepper to taste.

Green Beans and Cauliflower with Red Onion

Red, green and white combine for a colourful vegetable medley.

Steam 1 cup (250 mL) whole green beans and 1 cup (250 mL) cauliflower florets for 5 to 7 minutes or until tender but firm. Drain and transfer to serving dish. Meanwhile, in small microwave-safe dish, combine 1 tsp (5 mL) vegetable oil and 1/3 cup (75 mL) chopped red onion. Microwave on 100% power for 1 minute or just until tender. Stir in 1 tbsp (15 mL) finely chopped parsley. Season with salt and pepper to taste.

Lettuces with Ranch Dressing

Ranch dressing was first served at a California ranch in the 1950s. It has since come to refer to any dressing with a buttermilk flavour.

In salad bowl, combine about 3 cups (750 mL) assorted lettuces such as red oak and green leaf. Toss with dressing.

Dressing: In small bowl, whisk together 1/4 cup (50 mL) buttermilk or yogurt, 1 tbsp (15 mL) light mayonnaise, 1 tbsp (15 mL) chopped parsley, 1 tsp (5 mL) lemon juice, 1 small minced clove garlic and salt and ground black pepper to taste.

Clean and Separate for Food Safety

Raw poultry as well as all raw meats and seafood contain naturally occurring bacteria. When cutting these foods, be sure to wash the cutting board and knives in very hot soapy water to avoid spreading these bacteria. And keep raw poultry, meat and seafood well away from other foods, especially any that will be served uncooked. When it is properly cooked, chicken has no traces of pink.

PER SERVING
WITH ROUND OUTS

Calories 605
Protein 46 g
Total Fat 13 g
  saturated 1.9 g
  monounsaturated 6.7 g
  polyunsaturated 3.6 g
Carbohydrate 77 g
  fibre 7 g
Calcium 187 mg
Folacin 109 mcg
Sodium 686 mg

FOOD GUIDE SERVINGS

1 1/2   4   1 1/2

Sesame Baked Chicken

PER SERVING
OF MAIN DISH

Calories 330
Protein 47 g
Total Fat 7 g
  saturated 1.8 g
  monounsaturated 2.4 g
  polyunsaturated 2.2 g
Carbohydrate 17 g
  fibre 1 g
Calcium 168 mg
Folacin 29 mcg
Sodium 494 mg

Sesame seeds add a pleasing crunch to this popular yogurt-crumb coating for chicken.

1/3 cup	**fine dry bread crumbs**	75 mL
1 tbsp	**sesame seeds**	15 mL
1/3 cup	**plain yogurt**	75 mL
1 tbsp	**Dijon mustard**	15 mL
1/8 tsp	**salt**	0.5 mL
2	**skinless chicken breast halves or legs, about 12 oz (375 g) total**	2

1. In a shallow bowl, combine crumbs and seeds.

2. In a second shallow bowl, combine yogurt, mustard and salt.

3. Dip chicken into mustard mixture and roll in crumb mixture.

4. Place chicken in a flat baking dish. Bake, uncovered, in 375°F (190°C) oven for 40 to 50 minutes or until chicken is no longer pink in the centre.

Makes 2 servings.

The Sesame Touch

The touch of sesame seed adds a unique flavour as well as valuable iron and fibre. The fat content of sesame seeds is not negligible, but most of it is unsaturated. Calcium is also present in good quantity in sesame seeds, but to a large extent is unavailable to the body.

Rounding Out the Meal

Roasted Potatoes

Roast potatoes to a fragrant crispness alongside the chicken.

Peel 2 potatoes and cut each into 4 to 6 pieces. Place potatoes in a small bowl. Add 1 tsp (5 mL) vegetable oil and 1/2 tsp (2 mL) dried thyme; mix well. Place potatoes on baking sheet to roast in 375°F (190°C) oven for 30 minutes alongside the chicken.

Carrots Provençales

The fruity flavour of black olives, a hint of garlic and olive oil transform ordinary carrots into a rewarding side dish.

Cook 8 oz (250 g) baby carrots in 1/4 cup (50 mL) water for 6 to 7 minutes or until tender. Drain. Add 4 chopped black olives, 1 tsp (5 mL) olive oil, 1 minced clove garlic and a pinch of salt and ground black pepper; stir and heat through.

Cabbage Toss

Toss a simple yogurt dressing with your choice of cabbage. Savoy and napa are considered to be the sweetest and most flavourful members of the cabbage family, but use green or red if they are young and mild.

In salad bowl, combine 2 cups (500 mL) finely sliced cabbage, 1/4 cup (50 mL) chopped celery and 1/4 cup (50 mL) chopped sweet red pepper. Toss with dressing.

Dressing: In small bowl, whisk together 2 tbsp (25 mL) plain yogurt, 1 tbsp (15 mL) light mayonnaise, 1/4 tsp (1 mL) dried tarragon, 1/4 tsp (1 mL) granulated sugar, 1/4 tsp (1 mL) wine vinegar and a pinch salt.

PER SERVING
WITH ROUND OUTS

Calories 575
Protein 53 g
Total Fat 16 g
  saturated 2.9 g
  monounsaturated 7.5 g
  polyunsaturated 4.3 g
Carbohydrate 57 g
  fibre 5 g
Calcium 297 mg
Folacin 113 mcg
Sodium 701 mg

FOOD GUIDE SERVINGS

1/2   3 1/2   1 1/2

Roasted Chicken and Vegetables

A flavourful marinade transforms chicken and assorted vegetables into an aromatic feast that requires no attention once you have it in the oven.

Marinade

1	**clove garlic, minced**	1
1/3 cup	**dry white wine or sherry**	75 mL
2 tbsp	**vegetable oil**	25 mL
1 tbsp	**balsamic vinegar**	15 mL
1 tbsp	**Dijon mustard**	15 mL
1/2 tsp	**dried marjoram**	2 mL
1/2 tsp	**dried thyme**	2 mL
1/2 tsp	**dried oregano**	2 mL
1/8 tsp	**salt**	0.5 mL
1/8 tsp	**ground black pepper**	0.5 mL

Chicken and Vegetables

2	**skinless chicken breasts, halves or legs, about 12 oz (375 g)**	2
4	**small whole onions**	4
1	**sweet potato, cut into large chunks**	1
1	**white potato, cut into quarters**	1
1	**sweet red or green pepper, cut in quarters**	1
1	**small zucchini, cut in half lengthwise**	1
2	**Belgian endive, cut in half (optional)**	2

1. Marinade: In small bowl, whisk together garlic, wine, oil, vinegar, mustard, marjoram, thyme, oregano, salt and pepper.

2. Chicken and Vegetables: Place chicken in a small plastic bag; pour in marinade. Refrigerate up to 4 hours, turning bag at least once.

3. Remove chicken from marinade; place on shallow baking pan. Pour marinade into a small saucepan. Bring to a boil; reduce heat and simmer for 5 minutes.

4. Meanwhile, place onions, sweet potato, white potato and pepper into a large bowl. Pour marinade over; toss to coat evenly. Lift vegetables from marinade and place on baking pan. Brush zucchini and endive with remaining marinade and place on pan.

5. Bake in 375°F (190°C) oven for 40 to 50 minutes or until potatoes are soft and chicken is no longer pink. Brush with marinade once during baking.

Note: If chicken pieces are large, bake them for 10 to 15 minutes before adding vegetables to pan.

Makes 2 servings.

Rounding Out the Meal
Greens with Red Cabbage and Roquefort Dressing

Red cabbage adds colour and texture to a green salad. Part of the remaining head can be steamed and tossed with a bit of currant jelly and caraway seeds for a tasty side dish.

In salad bowl, combine 2 cups (500 mL) assorted lettuces and 1/2 cup (125 mL) thinly sliced red cabbage. Toss with dressing.

Dressing: In small bowl, break up 2 tbsp (25 mL) Roquefort or other blue cheese; stir in 1/4 cup (50 mL) plain yogurt and 1 small minced shallot. Add ground black pepper to taste.

Vitamin A Ups and Downs

For most of us, our daily intake of vitamin A fluctuates quite a bit. We rely to a large extent on a few star sources to give us our fill. Sweet potatoes are one of them. In this meal they provide well above the daily requirement of vitamin A. The range of vitamin A that you will find in the dinners in this book is wide, going from about one-fifth to two-and-a-half times the amount we need. Most of our dinners attain a near perfect score of well over 80% of the day's requirement for this vitamin.

PER SERVING
WITH ROUND OUTS

Calories 640
Protein 54 g
Total Fat 23 g
  saturated 5.0 g
  monounsaturated 10.4 g
  polyunsaturated 6.0 g
Carbohydrate 52 g
  fibre 7 g
Calcium 282 mg
Folacin 101 mcg
Sodium 585 mg

FOOD GUIDE SERVINGS

4 🍓   1/2 🥛   1 1/2 🥦

Ground Turkey with Vegetables and Rice

PER SERVING
OF MAIN DISH

Calories 470
Protein 28 g
Total Fat 13 g
    saturated 3.0 g
    monounsaturated 5.1 g
    polyunsaturated 3.9 g
Carbohydrate 62 g
    fibre 5 g
Calcium 162 mg
Folacin 73 mcg
Sodium 1033 mg

In this easy one-dish meal, lean ground turkey simmers with squash and broccoli for a tantalizing flavour, leaving you lots of time to fill a tall glass with soda water and cranberry juice or white wine to enjoy while your dinner cooks. Another time, use rutabagas and green beans or carotene-rich sweet potatoes and green peas.

1 tsp	**vegetable oil**	5 mL
1	**small onion, chopped**	1
1	**clove garlic, minced**	1
1/2 lb	**lean ground turkey**	250 g
2 cups	**cubed, peeled butternut squash, rutabaga or sweet potato, about 10 oz (300 g)**	500 mL
1 1/3 cups	**chicken broth or white wine**	325 mL
1/2 cup	**long-grain white rice**	125 mL
1 tsp	**dried thyme**	5 mL
1 1/2 cups	**fresh or frozen broccoli florets**	375 mL
	Salt and ground black pepper	

1. In medium nonstick skillet, heat oil over medium heat. Add onion and garlic; cook, stirring often, for 3 minutes or until onion is soft. Add turkey; cook, stirring, for 5 minutes or until no pink remains.

2. Add squash, broth, rice and thyme. Bring to a boil over high heat; reduce heat, cover and simmer for 20 minutes. Add broccoli; return to a boil, cover and simmer for 8 minutes or until the broccoli is tender-crisp and the liquid is absorbed. Season with salt and pepper to taste.

Makes 2 servings.

Rounding Out the Meal
Oak Leaf Salad with Herb Dressing

Oak leaf lettuce is a tender, colourful green. This simple vinaigrette goes with any salad of mixed greens.

In salad bowl, place about 3 cups (750 mL) torn red oak leaf lettuce leaves. Toss with dressing.

Dressing: In small bowl, whisk together 1 tbsp (15 mL) cider vinegar, 1 tbsp (15 mL) vegetable oil and 1 tbsp (15 mL) chicken broth. Add 1 tsp (5 mL) chopped parsley or any fresh herb, 1/4 tsp (1 mL) granulated sugar, 1/4 tsp (1 mL) Dijon mustard and salt and pepper to taste.

Rutabaga or Turnip?

Also known as Swede turnips, large, yellow-fleshed rutabagas are sometimes confused with the white, purple-topped turnips. As you might expect, the yellow rutabagas have more beta carotene and vitamin C than do their paler relatives.

PER SERVING
WITH ROUND OUTS

Calories 550
Protein 29 g
Total Fat 21 g
  saturated 3.5 g
  monounsaturated 9.3 g
  polyunsaturated 6.1 g
Carbohydrate 66 g
  fibre 6 g
Calcium 218 mg
Folacin 105 mcg
Sodium 1071 mg

FOOD GUIDE SERVINGS

1 1/2  4   1 1/2

Turkey Stuffed Peppers

In this recipe, stuffed peppers are given a modern twist with ground turkey filling a sweet red pepper. Cooking in the microwave greatly reduces the preparation time and eliminates the need to parboil the pepper. No peppers on hand? Simply microwave the filling in two small cups or cook as a small skillet loaf.

6 oz	**lean ground turkey**	180 g
1	**small onion, chopped**	1
1/4 cup	**quick-cooking rolled oats**	50 mL
2 tbsp	**salsa**	25 mL
1 tbsp	**ground flax seed**	15 mL
1 tbsp	**chopped fresh parsley**	15 mL
1/4 tsp	**salt**	1 mL
1	**large red pepper**	1

1. In medium bowl, combine turkey, onion, oats, salsa, flax seed, parsley and salt. Mix well.

2. Cut pepper in half lengthwise and remove seeds. Pack half the turkey mixture into each half pepper; place in a 9 x 5-inch (2 L) microwave-safe loaf pan. Cover with plastic wrap and microwave at 70% power for 6 minutes or until turkey is no longer pink. Release steam from under wrap, recover and let stand for 2 minutes before serving.

Makes 2 servings.

Variation:
Turkey Skillet Loaf

Form turkey mixture into a flat patty about 1 inch (2.5 cm) thick. Heat a small nonstick skillet over medium heat; cook patty for 6 minutes a side or until centre is no longer pink. Serve with your choice of salsa or chutney.

Rounding Out the Meal
Mango Cilantro Salsa

This refreshing salsa will complement the turkey and pepper.

In small bowl, combine 1 chopped and peeled mango, 1 tbsp (15 mL) chopped fresh cilantro or parsley, 1 chopped green onion, 1 tbsp (15 mL) finely chopped jalapeño pepper, 1 tsp (5 mL) lime juice, 1/2 tsp (2 mL) granulated sugar and a pinch of salt.

Spinach with Orzo

A star of the vegetable world, spinach blends with the rice-shaped pasta for a pleasing taste and texture contrast.

In small saucepan, cook 1/3 cup (75 mL) orzo in boiling salted water for 10 minutes or until tender but still firm. Meanwhile, in a small nonstick skillet, heat 1 tsp (5 mL) olive oil over medium-high heat. Add 1 chopped small shallot and 1 minced clove garlic; cook for 5 minutes or until soft. Stir in 2 cups (500 mL) finely chopped spinach; cover and cook for 2 to 3 minutes or until spinach is wilted. Drain orzo and stir into spinach; season with salt and pepper to taste.

Mexican Salad Toss

A sprinkle of corn and chili powder gives an ordinary green salad a Mexican flair.

In salad bowl, top 3 cups (750 mL) assorted torn greens with 1 tomato, cut in wedges, 2 sliced green onions and 1 tbsp (15 mL) defrosted frozen corn. Sprinkle with chili powder. Toss with dressing.

Dressing: In small bowl, whisk together 1 tbsp (15 mL) tomato sauce, 1 tbsp (15 mL) red wine vinegar, 1 tbsp (15 mL) olive oil, 1/4 tsp (1 mL) dried basil and a pinch dry mustard.

Reach for the Red

Gram for gram, red pepper contains three times as much vitamin C as the well-regarded fruit of the orange tree. Red pepper also has the edge on green pepper for both beta carotene and vitamin C content.

PER SERVING
WITH ROUND OUTS

Calories 555
Protein 26 g
Total Fat 20 g
 saturated 3.7 g
 monounsaturated 10.3 g
 polyunsaturated 4.3 g
Carbohydrate 72 g
 fibre 11 g
Calcium 213 mg
Folacin 205 mcg
Sodium 404 mg

FOOD GUIDE SERVINGS

1 1/2  5 1

Schnitzel with Salsa

Slices of lean pork team with salsa for a fine-flavoured, easy meal. If you can find very thin slices of pork loin labelled scallopine, you can eliminate the pounding.

8 oz	**thin slices pork loin or butterfly pork chops, cut in half**	250 g
1	**egg white**	1
3 tbsp	**fine dry bread crumbs**	50 mL
1/4 tsp	**dried oregano**	1 mL
1 tsp	**vegetable oil**	5 mL
1/4 cup	**mild or hot salsa**	50 mL

PER SERVING OF MAIN DISH

Calories 205
Protein 24 g
Total Fat 8 g
  saturated 2.1 g
  monounsaturated 3.7 g
  polyunsaturated 1.3 g
Carbohydrate 9 g
  fibre 1 g
Calcium 59 mg
Folacin 16 mcg
Sodium 232 mg

1. Trim all visible fat from pork. Place on wax paper; pound with a wooden mallet until slices are very thin.

2. In shallow dish, lightly beat egg white. In a second shallow dish, combine bread crumbs and oregano.

3. Dip pork first into egg white, then press into crumbs to coat both sides.

4. Heat oil in a nonstick skillet over medium-high heat. Brown schnitzel on both sides and cook for 2 minutes or until just barely pink in the centre. Place pork on serving plates and top with salsa.

Makes 2 servings.

Rounding Out the Meal
Orange-Glazed Brussels Sprouts

A hint of orange and lemon brightens these "little cabbages."

Steam 2 cups (250 mL) fresh or frozen Brussels sprouts for 6 to 8 minutes or until just tender; drain. In small bowl, combine 1 tbsp (15 mL) orange marmalade and 1 tsp (5 mL) lemon juice. Pour over sprouts and toss to mix.

Mashed Parsnip and Potatoes

If it is not cut or pressed before cooking, garlic develops a pleasant sweet flavour that wonderfully enhances a combo of parsnip and potatoes.

Cut 2 small peeled white or yellow potatoes into quarters; place in a medium saucepan. Add 1 to 2 peeled parsnips, cut into large pieces, and 2 large peeled cloves garlic. Cover with salted water. Bring to a boil; reduce heat, cover and simmer for 15 to 20 minutes or until vegetables are tender. Drain and mash until smooth with potato masher. Stir in 1/4 cup (50 mL) yogurt; add salt and pepper to taste.

Mixed Greens with Favourite Vinaigrette

A traditional dressing you may want to make up in larger quantities to keep on hand in the refrigerator.

In salad bowl, combine 3 cups (750 mL) mixed greens, 2 thin slices red onion and 1 tomato, cut in wedges. Toss with dressing and sprinkle with 3 tbsp (45 mL) shredded Cheddar cheese.

Dressing: In small bowl, whisk together 1 tbsp (15 mL) olive oil, 1 tsp (5 mL) red wine vinegar, 1 tsp (5 mL) balsamic vinegar, 1/4 tsp (1 mL) Dijon mustard, 1/4 tsp (1 mL) granulated sugar, 1/2 small minced clove garlic and salt and pepper to taste.

PER SERVING
WITH ROUND OUTS

Calories 605
Protein 40 g
Total Fat 20 g
  saturated 5.8 g
  monounsaturated 10.1 g
  polyunsaturated 2.6 g
Carbohydrate 73 g
  fibre 15 g
Calcium 364 mg
Folacin 202 mcg
Sodium 705 mg

FOOD GUIDE SERVINGS

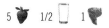

5   1/2   1

Fibre Bounty

There are an amazing 15 grams of fibre in this meal, more than half coming from Brussels sprouts, which are also responsible for boosting the iron content.

Pork Chops with Pears and Ginger

Pears and a hint of ginger wonderfully set off the mild taste of pork. Choose either regular chops with bone, or a large butterfly chop cut in half to make two servings.

1 tsp	**vegetable oil**	5 mL
2	**centre-cut pork chops, about 5 oz (150 g each)**	2
1/4 cup	**dry white wine**	50 mL
1/4 cup	**chicken bouillon**	50 mL
1 tsp	**balsamic vinegar**	5 mL
1	**pear, peeled and cut in 8 wedges**	1
1 tsp	**finely chopped gingerroot**	5 mL
2	**green onions, cut into slivers 2 in (5 cm) long**	2
1 tsp	**cornstarch**	5 mL
2 tsp	**water**	10 mL

1. In small nonstick skillet, heat oil over medium-high heat. Cook chops for 4 minutes a side or until just barely pink in the centre. Remove to a plate and keep warm.

2. Add wine, bouillon and vinegar to skillet, stirring to dissolve any brown bits; bring to a boil.

3. Add pear and gingerroot; reduce heat and simmer, uncovered, for 3 minutes. Stir in green onions.

4. Combine cornstarch and water; stir into pan. Cook, stirring constantly, for 1 minute or until thickened and bubbly. Pour over chops.

Makes 2 servings.

Rounding Out the Meal
Swiss Chard Sauté

Seed catalogues often call this leafy green "'silver beet." But whatever the name, its mild taste and abundant nutrients should earn it a frequent place at your table.

Wash and slice 8 oz (250 g) Swiss chard. In small saucepan, heat 1 tsp (15 mL) olive oil. Add Swiss chard to pan with water clinging to leaves; cook, covered, for 2 to 3 minutes or until chard is just tender. Season with a splash of wine vinegar and salt and pepper.

Two Potato Bake

Sweet potato adds colour and lots of beta carotene to a foil-baked potato.

Peel and slice 1 white and 1 sweet potato; place overlapping slices on a sheet of foil. Sprinkle with 1 small chopped onion and salt and ground black pepper to taste. Drizzle with 2 tsp (10 mL) olive oil and fold into small package. Bake in 400°F (200°C) oven for 40 minutes or until potato is soft.

Salad with Chutney Dressing

Just a dollop of any chutney with a bit of yogurt makes a quick flavourful salad topping.

In small bowl, combine 3 cups (750 mL) assorted greens such as lettuce, spinach or arugula. Toss with dressing.

Dressing: In small bowl, stir together 2 tbsp (25 mL) plain yogurt and 1 tbsp (15 mL) fruit chutney.

TLC for Sweet Potatoes

Sweet potatoes bruise easily and tend to spoil rapidly. Never store them in the refrigerator, where they may develop a hard core and off taste. If kept in a dry, cool place away from the light, they will keep for a month or so. Left at room temperature, they should be used within a week.

PER SERVING
WITH ROUND OUTS

Calories 485
Protein 27 g
Total Fat 16 g
  saturated 3.2 g
  monounsaturated 8.7 g
  polyunsaturated 2.2 g
Carbohydrate 58 g
  fibre 8 g
Calcium 210 mg
Folacin 123 mcg
Sodium 432 mg

FOOD GUIDE SERVINGS

5   1

Orange Beef Stir-Fry

Mandarin oranges add bright colour and refreshing taste to a quick beef stir-fry. To cut beef into thin slices more easily, first place in the freezer for 20 to 30 minutes.

PER SERVING
OF MAIN DISH

Calories 575
Protein 30 g
Total Fat 18 g
  saturated 4.8 g
  monounsaturated 8.7 g
  polyunsaturated 2.7 g
Carbohydrate 73 g
  fibre 4 g
Calcium 111 mg
Folacin 69 mcg
Sodium 1182 mg

8 oz	**sirloin or top round steak**	250 g
1/2 cup	**orange juice**	125 mL
2 tbsp	**soy sauce**	25 mL
2 tsp	**finely chopped gingerroot, or 1/4 tsp (1 mL) ground ginger**	10 mL
1 tbsp	**vegetable oil**	15 mL
1	**small onion, thinly sliced**	1
1	**clove garlic, minced**	1
6 oz	**green beans, cut in 1-inch (2.5 cm) lengths**	180 g
1/2 cup	**beef broth or water**	125 mL
1 tbsp	**cornstarch**	25 mL
2	**green onions, cut in 1-inch (2.5 cm) pieces**	2
1	**can (10 oz/284 mL) mandarin oranges, drained**	1
2 cups	**hot cooked rice**	500 mL

1. Cut beef into thin slices across the grain.

2. In medium bowl, combine orange juice, soy sauce and gingerroot. Add beef; let stand for 30 minutes.

3. In nonstick skillet or wok, heat oil over high heat. Drain beef, reserving marinade. Stir-fry beef, onion and garlic for 2 minutes or until beef is no longer pink. Remove beef mixture from skillet and set aside.

4. Add beans and broth to skillet. Heat to boiling, reduce heat, cover and boil gently for 3 minutes.

5. Combine cornstarch with remaining marinade and stir into skillet. Add green onions and bring to a boil, stirring constantly. Gently fold in reserved beef and oranges; return to a boil. Serve over rice.

Makes 2 servings.

Rounding Out the Meal
Cucumbers with Yogurt Topping

A simple version of raita, the popular Indian salad. Add spices such as black mustard or cumin seeds for different flavours.

Place slices of English cucumber on a serving dish. In small bowl, combine 1/4 cup (50 mL) plain yogurt with a splash of a flavoured vinegar and a pinch of salt and sugar; mix with cucumbers.

Zinc, Part of the Beef Bonus

Meat is a prime source of zinc. Zinc is also found in plant foods, but is poorly absorbed, so shying away from meat may leave you short of this mineral. This is often a problem for young women, vegetarians and the not-so-young who may need extra zinc to fulfill their needs. Given the importance of zinc for wound healing and proper functioning of the immune system, you need to ensure you receive enough zinc from your diet or supplements.

PER SERVING
WITH ROUND OUTS

Calories 600
Protein 32 g
Total Fat 19 g
  saturated 5.1 g
  monounsaturated 9.0 g
  polyunsaturated 3.0 g
Carbohydrate 77 g
  fibre 4 g
Calcium 173 mg
Folacin 78 mcg
Sodium 1204 mg

FOOD GUIDE SERVINGS

2  2 1

Two-Pepper Beef Stew with Farfalle

Peppers and savoury spicing give a rich flavour to this superb stew. The bow-tie pasta makes a perfect companion. Note that this recipe makes four servings. Freeze the extra or keep in the refrigerator for up to three days.

2 tsp	**vegetable oil**	10 mL
1 lb	**lean stewing beef, cubed**	500 g
1/2 cup	**coarsely chopped onion**	125 mL
2	**cloves garlic, minced**	2
1	**can (19 oz/540 mL) tomatoes**	1
1	**sweet green pepper, cubed**	1
1	**sweet red pepper, cubed**	1
1 1/2 tsp	**dried oregano**	7 mL
1/2 tsp	**ground cumin**	2 mL
1/2 tsp	**salt**	2 mL
1 tbsp	**cornstarch**	15 mL
1 tbsp	**water**	15 mL
12 oz	**farfalle (bow-tie pasta) or other pasta**	375 g

1. In Dutch oven or large heavy-bottomed saucepan, heat oil over high heat. Brown beef. Add onion and garlic; cook for 2 to 3 minutes or until soft.

2. Add tomatoes, peppers, oregano, cumin and salt. Bring to a boil, reduce heat, cover and simmer for 2 hours or until meat is tender.

3. In a large pot of salted water, cook pasta for 8 to 10 minutes or until tender but firm. Drain, rinse in hot water, drain well.

4. Meanwhile, in a small dish, combine cornstarch and water. Stir into stew; cook, stirring constantly, for 1 to 2 minutes or until thickened and bubbly. Serve over hot pasta.

Makes 4 servings.

Rounding Out the Meal
Mixed Salad with Parmesan Dressing

This yogurt-based dressing is perfect on a mixed vegetable salad.

In salad bowl, combine 3 cups (750 mL) tender lettuces such as red oak or green leaf. Toss with dressing and garnish with 6 halved cherry tomatoes and 1/2 cup (125 mL) small cauliflower florets.

Dressing: In small bowl, whisk together 2 tbsp (25 mL) plain yogurt, 1 tbsp (15 mL) grated Parmesan cheese, 1 tbsp (15 mL) light mayonnaise, 1 tbsp (15 mL) milk, 1/2 minced clove garlic and salt and pepper to taste.

An Iron-B_6 Benefit

Brimming with iron and B_6, this meal provides you with more than half of your daily needs for these nutrients.

Browning Beef

When browning beef, add meat slowly to keep the pan from cooling down. A hot surface is needed for the dark colour to develop.

PER SERVING
WITH ROUND OUTS

Calories 680
Protein 42 g
Total Fat 18 g
  saturated 5.5 g
  monounsaturated 7.5 g
  polyunsaturated 2.8 g
Carbohydrate 88 g
  fibre 8 g
Calcium 251 mg
Folacin 264 mcg
Sodium 701 mg

FOOD GUIDE SERVINGS

3   4   1

Steak with Mushroom Wine Sauce

PER SERVING
OF MAIN DISH

Calories 245
Protein 22 g
Total Fat 9 g
  saturated 2.5 g
  monounsaturated 3.8 g
  polyunsaturated 1.0 g
Carbohydrate 10 g
  fibre 2 g
Calcium 30 mg
Folacin 28 mcg
Sodium 46 mg

Steak enhanced with mushrooms and wine is a perfect choice for celebrating a special occasion or simply beginning the weekend.

1 tsp	**vegetable oil**	5 mL
1	**onion, sliced thinly**	1
6 oz	**mushrooms, sliced, about 2 cups (500 mL)**	180 g
1 tbsp	**chopped fresh parsley, or 1 tsp (5 mL) dried**	15 mL
1/4 tsp	**dried thyme**	1 mL
8 oz	**sirloin or strip loin steak**	250 g
1/2 cup	**dry red wine or beef stock**	125 mL
	Salt and ground black pepper	

1. In medium nonstick skillet, heat oil over medium heat. Add onions; cook for 5 to 7 minutes or until golden brown, stirring occasionally.

2. Add mushrooms, parsley and thyme. Increase heat to medium-high and cook for 7 minutes or until soft and browned. Remove onion-mushroom mixture to bowl and keep warm.

3. Cook steak in skillet, turning once, for 6 minutes or until well browned and of desired rareness. Transfer to bowl with mushrooms and keep warm.

4. Add wine to skillet; boil gently, stirring to dissolve brown bits in pan, for 3 to 4 minutes or until liquid has been reduced by half. Cut steak into two pieces and place on warmed plates. Stir mushroom mixture into sauce and spoon over steaks. Season with salt and pepper to taste.

Makes 2 servings.

Rounding Out the Meal
Creamed Noodles with Parsley

Evaporated milk makes a simple creamy sauce for pasta.

In a large pot of salted water, cook 4 oz (120 g) small egg noodles and 1 tbsp (15 mL) dried onion flakes for 6 to 8 minutes or until pasta is tender but firm. Drain. Stir in 1 tbsp (15 mL) evaporated milk; mix in 2 tbsp (25 mL) chopped parsley and salt and pepper to taste.

Peas with Mint and Lemon

Another time, replace the mint with basil for a savoury variation.

Steam 1 cup (250 mL) frozen or fresh peas just until tender. Transfer to serving dish; stir in 1 tsp (5 mL) butter or margarine, 1 tsp (5 mL) chopped fresh mint and 1/4 tsp (1 mL) grated lemon zest.

Romaine Salad with Watercress and Dijon Yogurt Dressing

The peppery taste of watercress is a nice addition to the romaine.

In salad bowl, combine 3 cups (750 mL) coarsely torn romaine lettuce, 1/2 bunch trimmed watercress and 1 thinly sliced pear. Toss with dressing and garnish with 1 tsp (5 mL) toasted pecans.

Dressing: In small bowl, whisk together 1/4 cup (50 mL) yogurt, 1 tsp (5 mL) granulated sugar, 1 tsp (5 mL) white wine vinegar, 1 tsp (5 mL) minced shallot, 1/2 tsp (2 mL) Dijon mustard and 1/4 tsp (1 mL) dried tarragon or basil.

Mushrooms

More varieties of mushrooms are becoming available in our stores. Look for creminis with a dark, rich brown cap, an earthy flavour and more solid texture than the common white button. The large portobello mushrooms can be sliced and used as any mushroom, or try them grilled, brushed with a bit of oil and served in a toasted bun. Chanterelles are prized for their more intense flavour; Shiitake are another darker, meaty mushroom. The long-stemmed oyster mushrooms are mild in flavour with a silky texture.

PER SERVING
WITH ROUND OUTS

Calories 650
Protein 38 g
Total Fat 15 g
    saturated 4.8 g
    monounsaturated 5.8 g
    polyunsaturated 2.3 g
Carbohydrate 83 g
    fibre 1 g
Calcium 204 mg
Folacin 309 mcg
Sodium 260 mg

FOOD GUIDE SERVINGS

2   4 1/2   1

Hot Taco Beef with Rice

PER SERVING
OF MAIN DISH

Calories 520
Protein 25 g
Total Fat 20 g
  saturated 7.6 g
  monounsaturated 8.7 g
  polyunsaturated 1.5 g
Carbohydrate 61 g
  fibre 5 g
Calcium 152 mg
Folacin 36 mcg
Sodium 903 mg

A fast and satisfying main dish that will soon become a favourite if you enjoy Mexican flavours.

6 oz	**lean ground beef**	180 g
1	**small onion, chopped**	1
3/4 cup	**hot salsa**	175 mL
1/2 cup	**tomato sauce**	125 mL
1/2 tsp	**beef bouillon granules**	2 mL
1/2 tsp	**ground cumin**	2 mL
1	**tomato, chopped**	1
2 tbsp	**shredded Cheddar cheese**	25 mL
2 cups	**hot cooked rice**	500 mL
16	**tortilla chips**	16

1. In a medium nonstick skillet over medium-high heat, brown beef and onion until beef is no longer pink.

2. Add salsa, tomato sauce, bouillon and cumin. Bring to a boil; reduce heat, cover and simmer for 5 minutes.

3. Mound rice on 2 serving plates and top with beef mixture. Top with chopped tomato and shredded cheese; arrange tortilla chips on side.

Makes 2 servings.

Rounding Out the Meal
Grapefruit Salad with Currant Glaze

Currant jelly makes a colourful and tasty topping for a grapefruit salad. The addition of a few pomegranate seeds adds special interest.

Line 2 salad plates with lettuce leaves. Remove outside rind from 1 large pink grapefruit with a sharp knife, exposing the pulp. Carefully cut on both sides of each inner membrane and lift out fruit sections. Arrange sections on each plate. Drizzle with dressing and garnish with a few pomegranate seeds if desired.

Dressing: In small bowl, whisk together 1 tbsp (15 mL) currant jelly and 1/2 tsp (2 mL) lemon juice.

Rice

White rice has all the bran removed and requires a shorter cooking time than does brown rice, which has some of the bran layer still remaining. Converted, or parboiled, rice is steamed before milling, which causes the B vitamins in the bran to diffuse into the rice kernel. Long-grain white rice is generally fortified with a vitamin coating applied to the outside of the grain. For that reason, it should not be rinsed before cooking.

Go Pink

Pink and white grapefruit are equal on the vitamin C and calorie fronts, but pink has 25% more beta carotene as well as some lycopene.

Wine-Poached Salmon with Capers

Poaching is a good choice for salmon fillets. Not only is it an easy way to cook any fish, but the wine lets the delectable flavour of the fish come through and prevents it from becoming dry. A few capers add an interesting subtle taste. This recipe also works well with a salmon steak; just increase the cooking time to compensate for the extra thickness.

2	salmon fillets, about 12 oz (350 g)	2
1/4 cup	white wine	50 mL
2 tsp	drained capers	10 mL

Place salmon, wine and capers in a medium-size frying pan. Bring to a gentle boil; reduce heat, cover and boil gently for 4 minutes, depending on thickness or until fish is opaque and flakes easily with a fork. Remove salmon to serving plates. Boil liquid uncovered until slightly reduced; pour over fillets.

Makes 2 servings.

Salmon, a Jewel of Canadian Cuisine

Omega-3 fatty acids, known to foster cardio-vascular health, constitute a good portion of the fat in this meal. The omega-3s present in fish may lessen the risk of a heart attack by reducing the likelihood of blood clotting. Eating fish once or twice a week is a wise choice; featuring salmon twice a month is real savoury wisdom.

Rounding Out the Meal
Broccoli with Sun-Dried Tomatoes

The unique flavour of sun-dried tomatoes adds a pungent flavour to broccoli.

In small saucepan, steam 2 cups (500 mL) broccoli florets for 5 minutes or until just tender-crisp. Meanwhile, in a small microwave-safe dish, place 1 tsp (5 mL) olive oil and 1 minced clove garlic. Microwave on 100% power for 30 seconds or until garlic is soft. Add 1 thinly sliced sun-dried tomato. Toss with broccoli.

Lemon Rice

A new twist on the lemon traditionally served with fish.

In small saucepan, bring 1 cup (250 mL) chicken broth to a boil. Stir in 1/2 cup (125 mL) long-grain rice; reduce heat, cover and simmer for 20 minutes or until liquid is absorbed. Stir in grated zest of 1 lemon and a bit of chopped fresh or dried dill.

Mandarin Orange Salad

Add spinach to torn greens for extra flavour and nutrients. Orange pieces with an orange-based vinaigrette complete the salad.

In salad bowl, combine 2 cups (500 mL) torn assorted greens and 1 cup (250 mL) torn spinach. Toss with dressing and garnish with 1/2 cup (125 mL) mandarin orange pieces and 2 thin sweet onion slices.

Dressing: In small bowl, whisk together 2 tbsp (25 mL) orange juice, 1 tbsp (15 mL) white wine vinegar, 1 tbsp (15 mL) vegetable oil, 1 tsp (5 mL) lemon juice, 1/2 tsp (2 mL) granulated sugar and salt and pepper to taste.

PER SERVING
WITH ROUND OUTS

Calories 725
Protein 49 g
Total Fat 32 g
  saturated 5.4 g
  monounsaturated 13.5 g
  polyunsaturated 10.3 g
Carbohydrate 56 g
  fibre 6 g
Calcium 135 mg
Folacin 191 mcg
Sodium 583 mg

FOOD GUIDE SERVINGS

1 1/2  2 1/2 1 1/2

Halibut Steak with Roasted Red Peppers

PER SERVING
OF MAIN DISH

Calories 185
Protein 30 g
Total Fat 6 g
 saturated 0.7 g
 monounsaturated 2.4 g
 polyunsaturated 2.0 g
Carbohydrate 3 g
 fibre 1 g
Calcium 69 mg
Folacin 16 mcg
Sodium 104 mg

Roasted red peppers make an exceptional accompaniment for halibut steak. Use bottled peppers for maximum convenience.

1 tsp	**oil**	5 mL
1	**halibut steak, about 10 oz (300 g)**	1
1 tsp	**Dijon mustard**	5 mL
1/2	**roasted sweet red pepper, cut in strips**	1/2

1. In medium nonstick skillet, heat oil over medium-high heat. Add halibut and cook for 3 minutes. Turn fish and cook for 4 minutes or until fish flakes easily.

2. Spread mustard over halibut and top with peppers. Cook for 1 minute longer to heat through.

Makes 2 servings.

Roasted Red

When sweet red peppers are plentiful, roast them on your barbecue grill or on a rack under the broiler until skins are blackened. Place in a paper bag until cool enough to handle; then peel off skin, cut peppers in half and remove seeds. To freeze for use all year, place the peeled, seeded pepper halves on a baking sheet and set in the freezer. When frozen, pack into sealable plastic bags to be removed as needed.

Rounding Out the Meal
Butternut and Greens

Frozen cubes of butternut squash are handy to keep in the freezer. The sweet squash partners beautifully with spinach for good flavour and colour. Another time, use Swiss chard, turnip greens or kale in the quest for variety.

In medium nonstick skillet, heat 2 tsp (10 mL) vegetable oil over medium-high heat. Add 1 small chopped onion; cook for 2 minutes or until soft. Add 1 cup (250 mL) fresh or frozen butternut squash cubes and 1/4 cup (50 mL) chicken broth. Bring to a boil; reduce heat, cover and simmer for 8 minutes (less for frozen) or until squash is just tender. Stir in 1/2 package (about 5 oz/150 g) sliced spinach. Return to boil; cover and simmer for 5 minutes. Season with salt and ground black pepper to taste.

Rice Quinoa Pilaf

Quinoa, a staple grain of the ancient Incas, can be found in most health-food stores. Its protein is of higher quality than that of other grains as it provides a greater quantity of lysine, an essential amino acid.

In medium saucepan, bring 1 1/4 cup (300 mL) chicken broth to a boil. Stir in 1/3 cup (75 mL) long-grain brown rice, 3 tbsp (45 mL) quinoa, 1/2 tsp (2 mL) dried chives, 1/4 tsp (1 mL) dried marjoram and 1/8 tsp (0.5 mL) salt. Bring to a boil; reduce heat, cover and simmer for 40 minutes or until grains are tender and liquid is absorbed. Stir in 2 tbsp (25 mL) chopped parsley.

Cherry Tomatoes with Basil

The small red tomatoes make an attractive salad, but this dressing is equally good to top slices of the larger variety.

Cut 1 cup (250 mL) cherry tomatoes in half; place in serving bowl together with 4 to 5 fresh chopped basil leaves. Just before serving, toss with dressing.

Dressing: In small bowl, whisk together 1/2 minced clove garlic, 1 tbsp (15 mL) olive oil, 1 tsp (5 mL) balsamic vinegar and 1/8 tsp (0.5 mL) salt.

PER SERVING
WITH ROUND OUTS

Calories 580
Protein 42 g
Total Fat 21 g
  saturated 2.6 g
  monounsaturated 11.3 g
  polyunsaturated 5.1 g
Carbohydrate 60 g
  fibre 8 g
Calcium 212 mg
Folacin 173 mcg
Sodium 1157 mg

FOOD GUIDE SERVINGS

1 1/2   2   1

Fish Baked with Vegetables En Papillote

En papillote refers to food baked inside a wrapping of parchment or foil. The flavours blend beautifully, and each person can savour the wonderful aroma when the individual package is opened. Use frozen and defrosted fillets if you prefer.

1	**carrot, very thinly sliced**	1
2	**fresh fish fillets, such as sole or flounder, about 12 oz (375 g)**	2
4	**green onions, sliced**	4
4	**mushrooms, sliced**	4
1	**small zucchini, sliced**	1
1 tbsp	**fresh lemon juice**	15 mL
2 tsp	**olive or vegetable oil**	10 mL
1/4 tsp	**dried thyme**	1 mL
	Salt and pepper	

1. Cut two sheets of parchment or aluminum foil into rectangles about 12 x 15 in (30 x 37 cm).

2. Place half the carrots in a mound in the centre of each rectangle. Layer half the fish over each mound. Cover with half the green onions, mushrooms and zucchini.

3. In small bowl, whisk together the lemon juice, oil, thyme and salt and pepper to taste; drizzle over vegetables.

4. Bring short sides of paper together, folding the edges twice to seal tightly. Roll remaining ends together tightly to seal.

5. Place on a baking sheet. Bake in 400ºF (200ºC) oven for 25 minutes or until fish flakes easily with a fork and vegetables are tender. Place unopened packet on plate for each person.

Makes 2 servings.

Rounding Out the Meal
Quick Baked Tomatoes

Set these tomatoes to bake alongside the fish packages.

Cut 2 tomatoes in half; set in a baking dish. Sprinkle each with 1 tsp (5 mL) Italian-flavoured dry bread crumbs and 1 tsp (5 mL) grated Parmesan cheese. Bake in 400°F (200°C) oven for 15 minutes or until tomatoes are just soft.

Couscous with Lemon and Herbs

Couscous with a hint of lemon and fresh herbs is a perfect accompaniment to fish. Garnish with currants or sunflower seeds if you desire.

In small saucepan, heat 1 tsp (5 mL) vegetable oil over medium heat; cook 1 minced shallot for 2 minutes or until soft. Add 3/4 cup (175 mL) chicken broth; bring to a boil. Stir in 1/2 cup (125 mL) couscous and grated zest of 1/2 lemon. Remove from heat; cover and let stand for 5 minutes. Stir in 1 tbsp (15 mL) chopped fresh herbs such as basil, oregano, thyme or rosemary.

Spinach Sprout Salad

Fresh sprouts and sesame seeds garnish this Japanese-inspired salad.

In salad bowl, combine 2 cups (500 mL) torn spinach leaves and 1/2 cup (125 mL) fresh bean sprouts. Toss with dressing and sprinkle with 1 tbsp (15 mL) toasted sesame seeds. (See p. 124 for instructions on toasting.)

Dressing: In small bowl, whisk together 2 tbsp (25 mL) rice vinegar, 2 tbsp (25 mL) pineapple or orange juice, 1 tsp (5 mL) granulated sugar, 1 tsp (5 mL) soy sauce, 1/2 tsp (1 mL) sesame oil and a pinch ground black pepper.

Couscous

Couscous is a perfect food for two since it requires little cooking and is easy to prepare in small quantities. Made from semolina wheat much as pasta is, it is a staple of North African cuisine. The traditional way to prepare it is to steam it in the top of a special pot called a couscoussière while pieces of meat and vegetables cook below. This method produces couscous that is the most fluffy, but stirring it into boiling broth works just fine.

PER SERVING
WITH ROUND OUTS

Calories 580
Protein 47 g
Total Fat 15 g
  saturated 2.9.g
  monounsaturated 7.1 g
  polyunsaturated 3.8 g
Carbohydrate 65 g
  fibre 7 g
Calcium 246 mg
Folacin 187 mcg
Sodium 819 mg

FOOD GUIDE SERVINGS

1 1/2   3   1

Citrus Shrimp with Asian Noodles

PER SERVING
OF MAIN DISH

Calories 485
Protein 30 g
Total Fat 9 g
  saturated 1.3 g
  monounsaturated 5.0 g
  polyunsaturated 2.0 g
Carbohydrate 69 g
  fibre 0 g
Calcium 100 mg
Folacin 25 mcg
Sodium 483 mg

Sautéing seafood is one of the fastest ways to get dinner on the table. A hint of orange and lemon enhance the succulent flavour of shrimp wonderfully without overwhelming it.

10 oz	**large shrimp**	300 g
1 tsp	**grated orange zest**	5 mL
1 tsp	**grated lemon zest**	5 mL
1/3 cup	**orange juice**	75 mL
2 tbsp	**fresh lemon juice**	25 mL
2 tsp	**olive oil**	10 mL
1/2 tsp	**minced gingerroot**	2 mL
1/4 tsp	**salt**	1 mL
1 tsp	**vegetable oil**	5 mL
5 oz	**Asian noodles such as cellophane or rice stick, cooked according to package directions**	150 g
1 tbsp	**chopped fresh parsley**	15 mL

1. Peel and devein shrimp, leaving tail if desired.

2. In small bowl, combine orange zest, lemon zest, orange juice, lemon juice, olive oil, gingerroot and salt. Set aside.

3. In medium nonstick skillet, heat vegetable oil over medium-high heat. Add shrimp; cook for 4 minutes or until shrimp are no longer pink. Add citrus mixture; bring just to a boil. Arrange shrimp over noodles and pour sauce over top. Sprinkle with parsley.

Makes 2 servings.

Zest for Flavour

Zest is the term used for the fragrant thin outer layer of citrus fruits. Sometimes called rind, it contains the aromatic oils that offer so much flavour to food. Don't confuse this colourful layer with the white one hiding underneath. A zester is a handy tool for removing this perfumy skin, but you can also use a fine grater or vegetable peeler. Be sure to take only the coloured part, leaving the bitter-tasting white layer behind.

Rounding Out the Meal
Oriental Beans

Just a splash of soy sauce adds flavour without fat. Use the light version for less salt.

In small saucepan, cook 1 1/2 cups (375 mL) whole green beans with a small amount of water for 7 minutes or until tender but firm. Drain and toss with 1 minced clove garlic and 1 tsp (5 mL) soy sauce.

Quick Coleslaw

Here's a light coleslaw that doesn't mask the taste of sweet fresh cabbage.

In medium bowl, whisk together 1/2 minced clove garlic, 1 tbsp (15 mL) olive oil, 1 tbsp (15 mL) white wine vinegar, 1 tbsp (15 mL) water, 2 tsp (10 mL) granulated sugar and 1/2 tsp (2 mL) Dijon mustard. Add 2 cups (500 mL) shredded savoy or other cabbage; toss to mix.

Noodles of Asia

Asian noodles are produced from a variety of flours. Two popular types are cellophane or bean thread noodles, which use mung-bean starch, and rice stick or rice vermicelli, which are made from rice flour. These translucent noodles have a very mild taste, allowing the subtle flavour of the citrus shrimp in this recipe to come through. Soba noodles, made from buckwheat flour, have a slightly nutty flavour and are also good in this recipe.

PER SERVING
WITH ROUND OUTS

Calories 655
Protein 34 g
Total Fat 17 g
   saturated 2.3 g
   monounsaturated 10.2 g
   polyunsaturated 2.8 g
Carbohydrate 93 g
   fibre 5 g
Calcium 206 mg
Folacin 105 mcg
Sodium 660 mg

FOOD GUIDE SERVINGS

2 1/2  3 ❧ 1 ❧

Quick Ways with Fillets

Fish fillets cook in just minutes in a microwave, making a great meal for two. With a variety of ways to prepare them, it is easy to have fish more often. One serving of each recipe provides one serving of the Meat & Alternatives food group. Use 8 to 12 oz (250 to 350 g) fresh or individually frozen fillets of sole, red snapper, cod or blue fish to prepare any of the following:

Florentine Fillet Cups

Cut fillets into strips about 1 1/2 inches (4 cm) wide; arrange around the inside of 2 lightly oiled 10 oz (300 g) custard or baking cups. In small bowl, combine 1 cup (250 mL) finely chopped fresh spinach, 1 tbsp (15 mL) grated Parmesan cheese, 1 slice crumbled bread, a pinch of salt and a pinch of ground black pepper. Spoon mixture into fish cups. Place cups in microwave, cover with a paper towel; microwave on 100% power for 2 to 2 1/2 minutes or until fish flakes easily with a fork.

Vegetable-Topped Fillets

In small flat microwave-safe dish, place 1 very thinly sliced small carrot, 1 diced stalk celery, 3 sliced mushrooms and 2 sliced green onions. Cover with plastic wrap and microwave on 100% power for 3 to 4 minutes or until vegetables begin to soften. Add fillets, spooning vegetables over fish. Drizzle with 1 tsp (5 mL) olive oil and sprinkle with salt and pepper. Cover with plastic wrap; microwave on 100% power for 2 to 3 minutes or until fish flakes easily with a fork.

Fillets Chinese-Style

Place fillets in small flat microwave-safe dish; top with 4 green onions sliced lengthwise, 1 tsp (5 mL) finely chopped gingerroot or 1/4 tsp (1 mL) ground ginger and 1 tbsp (15 mL) soy sauce. Cover with plastic wrap; microwave on 100% power for 2 to 3 minutes or until fish flakes easily with a fork.

Fillets Parmesan

On flat plate or piece of wax paper, combine 2 tbsp (25 mL) Italian-flavoured bread crumbs and 1 tbsp (15 mL) grated Parmesan cheese. Coat fillets with crumbs and transfer to a small flat microwave-safe dish. Cover with paper towel; microwave on 100% power for 2 to 3 minutes or until fish flakes easily with a fork.

Fillets with Mustard Sauce

In small bowl, combine 1/4 cup (50 mL) plain yogurt, 1 tsp (25 mL) Dijon mustard, 1/2 tsp (2 mL) honey and 1/4 tsp (1 mL) chicken bouillon granules. Place fillets in a small flat microwave-safe dish; spread mustard mixture over top. Sprinkle with 1 tbsp (15 mL) dry bread crumbs. Cover with plastic wrap; microwave on 100% power for 2 to 3 minutes or until fish flakes easily with a fork.

Fillets Almondine

In small microwave-safe dish, combine 2 tbsp (25 mL) slivered almonds and 1 tbsp (15 mL) butter. Microwave on 100% power, stirring once, for 40 seconds to 1 minute or until almonds are golden brown. Place fillets in a small flat microwave-safe dish. Drain butter from almonds and pour over fish. Cover with plastic wrap; microwave on 100% power for 2 to 3 minutes or until fish flakes easily with a fork. Sprinkle almonds over fillets before serving.

Creole Fillets

In small microwave-safe dish, combine 1/4 cup (50 mL) sliced celery, 1/4 cup (50 mL) chopped sweet green pepper, 2 tbsp (25 mL) chopped onion and 1 tsp (5 mL) vegetable oil. Cover with plastic wrap; microwave on 100% power for 1 to 1 1/2 minutes or until vegetables are almost tender. Meanwhile, place fillets in a small flat microwave-safe dish. Add 1/3 cup (75 mL) tomato sauce, 1/4 tsp (1 mL) chili powder and a pinch of salt to vegetable mixture; pour over fillets. Cover with plastic wrap; microwave on 100% power for 3 to 4 minutes or until fish flakes easily with a fork.

Pasta Layers with Spinach and Ricotta

Pasta forms a base supporting a filling of spinach and a trio of calcium- and vitamin A-rich cheeses.

1 1/2 cups	**small pasta, such as baby shells or macaroni**	375 mL
1	**egg**	1
1/4 cup	**grated Parmesan cheese**	50 mL
3 tbsp	**milk**	45 mL
1/4 tsp	**salt**	1 mL
3 cups	**packed chopped fresh spinach**	750 mL
1/2 cup	**ricotta cheese**	125 mL
1/4 tsp	**ground nutmeg**	1 mL
2-3	**plum tomatoes, thinly sliced**	2-3
1/4 cup	**shredded part-skim mozzarella cheese**	50 mL

1. In a large pot of salted water, cook pasta for 8 to 10 minutes or until tender but firm. Drain.

2. In medium bowl, whisk together egg, Parmesan cheese, milk and salt. Mix in pasta; spread on bottom of a lightly greased 9 x 5-inch (2 L) baking pan.

3. Rinse spinach; place in a glass measure or microwave-safe bowl. Cover with plastic wrap; microwave on 100% power for 1 1/2 to 2 minutes or until spinach is just wilted. Drain spinach, pressing to remove liquid. Stir in ricotta cheese and nutmeg.

4. Spread spinach mixture over pasta; top with tomato slices. Bake uncovered in 350°F (180°C) oven for 30 minutes. Sprinkle mozzarella over top; bake uncovered for 5 minutes or until cheese is melted. Let stand for 5 minutes before serving.

Makes 2 servings.

Rounding Out the Meal
Mixed Vegetable Salad

Raw veggies add extra crunch and fibre to a green salad.

In salad bowl, combine 2 cups (500 mL) torn assorted greens, 1/2 cup (125 mL) shredded red cabbage, 1/4 cup (50 mL) sliced cauliflower florets and 1/4 cup (50 mL) sliced celery. Toss with dressing.

Dressing: In small bowl, whisk together 2 tbsp (25 mL) light mayonnaise, 1 tbsp (15 mL) salsa and 1/4 tsp (1 mL) granulated sugar.

Ricotta Cheese

Ricotta cheese was originally made in Italy from the whey produced during the manufacture of cheeses such as mozzarella and provolone. In North America, whole or skim milk is added to the whey, greatly increasing the calcium content of ricotta compared to cottage cheese.

PER SERVING
WITH ROUND OUTS

Calories 650
Protein 35 g
Total Fat 24 g
  saturated 11.l g
  monounsaturated 7.9 g
  polyunsaturated 3.0 g
Carbohydrate 76 g
  fibre 7 g
Calcium 580 mg
Folacin 341 mcg
Sodium 862 mg

FOOD GUIDE SERVINGS

Caribbean Beans and Rice

The combination of beans and rice is traditional fare in many countries. Long before anything was known about amino acids, the building blocks of proteins, people took advantage of the complementary nature of these two foods. This robust one-dish meal is also a very high source of fibre, providing as well calcium and iron plus an amazing quantity of folate.

1 tsp	**vegetable oil**	5 mL
1	**onion, chopped**	1
1	**clove garlic, minced**	1
1/2 cup	**chopped sweet green pepper**	125 mL
1/2 cup	**chopped celery**	125 mL
1 cup	**seasoned tomato sauce**	250 mL
1/2 cup	**chicken broth**	125 mL
1/4 cup	**long-grain white rice**	50 mL
1/2 tsp	**chili powder**	2 mL
1/2 tsp	**ground cumin**	2 mL
1/8 tsp	**salt**	0.5 mL
1/8 tsp	**ground black pepper**	0.5 mL
1	**can (19 oz/540 mL) black beans or chick-peas, drained and rinsed, or 2 cups/500 mL cooked beans**	1
1/4 cup	**grated Parmesan cheese**	50 mL

1. In large saucepan, heat oil over medium heat. Cook onion, garlic, green pepper and celery for 7 minutes or until very soft.

2. Add tomato sauce, broth, rice, chili powder, cumin, salt and pepper. Bring to a boil; reduce heat, cover and simmer for 20 minutes or until rice is cooked.

3. Add beans and cook for 5 minutes or until hot. Serve sprinkled with cheese.

Makes 2 servings.

Variation:
Lentils with Rice

Replace the beans with 1/4 cup (50 mL) lentils, adding lentils at the same time as the rice.

Rounding Out the Meal
Swiss Chard with Balsamic Vinegar

The dark leaves of Swiss chard make it a good choice for a nutritious vegetable. Just a splash of balsamic vinegar cuts the slight bitterness and adds a delicious pungent flavour.

Steam 8 oz (250 g) sliced Swiss chard just until tender. Splash with 1 tbsp (15 mL) balsamic vinegar.

Pineapple Carrot Salad with Creamy Dressing

An old-fashioned creamy dressing is perfect for a salad of sweet lettuces and carrot.

In salad bowl, combine 3 cups (750 mL) torn assorted lettuces, 1/4 cup (50 mL) pineapple tidbits and 1/4 cup (50 mL) shredded carrot. Toss with dressing.

Dressing: In small bowl, whisk together 2 tbsp (25 mL) light mayonnaise, 1 tbsp (15 mL) granulated sugar, 1 tbsp (15 mL) cider vinegar, 1 tbsp (15 mL) milk and salt and pepper to taste.

To Cook Beans

Canned beans are the ultimate in convenience. If you choose the longer and more economical route and cook dried beans, make a lot and freeze the extra beans in small containers for use another time.

Rinse dried beans; place in a large saucepan and cover with cold water by 2 inches (10 cm). Bring to a boil; reduce heat and boil gently for 2 minutes. Remove from heat and let stand for 1 hour. Or soak beans overnight in enough cold water to cover beans by 2 inches (10 cm).

Drain beans and cover with fresh cold water. Bring to a boil; reduce heat and simmer for 30 to 60 minutes or until beans are tender. Add a bit of salt during the last half of cooking time.

1 cup (250 mL) dry beans gives about 2 1/2 cups (625 mL) cooked beans.

PER SERVING
WITH ROUND OUTS

Calories 605
Protein 29 g
Total Fat 13 g
  saturated 3.4 g
  monounsaturated 5.4 g
  polyunsaturated 3.0 g
Carbohydrate 99 g
  fibre 20 g
Calcium 403 mg
Folacin 276 mcg
Sodium 1795 mg

FOOD GUIDE SERVINGS

1   5   1

Soybeans with Snow Peas and Pineapple

PER SERVING
OF MAIN DISH

Calories 510
Protein 21 g
Total Fat 13 g
  saturated 1.7 g
  monounsaturated 4.7 g
  polyunsaturated 6.1 g
Carbohydrate 80 g
  fibre 9 g
Calcium 170 mg
Folacin 73 mcg
Sodium 796 mg

Soybeans are becomingly increasingly favoured on Canadian dinner plates for their nutritional benefits as well as their nutty taste. A fruity, sweet-sour flavour perfectly complements this versatile legume.

2 tsp	vegetable oil	10 mL
1	small onion, chopped	1
1	clove garlic, minced	1
1/2	sweet green pepper, cut in cubes	1/2
1/2 cup	chopped celery	125 mL
1 tbsp	granulated sugar	15 mL
1 tbsp	cornstarch	15 mL
1/2 cup	chicken broth	125 mL
2 tbsp	cider vinegar	25 mL
1 tbsp	soy sauce	15 mL
1 cup	cooked soybeans (see page 107)	250 mL
3/4 cup	canned pineapple tidbits	175 mL
3/4 cup	snow peas, about 3 oz (90 g)	175 mL
2 cups	cooked rice	500 mL

1. In large saucepan, heat oil over medium-high heat. Add onion, garlic, green pepper and celery; cook for 3 minutes or until vegetables are tender-crisp.

2. In small bowl, combine sugar and cornstarch; blend in chicken broth. Stir broth into saucepan. Bring to a boil, stirring constantly; cook for 1 minute or until thickened and boiling. Blend in vinegar and soy sauce; stir in beans, pineapple and snow peas. Return to boil; cover and boil gently for 3 minutes or until peas are just tender. Serve over cooked rice.

Makes 2 servings.

Rounding Out the Meal
Romaine Salad with Beets and Blue Cheese Dressing

Blue cheese adds a robust note to a beet and lettuce salad.

In salad bowl, place 3 cups (750 mL) torn romaine lettuce leaves. Toss with dressing and garnish with 1/2 cup (125 mL) sliced beets and 1/2 cup (125 mL) sweet onion rings.

Dressing: In small bowl, mash together 2 tbsp (25 mL) blue cheese and 2 tbsp (25 mL) light mayonnaise. Stir in 2 tbsp (25 mL) milk and 1 small minced clove garlic.

Soy Nuts

These tasty snacks can become as addictive as their cousins, the peanut.

Soak dried soybeans overnight in cold water; drain and spread on a baking sheet. Bake in 350°F (180°C) oven for 40 to 50 minutes or until dry and slightly browned. Stir frequently.

Soy Sense

Soy Nuts contain 50% less fat but only 30% fewer calories than peanuts. Go easy on these tempting treats! Two tablespoons (25 mL) will set you back 130 calories.

PER SERVING
WITH ROUND OUTS

Calories 660
Protein 28 g
Total Fat 23 g
  saturated 5.0 g
  monounsaturated 8.6 g
  polyunsaturated 7.7 g
Carbohydrate 91 g
  fibre 12 g
Calcium 315 mg
Folacin 232 mcg
Sodium 1146 mg

FOOD GUIDE SERVINGS

2   4   1

Tofu Vegetable Stir-Fry

PER SERVING
OF MAIN DISH

Calories 330
Protein 23 g
Total Fat 18 g
  saturated 2.1 g
  monounsaturated 6.5 g
  polyunsaturated 7.9 g
Carbohydrate 25 g
  fibre 5 g
Calcium 789 mg
Folacin 67 mcg
Sodium 625 mg

Sometimes called the cheese of Asia, tofu is a versatile ingredient that readily takes on other flavours. Firm tofu works best in this colourful dish since the cubes brown without crumbling before the vegetables are added.

1 tbsp	**vegetable oil**	15 mL
1/2 lb	**firm tofu, cut into 1/2 inch (1 cm) cubes**	250 g
1	**small onion, chopped**	1
1	**clove garlic, minced**	1
1	**carrot, very thinly sliced**	1
1	**sweet yellow or orange pepper, cut in cubes**	1
1 tsp	**minced gingerroot**	5 mL
4 oz	**snow peas**	120 g
1/2 cup	**chicken broth**	125 mL
1 tbsp	**soy sauce**	15 mL
pinch	**red pepper flakes**	pinch
1 tbsp	**water**	15 mL
2 tsp	**cornstarch**	10 mL

1. In large nonstick skillet, heat oil over high heat. Add tofu; cook without stirring for 2 minutes or until nicely browned on one side. Carefully turn cubes to brown on other sides. Remove from pan.

2. Add onion, garlic, carrot, peppers and gingerroot; cook for 3 minutes over medium heat or until tender-crisp.

3. Stir in peas, broth, soy sauce and pepper flakes. Bring to a boil; cook for 2 minutes or until peas are just tender.

4. Combine water and cornstarch; stir into pan. Cook, stirring constantly, for 1 to 2 minutes or until thickened and bubbly. Stir in tofu and heat through before serving. Serve over bulgur or rice.

Makes 2 servings.

Rounding Out the Meal
Bulgur for Two

Bulgur delivers the nutritional benefits of a whole grain and cooks quickly in small quantities to make a simple pilaf.

In small pan or microwave container, bring 1 1/4 cups (300 mL) chicken broth to a boil. Remove from heat; stir in 3/4 cup (75 mL) bulgur and 1 tbsp (15 mL) chopped dried cranberries. Let stand for 10 minutes.

Mediterranean Tomato Slices

When field ripened tomatoes are available, this simple dressing is all that is needed for a memorable side dish.

Drizzle 2 sliced ripe tomatoes with 1 tsp (5 mL) balsamic vinegar and 1 tsp (5 mL) olive oil. Sprinkle with chopped fresh herbs such as oregano or basil.

Terrific Tofu

Tofu is made from soy beans to which is added either magnesium or calcium sulfate to form a curd. Magnesium sulfate gives a more mellow flavour, but tofu made with the calcium form of the salt is a much better source of this essential nutrient. Substituting magnesium-made tofu in this meal for tofu made with calcium reduces the calcium content by 500 mg.

Tofu Types

With little flavour of its own, tofu readily picks up the flavour of other foods. Tofu is available in several forms. Silken tofu is much more fragile than regular tofu and will blend to a smooth purée in a food processor. Regular tofu is labelled "soft," "firm" or "extra firm," depending on the amount of liquid that has been pressed from it during processing. You can make tofu firmer by placing the block of tofu on a cutting board over the sink with a second board balanced on top. To hasten the process, add a weight, such as a small can of food, to the top board. Freezing tofu removes even more moisture, making it suitable to crumble over soups or salads.

PER SERVING
WITH ROUND OUTS

Calories 585
Protein 34 g
Total Fat 22 g
    saturated 2.8 g
    monounsaturated 8.7 g
    polyunsaturated 8.7 g
Carbohydrate 73 g
    fibre 13 g
Calcium 823 mg
Folacin 103 mcg
Sodium 1130 mg

FOOD GUIDE SERVINGS

2 1/2   3   1

Tofu Tip

Store unopened tofu in the refrigerator in the original package; after opening, keep it in a container and cover it with cold water. Change the water frequently, and use the tofu within a week or before it begins to smell sour.

Barley Lentil Bake

Barley and quick-cooking red lentils team up to make a pleasing meat-alternative that is a very high source of fibre and an excellent source of vitamins A and C, folate and iron. As a savoury accompaniment with poultry or meat, this bake will serve four people. A double recipe requires the same cooking time, and any extra freezes well.

1 tsp	**vegetable oil**	5 mL
1 cup	**sliced mushrooms**	250 mL
2	**carrots, chopped**	2
1	**stalk celery, chopped**	1
1	**small onion, chopped**	1
1/3 cup	**pot or pearl barley, rinsed**	75 mL
1/3 cup	**red lentils**	75 mL
1 1/3 cups	**chicken broth**	325 mL
2 tbsp	**tomato paste**	25 mL
1/2 tsp	**dried oregano**	2 mL
1/4 tsp	**salt**	1 mL
1/4 tsp	**ground black pepper**	1 mL

1. In small nonstick skillet, heat oil over medium-high heat. Add mushrooms, carrots, celery and onion; cook for 8 minutes or until vegetables are soft. Transfer to a 1 qt (1 L) casserole.

2. Stir in barley, lentils, broth, tomato paste, oregano, salt and pepper.

3. Bake in 350°F (180°C) oven for 1 hour if using pearl barley or 1 1/4 hours if using pot barley or until liquid is absorbed and barley is tender.

Makes 2 servings.

Rounding Out the Meal
Broccoli with Peppers

A delightful colour combination for a favourite vegetable.

Steam 2 cups (500 mL) broccoli florets with 1/4 sweet yellow pepper cut in slivers for 5 minutes or until just tender-crisp. Add 1 tsp (5 mL) olive oil or butter as desired.

Orange Date Salad with Honey Mustard Dressing

Orange, dates and a sweet mustard dressing combine beautifully for a refreshing salad.

In salad bowl, place 2 1/2 cups (625 mL) torn assorted lettuces, 1/2 cup (125 mL) spinach leaves and a sliced peeled seedless orange. Toss with dressing and garnish with 2 tbsp (15 mL) chopped dates, 2 tbsp (15 mL) whole-wheat croutons and 1 tbsp (15 mL) toasted sesame seeds.

Dressing: In small bowl, whisk together 1 tbsp (15 mL) vegetable oil, 1 tbsp (15 mL) white wine vinegar, 1 tbsp (15 mL) honey, 1/2 tsp (2 mL) Dijon mustard and salt and pepper to taste.

Barley – Pot or Pearl?

Barley comes wrapped in very tough outer layers which must be removed before the grain can be eaten. Hulled barley has only the outer husk taken off. It is very much like brown rice and requires a long cooking time. Further abrasion of the grains removes the germ and some of the underlying bran layer, producing what is called pot barley. When all of the bran and the innermost aleurone layer are polished off, the remaining endosperm is known as pearl barley. Pearl is the most common form of barley since the cooking time is relatively short, but it is the least nutritious.

PER SERVING
WITH ROUND OUTS

Calories 610
Protein 23 g
Total Fat 17 g
    saturated 1.8 g
    monounsaturated 8.5 g
    polyunsaturated 5.1 g
Carbohydrate 103 g
    fibre 16 g
Calcium 268 mg
Folacin 279 mcg
Sodium 1367 mg

FOOD GUIDE SERVINGS

1   5   1

Pasta Toppings

Here's a trio of quickly prepared sauces to serve with your favourite pasta. Each recipe, served with 4 to 6 ounces (120 to 180 g) pasta, is enough for two people. These sauces are also excellent on top of cooked rice or spaghetti squash. A sprinkle of freshly grated Parmesan cheese adds a finishing touch and a green salad is the perfect companion.

Turkey Italian

A few vegetables and ground turkey blend wonderfully into a fresh-tasting sauce with Italian flavours. Another time, replace the ground turkey with a can of tuna.

PER SERVING
WITH 1 1/2 CUPS (375 mL)
COOKED PASTA AND 2 TBSP
(25 mL) GRATED PARMESAN

Calories 580
Protein 34 g
Total Fat 15 g
 saturated 4.6 g
 monounsaturated 5.0 g
 polyunsaturated 3.6 g
Carbohydrate 78 g
 fibre 7 g
Calcium 243 mg
Folacin 207 mcg
Sodium 748 mg

FOOD GUIDE SERVINGS

3   2   1/2   1

1 tsp	**vegetable oil** 5 mL	
1	**small onion, chopped** 1	
1	**clove garlic, minced** 1	
6 oz	**lean ground turkey or chicken** 180 g	
1	**small zucchini, chopped** 1	
1/2	**sweet green pepper, cubed** 1/2	
2	**large tomatoes, peeled and chopped, or 1 cup (250 mL) canned** 2	
1 tbsp	**chopped fresh basil, or 1 tsp (5 mL) dried** 15 mL	
1 tbsp	**chopped fresh oregano, or 1 tsp (5 mL) dried** 15 mL	
1/4 tsp	**granulated sugar** 1 mL	
1/8 tsp	**salt** 0.5 mL	

1. In medium nonstick skillet, heat oil over medium-high heat. Add onion and garlic; cook, stirring often, for 5 minutes or until onion is soft. Add turkey; cook, stirring, until no pink remains.

2. Add zucchini, green pepper, tomatoes, basil, oregano, sugar and salt. Bring to a boil; reduce heat and simmer, uncovered, stirring occasionally for 20 minutes or until liquid is thickened.

Makes 2 servings.

Ham and Broccoli

Keep this recipe in mind the next time you have leftover baked ham. Evaporated milk makes a rich creamy sauce with double the calcium of regular milk.

3 cups	**small broccoli florets**	750 mL
2 tsp	**vegetable oil**	10 mL
1	**leek, thinly sliced**	1
1 cup	**sliced mushrooms**	250 mL
3/4 cup	**2% evaporated milk**	175 mL
1/4 cup	**dry white wine**	50 mL
1 tbsp	**all-purpose flour**	15 mL
3/4 cup	**cubed cooked ham, about 6 oz (180 g)**	175 mL
1/2 tsp	**dried basil**	2 mL
1/4 tsp	**salt**	1 mL
pinch	**ground black pepper**	pinch

1. In large pot of boiling water, cook broccoli for 5 minutes or until tender-crisp. Drain and set aside.

2. Meanwhile, in nonstick skillet, heat oil over medium-high heat. Add leek and mushrooms; cook for 3 minutes or until slightly soft.

3. In small bowl, whisk together milk, wine and flour; stir into skillet. Bring to a boil, stirring constantly; cook for 1 minute or until thickened and bubbly. Add ham, basil, salt, pepper and broccoli; cook until sauce just returns to a boil.

Makes 2 servings.

Broccoli Perfection

A star among vegetables, broccoli delivers a remarkable dose of vitamin C and beta carotene, as well as valuable sulforafan, a phytochemical believed to have cancer-fighting attributes. Broccoli also tops up your calcium intake nicely.

PER SERVING
WITH 1 CUP (250 mL)
COOKED PASTA AND 1 TBSP
(15 mL) GRATED PARMESAN

Calories 570
Protein 35 g
Total Fat 15 g
 saturated 4.4 g
 monounsaturated 6.0 g
 polyunsaturated 2.8 g
Carbohydrate 73 g
 fibre 8 g
Calcium 462 mg
Folacin 235 mcg
Sodium 1524 mg

FOOD GUIDE SERVINGS

2 2 1 1

Red Lentils

Red lentils cook to a thick purée making a luscious sauce for topping pasta. This version is based on the earthy flavours of Italian sauces. Add a bit of cooked sausage, chopped ham or a few anchovy fillets if you have them on hand.

1 tsp	**olive or vegetable oil** 5 mL
1	**onion, finely chopped** 1
1	**clove garlic, minced** 1
1 1/4 cups	**chicken or vegetable broth** 300 mL
1/3 cup	**red lentils, rinsed** 75 mL
2 tbsp	**tomato paste** 25 mL
1/4 cup	**finely chopped fresh basil, or 1 tbsp (15 mL) dried** 50 mL
1/4 cup	**finely chopped fresh parsley, or 1 tbsp (15 mL) dried** 50 mL
1/4 cup	**chopped black olives (optional)** 50 mL
1 tbsp	**drained capers, rinsed** 15 mL
	Salt and ground black pepper

1. In medium saucepan, heat oil over medium heat. Add onion and garlic; cook for 5 minutes or until soft

2. Add broth, lentils and tomato paste. Bring to a boil; reduce heat, cover and simmer for 15 minutes or until lentils are very soft.

3. Add basil, parsley, olives (if using) and capers. Add salt and pepper to taste.

Makes 2 servings.

Pasta Measures

Two to three ounces (60 to 90 g) is generally considered a serving of pasta. If you don't have a scale, use a tape measure or measuring cup instead. For a 5 oz (150 g) bundle of spaghetti, wrap a soft tape measure around the spaghetti; the bundle should measure about 3 1/4 inches (8.5 cm) around. A 6 oz (180 g) bundle of spaghetti will measure 3 1/2 inches (9 cm). For shaped pasta, the volume depends on the size of pasta. Small pasta such as macaroni will measure 1 1/4 cups (300 mL) for 5 oz (150 g) and 1 1/2 cups (375 mL) for 6 oz (180 g).

Meals to Share

Who's coming to dinner? Old or new friends, lovers of good food and wine? Children who have left the nest? Maybe a few colleagues coming up to the cottage? No matter what the answer or whether you are setting the table for four, six or eight, we have a number of savoury solutions. From casual dining around a Mexican Lasagne and Cauliflower Ensalada, to a more festive table featuring Baked Cornish Hens with Herbed Glaze, here are meals to please the eye and the palate and to keep the host and hostess worry free.

Our focus is on the main dish with its vegetable and starch accompaniments. If your style of serving permits, consider adding a first course, even a very simple one, to enhance the sense of celebration. The suggested salad may do very well as a meal starter, and in several instances it can be graced with a few shrimp or smoked salmon, all in keeping with savoury wisdom. The wonderful aroma of a homemade soup is also a great way to entice the appetite. Our soup selection includes a number of tantalizing combinations to appeal to your most critical guests. And by all means include a basket of whole grain rolls or bread, perhaps served with a flavoured butter or oil.

Eating with company is a time to celebrate, a time for indulgence. Our choice of ingredients is in harmony with this spirit. Keeping the main course moderate in calories and fat provides latitude for such splendid and healthful fares as Baked Vegetables Provence-Style or Curried Pasta Salad with Wild Rice and Lentils. These meals still leave room for your guests to partake of the extras the host or hostess may have to offer without guilt, be it a welcoming hors d'oeuvre or any of our Happy Endings.

Hors d'Oeuvres

Crudités with Fresh Herb Dip   118

Baked Dippers with Hummus   118

Hot Brie with Chutney   118

Cream Cheese with Chutney   119

Salmon Whirls   119

Tortilla Wedges   119

Meals for 4

Baked Cornish Hens with Herbed Glaze   120

Glazed Pork Tenderloins with Roasted Sweet Potatoes   122

Grilled Lamb Chops Dijon   124

Outback Flank Steak   126

Meals for 6

Chicken Bake with Wild Rice and Mushrooms   128

Herbed Loin of Pork with Roasted Potatoes   130

Seafood with Fennel in a Vermouth Sauce   132

Two-Cheese Pizza with Broccoli and Sun-Dried Tomatoes   134

Meals for 8

Mexican Lasagne   136

Premier Paella   138

Roast Vin Rouge   140

Polynesian Roasted Turkey Breast   142

Hors d'Oeuvres

A savoury bite makes for a warm welcome before the meal is served. These delicacies are usually offered away from the table and can range from something elegant either cold or hot to a more casual dip served with an assortment of crudités or crackers. We look for those requiring a minimum of last-minute preparation to allow time to be with guests before the main meal needs attention. At the table, a first-course appetizer of a light soup or an appealing salad will also whet the appetite before the star attraction.

Crudités with Fresh Herb Dip

Fresh veggies wait on a colourful platter for a dip into a savoury mixture of cheese and herbs.

Crudités: On large platter, arrange assorted fresh vegetables, such as florets of cauliflower and broccoli, strips of sweet red or orange pepper, mushrooms, slices of fennel, slices of cucumber.

Fresh Herb Dip: In small bowl, combine 1/2 cup (125 mL) plain yogurt and 1/4 cup (50 mL) ricotta cheese. Add 1 finely chopped green onion, 2 tbsp (25 mL) finely chopped parsley and 2 tbsp (25 mL) finely chopped fresh herb such as basil, fennel or dill.

Baked Dippers with Hummus

Baked tortilla triangles make a low-fat dipper to serve with hummus or your favourite dip.

Tortilla Dippers: With scissors, cut several flour tortillas into wedges. Bake in 350°F (180°C) oven for 20 minutes or until golden and crisp. Cool and store in a closed container.

Hummus: See recipe page 55.

Hot Brie with Chutney

When you have more than a few guests, a whole Brie cheese melted for spreading on crackers with a taste of chutney is a winner. While often sold in larger wheels, small Brie cheeses about 4 inches (10 cm) in diameter are usually available.

Place a small whole Brie cheese in a shallow baking pan. Top with 1/2 cup (125 mL) of any kind of chutney and 1/4 cup (50 mL) chopped pecans or almonds. Bake in 425°F (220°C) oven for 6 to 8 minutes or until cheese just begins to melt. Serve warm to spread on crackers garnished with slices of apple or pear. Choose crackers with a mild flavour in order not to mask the flavours of the Brie and chutney.

Cream Cheese with Chutney

One of the simplest hors d'oeuvres, yet one of the most tasty. Spoon soft cream cheese and a fruit chutney into separate small dishes. Offer an assortment of crackers for spreading with cheese and topping with a dollop of chutney.

Salmon Whirls

Smoked salmon and cream cheese combine for an easy ambrosial appetizer. Make ahead, refrigerate and slice when needed.

Spread large (about 9 in/23 cm) flour tortillas with cream cheese; sprinkle with chopped chives and a bit of dill. Layer thinly sliced smoked salmon over the cheese, leaving a rim of cheese uncovered so rolls will seal. Roll up each tortilla and wrap tightly in plastic wrap. Refrigerate until serving time, then cut into thin slices.

Tortilla Wedges

An easy appetizer for a warm welcoming bite.

Make half a recipe of Quesadillas (page 54), cutting each folded half into 4 wedges.

For a larger party, grate the cheese in the full recipe. Place 3 tortillas on a baking sheet; distribute cheese and peppers evenly over tortillas. Place remaining 3 tortillas on top and brush tops lightly with olive oil. Bake in 400°F (200°C) oven for 6 minutes or until lightly browned and cheese is melted. To serve, cut each stack into 8 wedges. Serve with salsa.

Fabulous!

Baked Cornish Hens with Herbed Glaze

PER SERVING
OF MAIN DISH

Calories 180
Protein 22 g
Total Fat 7 g
  saturated 1.4 g
  monounsaturated 3.7 g
  polyunsaturated 1.2 g
Carbohydrate 7 g
  fibre 1 g
Calcium 28 mg
Folacin 12 mcg
Sodium 90 mg

Roast Cornish hens on a bed of onions make an elegant dinner party entree. Another time, use chicken breast halves and, during grilling season, omit the onions and cook them outside on the barbecue. The Fresh Papaya Salsa is an attractive and refreshing accompaniment.

1 tbsp	**olive oil**	15 mL
1 tbsp	**balsamic vinegar**	15 mL
1	**small clove garlic, minced**	1
1 tbsp	**finely chopped fresh savoury or thyme, or 1 tsp (5 mL) dried**	15 mL
pinch	**salt**	pinch
2	**Cornish hens, about 1 1/2 lb (750 g) each**	2
2	**large onions, cut into rings**	2

1. In small bowl, whisk together oil, vinegar, garlic, herbs and salt.

2. Using kitchen shears or a heavy knife, cut hens into halves along back and breast bones. Layer onions in a 13 x 9-inch baking dish (3 L). Place hens over top; brush with oil mixture. Bake, uncovered, in 375°F (190°C) oven for 50 minutes or until hens are no longer pink.

Squeeze juice of an orange & zest over chicken. Fabulous!

Rounding Out the Meal

Fresh Papaya Salsa

The fresh taste of papaya wonderfully complements the Cornish hens.

In small bowl, combine 1 cup (250 mL) diced peeled papaya, 1/4 cup (50 mL) chopped sweet red pepper, 1 chopped green onion, 2 tsp (10 mL) lime juice and 1 tsp (5 mL) balsamic vinegar. Add salt and pepper to taste. Cover and let stand for about 1 hour. Refrigerate any unused salsa and use within a day.

Makes 1 1/4 cups (300 mL).

Mediterranean Green Beans

Fresh basil and lemon zest enhance fresh green beans for a savoury side dish.

In small saucepan, steam 1 lb (500 g) whole green beans for 7 minutes or until tender crisp. Meanwhile, in small skillet, heat 1 tbsp (15 mL) olive oil over medium heat; add 2 tbsp (25 mL) chopped onion. Cook for 5 minutes or until soft. Add 1 tbsp (15 mL) chopped fresh basil or 1 tsp (5 mL) dried basil, grated zest of 1 lemon and 1 tbsp (15 mL) fresh lemon juice; toss with beans.

PER SERVING
WITH ROUND OUTS

Calories 580
Protein 36 g
Total Fat 20 g
  saturated 3.1 g
  monounsaturated 12.8 g
  polyunsaturated 3.0 g
Carbohydrate 67 g
  fibre 9 g
Calcium 134 mg
Folacin 170 mcg
Sodium 269 mg

FOOD GUIDE SERVINGS

1   2 1/2   1

Curried Pasta Salad with Wild Rice and Lentils

The three types of carbohydrates cook together for this scrumptious make-ahead salad. Serve either with the meal or as a first course on individual salad plates lined with Boston lettuce.

1/3 cup	**wild rice**	75 mL
1/2 cup	**brown lentils**	125 mL
1/3 cup	**orzo pasta**	75 mL
1/4 cup	**dried currants**	50 mL
3 tbsp	**finely chopped red onion**	45 mL
1/4 cup	**chopped parsley**	50 mL
2 tbsp	**toasted slivered almonds**	25 mL

Dressing:

2 tbsp	**olive oil**	25 mL
2 tbsp	**white wine vinegar**	25 mL
2 tbsp	**cold tea**	25 mL
1 tsp	**Dijon mustard**	5 mL
1/2 tsp	**ground cumin**	2 mL
1/2 tsp	**curry powder**	2 mL
1/4 tsp	**granulated sugar**	1 mL
1/4 tsp	**salt**	1 mL

1. Bring a large pot of salted water to a boil. Add wild rice; reduce heat, cover and simmer for 10 minutes.

2. Add lentils, return to boil. Reduce heat, cover and simmer for 20 minutes.

3. Add orzo, return to boil. Reduce heat, cover and simmer for 5 minutes or until just tender; drain. Place in large serving bowl. Add currants and onion.

4. Dressing: In small bowl, whisk together oil, vinegar, tea, mustard, cumin, curry powder, sugar and salt. Pour over warm rice mixture; mix gently. Cover and refrigerate for at least 2 hours and up to 2 days. At serving time, stir in parsley and almonds.

To Toast Almonds

Place almonds in small microwave-safe dish. Microwave on 100 % power, stirring frequently, for 1 to 3 minutes or until lightly browned.

Glazed Pork Tenderloins with Roasted Sweet Potatoes

PER SERVING
OF MAIN DISH

Calories 350
Protein 36 g
Total Fat 7 g
  saturated 1.6 g
  monounsaturated 3.0 g
  polyunsaturated 1.2 g
Carbohydrate 35 g
  fibre 4 g
Calcium 34 mg
Folacin 18 mcg
Sodium 155 mg

The Balancing Act

Amazingly low in fat, pork tenderloin provides a counterbalance to this heavenly vegetable gratin. Should the spectre of saturated fats be raised over that marvellous Gruyère, remind your guests that the fatty acid balance of the meal is well maintained with the touch of olive oil.

Roasting tenderloins with sweet potatoes and a vegetable gratin tucked alongside leaves you time to enjoy an appetizer with your family and friends while the meal cooks.

1–2	**pork tenderloins, about 1 lb (500 g)**	1–2
1 tbsp	**liquid honey** 25 mL	
1 tsp	**soy sauce** 5 mL	
1 tsp	**Dijon mustard** 5 mL	
1/4 tsp	**dried thyme** 1 mL	
4	**sweet potatoes, about 1 1/2 pounds (750 g), cut into 1 1/2 inches (4 cm) pieces** 4	
2 tsp	**vegetable oil** 10 mL	
pinch	**ground black pepper** pinch	

1. Place tenderloins on large foil-covered baking sheet. If tip is thin, fold under to make an even thickness.

2. In small bowl, combine honey, soy sauce, mustard and thyme. Brush over tenderloins.

3. Place sweet potatoes in large bowl; add oil and black pepper. Mix until pieces are evenly coated with oil. Arrange potatoes around meat on baking sheet.

4. Bake in 375°F (190°C) oven for 40 minutes or until potatoes are soft and meat has just a hint of pink remaining.

Rounding Out the Meal
Broccoli and Cauliflower Gratin

Mornay sauce enhances a popular vegetable combination. Make the dish ahead and bake it alongside the tenderloins to simplify last-minute preparations.

2 cups	**fresh or frozen broccoli florets** 500 mL	
2 cups	**fresh or frozen cauliflower florets** 500 mL	

2 tbsp	**all-purpose flour**	25 mL
1 cup	**milk**	250 mL
1/4 cup	**shredded Gruyère or other cheese**	50 mL
1/4 tsp	**salt**	1 mL
1/8 tsp	**ground white pepper**	0.5 mL
2 tbsp	**grated Parmesan cheese**	25 mL
2 tbsp	**dry bread crumbs**	25 mL

1. In large pot of boiling water, cook broccoli and cauliflower for 2 to 4 minutes or just until barely tender. Drain and rinse immediately in cold water. Spread in bottom of 8-inch (2 L) square baking dish.

2. In 2-cup (500 mL) glass measuring cup, whisk together flour and milk until blended. Microwave at 100% power, stirring frequently, for 2 minutes or until thickened and boiling. Add Gruyère, salt and pepper, stirring until cheese melts. Pour over vegetables; sprinkle top with Parmesan and bread crumbs. At this point, dish may be covered and refrigerated for up to 3 hours.

3. Bake in 375°F (190°C) oven for 30 minutes or until bubbly and lightly browned on top.

Snow Pea Salad with Red Peppers

A colourful salad to add a bright note to your meal.

6 oz	**snow peas**	180 g
4 oz	**bean sprouts**	120 g
1/2	**sweet red pepper, cut in thin strips**	1/2
1	**clove garlic, minced**	1
2 tbsp	**orange juice**	25 mL
2 tbsp	**olive oil**	25 mL
2 tbsp	**red wine vinegar**	25 mL
1/4 tsp	**salt**	1 mL
1 tbsp	**toasted sesame seeds**	15 mL

1. In large pot of boiling water, blanch snow peas for 2 minutes or until barely tender. Drain and rinse in cold water. Place in large salad bowl. Add sprouts and red pepper.

2. In small bowl, whisk together garlic, orange juice, oil, vinegar and salt. At serving time, toss with salad and sprinkle with sesame seeds.

PER SERVING
WITH ROUND OUTS

Calories 580
Protein 47 g
Total Fat 20 g
  saturated 5.5 g
  monounsaturated 9.8 g
  polyunsaturated 2.7 g
Carbohydrate 56 g
  fibre 7 g
Calcium 300 mg
Folacin 106 mcg
Sodium 605 mg

FOOD GUIDE SERVINGS

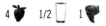

4 🍎 1/2 🥛 1 🍖

To Toast Sesame Seeds

Place sesame seeds in a small microwave-safe dish and microwave on 100% power, stirring frequently, for 1 to 2 minutes or until slightly brown. Or heat, stirring frequently, in a small ungreased skillet over medium heat until lightly browned.

Grilled Lamb Chops Dijon

A hint of mustard lends a pleasing overtone to lamb chops grilled either on the barbecue or under the broiler. This meal is bound to delight a fine palate that cannot indulge in calorie excess.

8	**loin lamb chops, about 1 1/2 lb (750 g)**	8
2 tsp	**grainy Dijon-style mustard**	10 mL
	Coarsely ground black pepper	

1. Trim off any excess fat from chops. Top each chop with 1/4 tsp (1 mL) mustard and a sprinkling of black pepper.

2. Preheat grill or broiler. Cook chops approximately 4 inches (10 cm) from heat for 5 to 6 minutes. Turn to other side and grill for 4 to 5 minutes, depending on thickness, or until chops are of desired doneness.

Rounding Out the Meal
Baked Vegetables Provence-Style

The tantalizing flavours from the French region of Provence make an aromatic accompaniment for the grilled lamb chops. This version includes potatoes, making a complete meal with grilled meat.

4	**unpeeled red potatoes, thinly sliced, about 1 lb (500 g)**	4
1/2 tsp	**salt, divided**	2 mL
	Ground black pepper	
1	**small eggplant, about 8 oz (250 g)**	1
3 tbsp	**minced fresh oregano or thyme, or 3 tsp (15 mL) dried, divided**	45 mL
1	**small zucchini, sliced**	1
1	**sweet red pepper, cut into strips**	1
1/2	**red onion, thinly sliced**	1/2
1	**large tomato, cut into thin wedges**	1
5-6	**mushrooms**	5-6
1 tbsp	**olive oil**	15 mL

1. Lightly oil a 3 qt (3 L) covered baking dish. Place potatoes in a layer on bottom; sprinkle with half the salt and pepper.

2. Cut unpeeled eggplant into 1/2-inch (1 cm) thick slices, then cut each round into quarters. Place on top of potatoes; sprinkle with one-third of oregano.

3. Layer zucchini, pepper and onion over eggplant; sprinkle with remaining salt, pepper and one-third of oregano.

4. Arrange tomato and mushrooms on top; sprinkle with remaining oregano and olive oil.

5. Cover casserole and bake in 375°F (190°C) oven for 1 hour; remove cover and bake for 15 minutes or until vegetables are tender.

Orange and Sweet Onion Salad

When Vidalia onions are in season, this is a great way to feature their succulent sweetness. At other times use Spanish or red onions sliced very thinly.

In large salad bowl, place 4 cups (1 L) torn romaine lettuce. Top with 1 cup (250 mL) chick-peas, 3 large peeled navel oranges cut into 1/4-inch (5 mm) slices and 1 sweet onion, cut into thin rings. At serving time, pour dressing over salad and toss. Garnish with 1/2 cup (125 mL) seasoned croutons.

Dressing: In small bowl, whisk together 2 tbsp (25 mL) orange juice, 2 tbsp (25 mL) olive oil, 1 tbsp (15 mL) balsamic vinegar and 1/8 tsp (1 mL) salt.

Romaine, a Green with a Difference

In the salad world, romaine lettuce offers great value in terms of taste, price and nutrition. Its folate content is particularly remarkable. This meal delivers over half of the amount of folate currently recommended with two-thirds coming almost equally from romaine and chickpeas.

Outback Flank Steak

The Australian flavours of kiwifruit and lime transform this extremely lean steak into a mouth-watering dish. Flank is the most flavourful of beef steaks, but it needs time in a marinade to become tender. As well as adding a lively fruit taste, kiwifruit contains an enzyme that aids the tenderizing process. This barbecue treat will please your most epicurean guests.

2	**kiwifruit, peeled and mashed**	2
1	**clove garlic, mashed**	1
3 tbsp	**fresh lime juice**	45 mL
2 tbsp	**white wine vinegar**	25 mL
2 tbsp	**water**	25 mL
1 tbsp	**finely chopped gingerroot**	15 mL
1 tbsp	**chopped fresh thyme, or 1 tsp (5 mL) dried**	15 mL
2 tsp	**granulated sugar**	10 mL
1/4 tsp	**ground black pepper**	1 mL
1 1/4 lb	**flank steak**	625 g

1. In a resealable plastic bag or flat dish, combine kiwifruit, garlic, lime juice, vinegar, water, gingerroot, thyme, sugar and pepper. Add steak. Seal bag or cover dish and refrigerate for 12 to 24 hours, turning several times.

2. Remove meat from marinade; broil or grill for 5 minutes on each side or until of desired doneness. Cut diagonally into thin slices across the grain.

Watch That Marinade

Marinades add great flavour to meats, and those containing an acid such as vinegar or wine help to tenderize tougher cuts. But after making contact with the meat they may be a source of bacteria. Before using the marinade to brush on food during grilling, bring it to a full boil for 5 minutes. Discard any unused marinade.

Rounding Out the Meal
Fennel with Carrots

The subtle taste of fennel blends nicely with carrots for an attractive vegetable combination. You may also cook the vegetables directly on the grill by placing them on a large sheet of heavy-duty foil, adding the herb and a little of the broth, then sealing tightly. Cook for 20 minutes or until tender.

1	**fennel bulb, about 12 oz (375 g)**	1
4	**large carrots**	4
1	**leek, sliced thinly**	1
1/3 cup	**chicken broth**	75 mL
1/2 tsp	**dried marjoram, oregano, thyme or basil**	2 mL

1. Trim stalks and root end of fennel. Slice bulb into 1/2 inch (1 cm) slices; then cut slices into 1/2-inch (1 cm) pieces, about 2 inches (5 cm) long. Slice carrots into similar-sized pieces.

2. Place fennel, carrots and leek in a medium saucepan. Add broth and marjoram; bring to a boil; reduce heat, cover and simmer for 15 minutes or until vegetables are tender.

Australian Bulgur Salad

Australians have their own refreshing version of the popular tabbouleh salad. Theirs is made with pineapple and melon rather than tomatoes.

1 1/4 cups	**chicken broth**	300 mL
1 cup	**bulgur**	250 mL
3 tbsp	**pineapple or orange juice**	45 mL
2 tbsp	**olive oil**	25 mL
2 tbsp	**liquid honey**	25 mL
1 tbsp	**fresh lemon juice**	15 mL
1/8 tsp	**salt**	0.5 mL
1 1/2 cups	**diced fresh pineapple**	375 mL
1 1/2 cups	**diced cantaloupe or honeydew melon**	375 mL
2 tbsp	**finely chopped red onion or shallots**	25 mL
1/3 cup	**finely chopped parsley**	75 mL
1/3 cup	**finely chopped mint**	75 mL

1. In small saucepan, bring broth to a boil. Stir in bulgur and remove from heat. Let stand for 15 minutes or until liquid has been absorbed.

2. In medium bowl, whisk together pineapple juice, oil, honey, lemon juice and salt. Blend in bulgur until well mixed. Add pineapple, melon, onion, parsley and mint; toss together. Chill until serving time.

PER SERVING
WITH ROUND OUTS

Calories 595
Protein 41 g
Total Fat 19 g
  saturated 5.6 g
  monounsaturated 9.5 g
  polyunsaturated 1.5 g
Carbohydrate 70 g
  fibre 10 g
Calcium 152 mg
Folacin 84 mcg
Sodium 503 mg

FOOD GUIDE SERVINGS

Meals for 6

Chicken Bake with Wild Rice and Mushrooms

**PER SERVING
OF MAIN DISH**

Calories 405
Protein 39 g
Total Fat 8 g
  saturated 2.2 g
  monounsaturated 3.0 g
  polyunsaturated 1.6 g
Carbohydrate 44 g
  fibre 2 g
Calcium 24 mg
Folacin 27 mcg
Sodium 452 mg

Wild rice adds a note of elegance as well as unique taste to this dish which will easily wait on a warming tray while you enjoy pre-dinner appetizers with your guests. Pre-soaking the wild rice ensures that the two types of rice cook in the same amount of time.

2 1/4 cups	**water**	550 mL
3/4 cup	**wild rice**	175 mL
6	**boneless chicken breasts, about 1 1/2 lb/750 g**	6
	Salt and ground black pepper	
1 tbsp	**vegetable oil**	15 mL
1 tbsp	**butter**	15 mL
4 cups	**sliced mushrooms, about 10 oz (300 g)**	1 L
1/2 cup	**chopped onion**	125 mL
1 cup	**long-grain white rice**	250 mL
2 cups	**chicken broth**	500 mL
1/2 tsp	**dried thyme**	2 mL
1/2 tsp	**salt**	2 mL

1. In large saucepan, bring water to boiling over high heat; stir in wild rice, reduce heat, cover and boil gently for 5 minutes. Remove from heat and let stand for 1 hour. Drain well.

2. Rinse chicken and pat dry. Season with salt and pepper to taste. In large nonstick skillet, heat oil over medium-high heat; add chicken. Cook for 5 to 7 minutes or until lightly browned. Remove from pan and set aside.

3. Add butter, mushrooms and onion. Cook on medium-low heat for 6 minutes or until vegetables are soft. Add long-grain rice; cook for 3 minutes or until rice is well coated and slightly browned. Add broth, thyme, salt and wild rice; bring to a boil.

4. Transfer rice mixture to a 13 x 9-inch (3.5 L) baking pan, spreading evenly. Arrange chicken pieces over top; cover tightly with foil. Bake in 350°F (180°C) oven for 30 minutes or until liquid is absorbed and chicken is no longer pink.

Rounding Out the Meal
Broccoli with Peppers and Pine Nuts

Strips of sweet orange pepper contrast with bright green broccoli and reflect the colour of the mango salad. Sprinkle on toasted pine nuts for an elegant note.

In small skillet, toast 1/4 cup (50 mL) pine nuts over medium heat until lightly browned; set aside. Cut 3 stalks of broccoli into florets. Peel and trim stems into 1 x 1/4-inch (2.5 cm x 5 mm) pieces. Steam broccoli for 4 minutes. To steamer, add 1 sweet orange pepper cut into thin slices; steam for 3 minutes or until vegetables are just tender. Drain broccoli and peppers and transfer to serving dish. Sprinkle with pine nuts.

Mango Salad with Mint and Honey Dressing

Only a very light dressing is needed to complement the fresh taste of mango. Be sure to use natural rice vinegar as the seasoned type is too strong.

On each of 6 salad plates place 1 cup (250 mL) torn romaine lettuce. Peel 3 mangoes and cut flesh into small cubes. Divide evenly among salad plates; sprinkle with chopped mint. Drizzle with dressing.

Honey Dressing: In small bowl, whisk together 2 tbsp (25 mL) vegetable oil, 2 tbsp (25 mL) rice vinegar, 1 tbsp (15 mL) liquid honey and 1 small minced shallot.

Wild Rice

Prized for its nutty flavour and chewy texture, wild rice is not really a rice at all but a long-grain marsh grass. It is sold in different grades, with the long grains being the best quality and the shorter broken grains making up the lesser quality. Wild rice can take up to an hour to cook, but soaking it first will shorten the cooking time.

PER SERVING
WITH ROUND OUTS

Calories 600
Protein 44 g
Total Fat 16 g
  saturated 3.2 g
  monounsaturated 7.0 g
  polyunsaturated 4.6 g
Carbohydrate 73 g
  fibre 9 g
Calcium 73 mg
Folacin 167 mcg
Sodium 479 mg

FOOD GUIDE SERVINGS

1 1/2   4   1

Herbed Loin of Pork with Roasted Potatoes

PER SERVING
OF MAIN DISH

Calories 325
Protein 33 g
Total Fat 10 g
  saturated 2.8 g
  monounsaturated 4.4 g
  polyunsaturated 1.3 g
Carbohydrate 26 g
  fibre 3 g
Calcium 55 mg
Folacin 19 mcg
Sodium 74 mg

Rubs give better flavour penetration to a roast than traditional marinades. A single loin roast offers more surface area for the rub and also cooks more quickly than does the usual double loin roast.

2	**cloves garlic, mashed**	2
1 tsp	**dried thyme**	5 mL
1 tsp	**dried basil**	5 mL
1/2 tsp	**ground ginger**	2 mL
1/8 tsp	**ground black pepper**	0.5 mL
	Finely grated zest of 1 orange	
2 lb	**boneless single loin pork roast**	1 kg
1 tbsp	**vegetable oil**	15 mL
1/2 tsp	**paprika**	2 mL
6	**potatoes, cut into quarters**	6

1. In small bowl, combine garlic, thyme, basil, ginger, pepper and orange zest. Rub evenly over surface of roast.

2. Place roast on a rack in a shallow roasting pan. Bake uncovered in 350ºF (180ºC) oven for 20 minutes.

3. Meanwhile, in large bowl, mix oil and paprika; add potatoes and toss to coat thoroughly. Place potatoes around roast in pan. Bake for another 50 minutes or until internal temperature of meat reads 160ºF (70ºC) and potatoes are tender. Cover loosely with foil and let stand for 10 minutes before slicing roast.

Rounding Out the Meal
Vegetable Sauté

A medley of vegetables makes a colourful side dish with delicious flavour.

3/4 cup	**chicken broth**	175 mL
2-3	**carrots, very thinly sliced**	2-3
4 cups	**broccoli florets**	1 L
2 cups	**thinly sliced napa cabbage**	500 mL
1 tbsp	**butter**	15 mL
2	**small onions, sliced**	2
1	**clove garlic, minced**	1
2 tsp	**minced gingerroot**	10 mL
1/2 tsp	**dried thyme**	2 mL
1/4 cup	**sliced water chestnuts**	50 mL
1 tbsp	**fresh lemon juice**	15 mL

1. In large saucepan, bring broth to a boil. Add carrots and place broccoli on top. Return to boil; reduce heat, cover and simmer for 6 minutes or until vegetables are almost tender. Add cabbage; steam for 2 minutes; drain.

2. In large nonstick skillet, heat butter over medium-high heat. Add onions, garlic and gingerroot; stir-fry for 1 minute. Sprinkle with thyme. Add water chestnuts and vegetables; sauté for 2 minutes or until vegetables are well mixed and heated through. Drizzle with lemon juice.

Greens with Pear and Poppy Seed Citrus Dressing

Slices of fresh pear add a refreshing note to a green salad.

Salad: In a large bowl, combine 6 cups (1.5 L) mixed salad greens (oak leaf lettuce, green leaf lettuce, butterhead lettuce), 1 thinly sliced red onion separated into rings and 2 sliced pears. Toss with dressing.

Dressing: In small glass measuring cup, combine 1/4 cup (50 mL) orange juice, 1 tbsp (15 mL) granulated sugar, 1 tsp (5 mL) lemon juice, 1/8 tsp (0.5 mL) dry mustard and 1/8 tsp (0.5 mL) salt. Microwave on 100% power for 30 seconds or until sugar is dissolved. Whisk in 2 tbsp (25 mL) vegetable oil and 2 tsp (10 mL) poppy seeds until well blended.

Chinese Cabbage

Chinese cabbage is the name given to two very different types of cabbage. Napa is pale in colour, and the head is very tightly closed, giving a boxy shape. Bok choy has quite a different appearance with its dark leaves and snow white stalks. Both have a more delicate taste and are more tender than traditional cabbage. They also require less cooking. Along with all members of the cabbage family, they contain nitrogen compounds called indoles which may play a role in reducing the risk of certain types of cancers.

PER SERVING
WITH ROUND OUTS

Calories 505
Protein 38 g
Total Fat 17 g
  saturated 4.5 g
  monounsaturated 7.9 g
  polyunsaturated 3.4 g
Carbohydrate 53 g
  fibre 9 g
Calcium 169 mg
Folacin 109 mcg
Sodium 273 mg

FOOD GUIDE SERVINGS

4   1 1/2

Seafood with Fennel in a Vermouth Sauce

A seafood mixture is always a favourite, and vermouth plus the subtle anise flavour of fennel make it even more appealing. Served over a bed of noodles, this makes an attractive buffet dish.

2 tbsp	**butter**	25 mL
1 tbsp	**vegetable oil**	15 mL
1	**fennel bulb, trimmed and chopped**	1
2 cups	**sliced mushrooms, about 6 oz (180 g)**	500 mL
1/2 cup	**finely chopped onion**	125 mL
2/3 cup	**dry vermouth**	150 mL
1 lb	**shrimp, shelled and deveined**	500 g
1/2 lb	**scallops, cut in half if large**	250 g
2 cups	**milk**	500 mL
1/3 cup	**all-purpose flour**	75 mL
3/4 tsp	**salt**	4 mL
3/4 cup	**shredded Emmenthal or Gruyère cheese, about 3 oz (90 g)**	175 mL
8 oz	**cooked crabmeat, cut in large pieces**	250 g
2 tbsp	**chopped fresh chives or parsley**	25 mL
12 oz	**noodles, cooked according to package directions**	375 g

1. In large nonstick skillet, heat butter and oil over medium heat. Add fennel, mushrooms and onion; cook for 6 minutes or until beginning to soften. Stir in vermouth; add shrimp and scallops. Bring to a boil; reduce heat and boil gently for 3 minutes or until fish is no longer opaque.

2. In small bowl, whisk together milk, flour and salt. Add to skillet; cook, stirring constantly for 1 to 2 minutes or until thickened and bubbly. Add cheese and crabmeat, stirring until cheese is melted.

3. Place noodles in a large shallow serving dish; pour seafood mixture over top or serve seafood and noodles separately. Garnish with chives.

Rounding Out the Meal
Asparagus with Orange Butter

Asparagus served with orange butter is not only a gourmet delicacy, but a fantastic source of folate bringing to the plate a quarter of what you should be aiming for in a day.

Snap the bottoms from 2 lb (1 kg) asparagus; steam until tender; drain. In small microwave-safe container, melt 1 tbsp (15 mL) butter. Whisk in zest of 1 large orange and 1 tbsp (15 mL) orange juice. Place asparagus on serving plate and drizzle orange butter over.

Fennel or Anise

Fennel, sometimes sold as anise, can be eaten raw or cooked. Cooking subdues the mild licorice taste of the raw vegetable. Trim off the stalks from the top of the fennel bulb and save them for soup, as they can be quite fibrous. Also save the fine green leaves to use as you would fresh dill. The base can be sliced or chopped. If you prefer the appearance of the slices when they hold together, keep a small amount of the core attached; otherwise, discard it. Slices of fennel make a delicious addition to a raw vegetable platter or to a vegetable stir-fry.

Surimi

Often sold as "imitation seafood," surimi is processed, usually from Pacific pollock, and designed to look like crabmeat. While the flavour is different from the real thing, it is quite acceptable, especially for adding to a casserole-type dish, and is much less expensive.

PER SERVING
WITH ROUND OUTS

Calories 650
Protein 49 g
Total Fat 19 g
  saturated 8.4 g
  monounsaturated 5.9 g
  polyunsaturated 2.9 g
Carbohydrate 64 g
  fibre 5 g
Calcium 370 mg
Folacin 274 mcg
Sodium 1001 mg

FOOD GUIDE SERVINGS

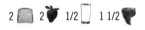

2   2   1/2   1 1/2

Meals for 6

Two-Cheese Pizza with Broccoli and Sun-Dried Tomatoes

The fabulous combination of flavours in this easy-to-make meal make it perfect for a casual evening.

1/2 cup	**sliced dry-packed sun-dried tomatoes**	125 mL
2 cups	**small broccoli florets**	500 mL
1 1/2 lb	**frozen or homemade pizza dough**	750 g
3 cups	**shredded provolone or mozzarella cheese, about 2/3 lb (350 g)**	750 mL
1/3 cup	**chopped sweet onion**	75 mL
1/4 cup	**chopped fresh basil, or 2 tsp (10 mL) dried**	50 mL
1/2 cup	**grated Parmesan cheese**	125 mL

1. In small bowl, cover tomatoes with hot water; let stand for 10 minutes. Drain and set aside.

2. Meanwhile, in large pot of boiling water, cook broccoli for 2 minutes to blanch. Drain and immediately place in cold water. Drain and set aside.

3. On lightly floured surface, roll out dough. Press into a nonstick or lightly greased 11 x 17-inch (28 x 43 cm) baking sheet, stretching dough to fit pan. Cover dough with cheese; add tomatoes, broccoli, onion and basil, distributing evenly. Sprinkle with Parmesan cheese.

4. Bake on bottom rack of 450°F (230°C) oven for 20 minutes or until cheese is bubbly and crust is golden.

Homemade Pizza Dough

In large bowl, stir together 1 1/4 cups (300 mL) warm water and 1 tsp (5 mL) dry yeast until yeast is dissolved. Add 1 tsp (5 mL) granulated sugar and 1 tsp (5 mL) salt. Stir in 1 2/3 cups (400 mL) all-purpose flour until mixture forms a smooth batter. Add approximately 1 1/3 cups (325 mL) more flour or enough to make a soft dough. Knead until smooth. Place in a lightly greased bowl, cover and let rise in a warm place for 1 hour. Makes about 1 1/2 lb (750 g) dough.

Rounding Out the Meal
Spinach, Grapefruit and Mushroom Salad with Raspberry Vinaigrette

Succulent dark leaves of spinach combine with sweet grapefruit for salad that is as delicious as it is nutritious.

On small microwave-safe plate, place 1 tbsp (15 mL) chopped pecans; microwave at 100% power for 30 seconds to 1 minute or until slightly browned. In large salad bowl, place 1 package (10 oz/284 g) stemmed and torn spinach. With sharp knife, remove the outside rind of 2 large grapefruit, exposing the pulp. Carefully cut on both sides of each inner membrane, lift out sections and add to spinach. Top with 2 cups (500 mL) sliced mushrooms. At serving time, toss with dressing and garnish with pecans.

Raspberry Vinaigrette Dressing: In small bowl or jar with tight-fitting lid, whisk or shake 3 tbsp (45 mL) olive oil, 2 tbsp (25 mL) raspberry vinegar, 2 tbsp (25 mL) cold tea, 1/2 tsp (2 mL) granulated sugar, 1/2 tsp (2 mL) Dijon mustard, 1/8 tsp (0.5 mL) salt and a pinch of ground black pepper.

Spinach, a Wealth of Vitamins

Spinach abounds in well-known beta carotene, the precursor of vitamin A, and the much sought-after folate. Newer on the list of spinach nutritional virtues is lutein, a compound associated with a lower risk of cataracts and colon cancer.

PER SERVING
WITH ROUND OUTS

Calories 565
Protein 30 g
Total Fat 21 g
  saturated 9.0 g
  monounsaturated 9.2 g
  polyunsaturated 1.6 g
Carbohydrate 65 g
  fibre 4 g
Calcium 586 mg
Folacin 196 mcg
Sodium 986 mg

FOOD GUIDE SERVINGS

3   2 1/2   1 1/2

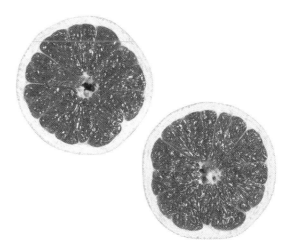

Mexican Lasagne

Excellence on All Fronts

This meal leaves no nutrition stone unturned. It brims with fibre and vitamin C and is an excellent source of vitamin A, folate, calcium, iron and zinc.

Lasagne is a favourite dish to serve a gathering of friends since it can be prepared well ahead of time and waits happily until people are ready to eat. This Mexican version brings welcome variety, and the corn tortillas eliminate the need for cooking the traditional lasagne pasta. For even greater time saving, replace the fresh spinach with frozen chopped spinach.

1/2 lb	**lean ground beef**	250 g
2	**jalapeño peppers, diced**	2
1	**large onion, chopped**	1
1	**can (19 oz/540 mL) kidney beans, drained and rinsed**	1
1	**can (14 oz/398 mL) tomato sauce**	1
1 cup	**medium or hot salsa**	250 mL
1 tsp	**ground cumin**	5 mL
1/2 tsp	**salt**	2 mL
1 1/2 cups	**light ricotta cheese**	375 mL
1 cup	**shredded Monterey Jack cheese**	250 mL
1	**egg, lightly beaten**	1
1	**pkg (10 oz/284 g) fresh spinach, rinsed**	1
18	**small (about 6-inch/15 cm) corn tortillas**	18
6	**green onions, chopped**	6
1	**tomato, chopped**	1

1. In large nonstick skillet, cook beef over medium-high heat until no longer pink. Add peppers and onion; cook for 5 minutes or until soft. Stir in beans, tomato sauce, salsa, cumin and salt. Bring to a boil; reduce heat and simmer for 10 minutes.

2. Meanwhile, in medium bowl, combine ricotta cheese, Monterey Jack cheese and egg.

3. Place spinach with rinse water clinging to leaves in microwave-safe container; cover and microwave on 100% power for 3 minutes or until wilted. Transfer to a colander; press to remove as much moisture as possible. Place on cutting board and chop coarsely.

4. Cut 6 tortillas in half; arrange over bottom of a lightly greased 13 x 9-inch (3 L) baking dish. Spread half the beef mixture over tortillas; top with 6 more tortillas, cut in half. Spread cheese mixture over second layer of tortillas; arrange spinach over cheese. Place remaining 6 tortillas, cut in half, over spinach; top with remaining beef mixture. Cover pan with foil.

5. Bake in 350°F (180°C) oven for 1 hour or until layers are set and heated through. Remove from oven; scatter green onions and tomato over top. Cover again; let stand for 10 minutes before cutting.

Rounding Out the Meal
Mexican Cauliflower Ensalada

Snowy white cauliflower topped with guacamole makes an attractive salad with a Mexican flair.

1	**cauliflower, separated into florets**	1
1/2 tsp	**cumin seed**	2 mL
1/4 cup	**chopped cilantro or parsley**	50 mL
1	**ripe avocado, peeled**	1
1	**small ripe tomato, finely chopped**	1
1	**jalapeño pepper, seeded and finely chopped (optional)**	1
1/4 cup	**finely chopped red onion**	50 mL
1 tbsp	**fresh lime juice**	15 mL
1/8 tsp	**salt**	0.5 mL
6-8	**leaves romaine lettuce**	6-8
1-2	**roasted sweet red peppers, thinly sliced, or pimientos**	1-2

1. Bring a large pot of salted water to a boil; add cauliflower. Cover and return to a boil. Boil gently for 4 minutes; drain and put immediately in cold water. Drain well and place in large bowl.

2. Sprinkle cumin and cilantro over cauliflower. Toss to mix. Chill at least 1 hour.

3. In small bowl, mash avocado; stir in tomato, jalapeño pepper (if using), onion, lime juice and salt. Cover and chill until serving time.

4. Arrange romaine lettuce on serving plate. Place cauliflower in centre. Spoon avocado mixture over top. Garnish with red peppers.

PER SERVING
WITH ROUND OUTS

Calories 505
Protein 29 g
Total Fat 19 g
   saturated 8.0 g
   monounsaturated 7.3 g
   polyunsaturated 2.1 g
Carbohydrate 61 g
   fibre 10 g
Calcium 449 mg
Folacin 265 mcg
Sodium 1150 mg

FOOD GUIDE SERVINGS

1 1/2   3   1/2   1

Premier Paella

PER SERVING
OF MAIN DISH

Calories 430
Protein 29 g
Total Fat 14 g
  saturated 3.6 g
  monounsaturated 6.4 g
  polyunsaturated 2.3 g
Carbohydrate 46 g
  fibre 2 g
Calcium 49 mg
Folacin 23 mcg
Sodium 967 mg

Traditionally made with a variety of seafood, paella can be as simple or as elaborate as you choose. Since it is easy to prepare and can be made ahead, it is a perfect choice for casual entertaining. A salad and crusty bread are all you need to complete the meal. The essential ingredients for paella are rice, chicken broth, garlic and saffron. Add others such as lobster or salmon pieces, steamed fresh mussels, artichoke hearts or hot chile peppers as you wish.

2 tbsp	**olive or vegetable oil**	25 mL
8	**skinless chicken thighs, or 4 boneless breasts, cut in strips**	8
1 tsp	**salt**	5 mL
1/4 tsp	**ground black pepper**	1 mL
1	**spicy smoked fresh or frozen sausage, about 4 oz (120 g), sliced thinly**	1
3 oz	**ham, cut in thin strips**	90 g
2	**cloves garlic, minced**	2
1 cup	**sliced onions**	250 mL
1	**sweet green pepper, cut in strips**	1
2 cups	**long-grain white rice**	500 mL
4 cups	**chicken broth**	1 L
3 tbsp	**tomato sauce**	45 mL
1/4 tsp	**saffron threads**	1 mL
8 oz	**frozen ready-to-eat shrimp with tails attached, defrosted**	250 g
1 cup	**frozen peas**	250 mL
3	**pimientos or roasted sweet red peppers, cut in strips**	3
2 tbsp	**chopped fresh parsley**	25 mL

1. In large covered skillet or Dutch oven, heat oil over medium-high heat. Brown chicken for 3 to 4 minutes. Sprinkle with salt and pepper and push to one side of pan. Add sausage, ham, garlic, onions and green pepper; cook for 5 minutes or until onions are softened. Add rice; stir for several minutes or until coated with oil.

2. Stir in chicken broth, tomato sauce and saffron. Bring mixture to a boil; reduce heat, cover and simmer for 20 minutes or until liquid is almost absorbed. (If making ahead, cover and refrigerate at this step.)

3. Add shrimp, peas, pimientos and parsley; cook for 5 minutes or until shrimp and peas are hot.

Note: If you prefer to use fresh shrimp, remove shells and add during the last 5 minutes of the cooking time for the rice.

Variation:
Vegetarian Paella

Replace the chicken, sausage, ham and shrimp with 1 can (19 oz/540 mL) drained and rinsed chick-peas and 1 can (19 oz/540 mL) drained and rinsed black beans and replace chicken broth with vegetable broth.

Rounding Out the Meal
Lettuces with Green Goddess Dressing

Back in the Roaring Twenties, this dressing, honouring William Archer's play of that name, enjoyed great popularity in the United States and Canada. The proportions varied but always included mayonnaise, tarragon, parsley and anchovies.

In large salad bowl, place 8 cups (2 L) torn assorted lettuces. Top with rings of 1 sweet onion. At serving time, toss with dressing.

Dressing: In small bowl, whisk together 1/2 cup (125 mL) light mayonnaise, 1/2 cup (125 mL) plain yogurt, 1/4 cup (50 mL) chopped parsley, 2 tbsp (15 mL) tarragon or white wine vinegar, 1 tbsp (15 mL) minced chives and 1 tbsp (15 mL) anchovy paste.

PER SERVING
WITH ROUND OUTS

Calories 500
Protein 31 g
Total Fat 19 g
  saturated 4.1 g
  monounsaturated 9.2 g
  polyunsaturated 3.7 g
Carbohydrate 51 g
  fibre 3 g
Calcium 126 mg
Folacin 59 mcg
Sodium 1135 mg

FOOD GUIDE SERVINGS

1 1/2   2   1

Roast Vin Rouge

Instead of the usual standing rib roast for those special occasions, try a rump or sirloin enhanced with the flavours of red wine, brandy and vegetables. The initial bake in a very hot oven shortens the cooking time and brings a very tender roast to the table sooner.

3 lb	**rump or sirloin tip roast**	1.5 kg
1 tsp	**vegetable oil**	5 mL
1 tbsp	**butter**	15 mL
1	**clove garlic, minced**	1
1/2 cup	**chopped onions**	125 mL
1/4 cup	**chopped carrots**	50 mL
1 tbsp	**warm brandy**	15 mL
1 1/2 cups	**dry red wine**	375 mL
1	**bay leaf**	1
1/2 tsp	**dried thyme**	2 mL
2 tbsp	**chopped fresh parsley**	25 mL

1. In nonstick skillet, heat oil over medium-high heat. Cook roast on all sides until well browned. Remove from pan and set aside.

2. Add butter to pan; melt over medium-high heat. Add garlic, onions and carrots; cook for 10 minutes or until softened and browned. Transfer vegetables to heavy metal Dutch oven or covered casserole.

3. Place meat on top of vegetables. Pour brandy over top and set aflame. When flame subsides, add wine, bay leaf and thyme. Bake, covered, in 500°F (260°C) oven for 20 minutes. Reduce temperature to 325°F (160°C); bake for 40 minutes or until internal temperature reaches 145°F (63°C).

4. To serve, slice roast and place on warmed platter. Pour a bit of pan juice over top; sprinkle with parsley. Serve remaining pan juice separately.

Rounding Out the Meal
Baked Mashed Potatoes

Pour evaporated milk over mashed potatoes to bake in the oven until the roast is ready.

In large pot of salted water, cook about 3 lb (1.5 kg) peeled, cubed potatoes until tender. Drain thoroughly and return to pot. Shake pot over medium heat until potatoes are dry and mealy. Put potatoes through ricer or mash until smooth. Add about 1/2 cup (125 mL) milk, 1 tbsp (15 mL) butter and pepper to taste. Spoon potatoes into a buttered baking dish, smoothing the surface; pour 1/4 cup (50 mL) evaporated milk over top. Cover loosely with aluminum foil and place in 325°F (160°C) oven for the last 10 minutes of the roast's cooking time. Garnish with chopped parsley.

Brussels Sprout and Carrot Duo

This attractive vegetable combination offers both taste and nutritional benefits. The orange glaze with a hint of olive gives a finishing touch. Add a fresh herb such as basil or oregano if you have it on hand.

4	**carrots, julienned**	4
3 cups	**fresh or frozen Brussels sprouts**	750 mL
2 tbsp	**orange juice**	25 mL
1 tsp	**olive oil**	5 mL
1 tsp	**lemon juice**	5 mL
1 tsp	**granulated sugar**	5 mL
1/4 tsp	**Dijon mustard**	1 mL
1 tbsp	**toasted sesame seeds**	15 mL
1 tbsp	**toasted sunflower seeds**	15 mL
2 tbsp	**chopped fresh parsley**	25 mL

1. Fill a medium saucepan with about 1/2 inch (1 cm) water. Place carrots in bottom, then add Brussels sprouts. Bring to a boil; reduce heat, cover and simmer for 8 minutes or until vegetables are just tender. Drain, rinse with cold water and set aside.

2. In same saucepan, combine orange juice, oil, lemon juice, sugar and mustard. Bring to a boil. Add vegetables and toss to heat through. Place in serving dish and sprinkle with seeds and parsley.

Watercress Lettuce Salad with Asian Pear

Watercress is a pungent green with a peppery note that sets off the buttery texture of Boston or Bibb lettuce. Asian pear, also known as apple pear or Nashi fruit, adds an interesting taste.

In large salad bowl, combine 2 bunches trimmed and sliced watercress and 2 heads torn Boston or Bibb lettuce. Add 1 cubed unpeeled Asian pear; toss with dressing.

Dressing: In small bowl, whisk together 2 tbsp (25 mL) rice vinegar, 2 tbsp (25 mL) water, 2 tbsp (25 mL) olive oil, 1 tbsp (15 mL) lime juice, 1 tbsp (15 mL) honey and 1/4 tsp (1 mL) salt.

PER SERVING
WITH ROUND OUTS

Calories 525
Protein 41 g
Total Fat 18 g
  saturated 5.8 g
  monounsaturated 8.0 g
  polyunsaturated 1.9 g
Carbohydrate 46 g
  fibre 8 g
Calcium 161 mg
Folacin 106 mcg
Sodium 541 mg

FOOD GUIDE SERVINGS

4 1

Cruciferous Value

Brussels sprouts along with cabbage, cauliflower and broccoli, all vegetables from the cruciferous family, are considered among the top cancer-risk reducers. Here in tandem with carrots and orange juice, Brussels sprouts bring this meal to a vitamin A and C peak.

Polynesian Roasted Turkey Breast

Turkey is not just for the holidays; serve it anytime. To give a new twist to the usual bird, marinate either a whole breast or a boneless roll with island flavours of pineapple and gingerroot. Since the cooking time depends on the size and shape of the breast, it is important to use a meat thermometer. The pilaf bakes alongside the turkey to make a meal with little last-minute preparation.

1	**whole turkey breast, about 4 to 5 lb (2 to 2.5 kg)**	1
1 cup	**pineapple juice**	250 mL
1/2 cup	**liquid honey**	125 mL
1/4 cup	**Worcestershire sauce**	50 mL
1 tbsp	**finely chopped gingerroot**	15 mL
2	**cloves garlic, minced**	2
1/4 tsp	**salt**	1 mL

1. Place turkey in large resealable plastic bag.

2. In small bowl, combine pineapple juice, honey, Worcestershire sauce, gingerroot, garlic and salt. Pour over turkey; press bag to remove as much air as possible and seal. Turn to coat. Refrigerate for at least 8 but no more than 24 hours.

3. Remove turkey from marinade; place on rack in a shallow roasting pan. Pour marinade into small saucepan, bring to a boil and simmer for 5 minutes.

4. Brush turkey with marinade. Bake in 325°F (160°C) oven for 1 1/2 hours or until a thermometer inserted into the thickest part of the breast reads 170°F (77°C) and the juices are no longer pink when you slice into the meat. Brush with marinade several times during cooking.

5. Cover turkey with foil and let stand 10 minutes before slicing.

Rounding Out the Meal
Apple Glazed Carrot Parsnip Medley

The assertive flavour of parsnip and the sweetness of carrot are highlighted by an apple glaze in this colourful veggie side dish.

3 cups	**julienned carrots (about 6)**	750 mL
1 1/2 cups	**julienned parsnips (about 3)**	375 mL
1/2 cup	**apple juice or cider**	125 mL
2 tsp	**brown sugar**	10 mL
1/4 tsp	**ground ginger**	1 mL
2 tbsp	**chopped fresh parsley**	25 mL

1. In medium saucepan, combine carrots, parsnips and apple juice. Bring to a boil; reduce heat, cover and simmer for 10 minutes or until vegetables are just tender.

2. Pour vegetables and liquid into a large nonstick skillet. Stir in sugar and ginger; bring to a boil; reduce heat and boil rapidly for 5 minutes or until all liquid has evaporated and vegetables are glazed. Stir in parsley.

Two-Rice Pilaf Bake

Leeks and a few pecans give exceptional flavour to a pilaf of wild and brown rice.

2 tbsp	**vegetable oil**	25 mL
2 cups	**chopped leeks (white and light green parts)**	500 mL
1	**sweet orange pepper, chopped**	1
1 cup	**long-grain brown rice**	250 mL
1 cup	**wild rice**	250 mL
1/2 cup	**chopped pecans**	125 mL
3 cups	**chicken broth**	750 mL
1/2 tsp	**salt**	2 mL
1/4 cup	**chopped fresh parsley**	50 mL

1. In nonstick skillet, heat oil over medium-high heat. Add leeks and pepper; cook for 5 minutes or until soft. Stir in brown rice, wild rice and pecans; cook for 2 minutes.

2. Transfer to 3 qt (3 L) baking dish; stir in broth and salt. Cover and bake in 325ºF (160ºC) oven for 1 1/2 hours or until liquid is absorbed. Stir in parsley.

PER SERVING
WITH ROUND OUTS

Calories 675
Protein 47 g
Total Fat 24 g
 saturated 3.9 g
 monounsaturated 13.5 g
 polyunsaturated 4.6 g
Carbohydrate 69 g
 fibre 6 g
Calcium 113 mg
Folacin 107 mcg
Sodium 527 mg

FOOD GUIDE SERVINGS

1 1/2   3   1 1/2

Avocado Grapefruit Salad

Citrus and avocado combine to provide a pleasing flavour combination.

With sharp knife, remove the rind of 4 grapefruit, exposing the pulp. Carefully cut on both sides of each inner membrane and lift out fruit sections, catching juice in small bowl; set fruit aside and reserve juice. Peel and cut 2 avocados into wedges. Gently toss wedges with reserved juice to coat. Line 8 salad plates with leaf lettuce. Arrange alternating slices of avocado and grapefruit over lettuce; drizzle with dressing.

Dressing: In small bowl, combine 3 tbsp (45 mL) olive oil, 1 tbsp (25 mL) red wine vinegar, 1 tsp (5 mL) liquid honey and 1/2 tsp (2 mL) Dijon mustard.

Turkey Planovers

The leftovers are sometimes as good as the turkey's first appearance. Depending on the size of your turkey breast, you should have enough left to make sandwiches or to use to replace the tuna in the Tuna Rice Casserole (page 152) or Tuna Over Noodles (page 153). The nutritional analysis for this meal was calculated for 125 g portions of turkey per serving, or about 4 ounces.

It's All in the Cut

Cutting vegetables into even-sized pieces has the advantage of allowing them to cook all at the same time as well as giving a pleasing appearance. Slicing is the easiest way to cut root vegetables, but if you want a more elegant presentation, prepare them julienne. First cut the vegetable into 1/8-inch (3 mm) slices, then stack several slices together and cut again into 1/8-inch (3 mm) strips. The resulting matchstick-like pieces can be cut into whatever length you desire.

Shelf Solutions

With the refrigerator bare and the elements outside formidable, calling for a pizza may be one option, but others are at hand. Take a minute and consider the tasty and quick "shelf solutions" we propose in this section.

With these recipes, that can of salmon or flaked ham sitting on your shelf can be transformed into a delicious meal for two. Adding a soup, frozen vegetables and an available starch balances the meal; frozen berries topped by a dollop of yogurt provide a happy ending. Check the Food Guide pattern in these meals and complement them accordingly. You may even want to stock up with shrimp, crab, smoked oysters and fancy crackers just so you are ready for an impromptu candlelight dinner.

A carefully planned supply of non-perishable foods will guarantee access to nutritious meals any time, any day. To select the basics, think variety and be guided by the four food groups. Choose several kinds of canned fish or meat, from tuna and sardines to such seafood delights as shrimp and crab. Evaporated milk is a must among your staples for giving soups and sauces a nutritious boost. Include your favourite vegetables, fruits, legumes and soups and don't forget vitamin-rich tomato juice. Then round out your choices with dried pasta, rice and other grains, including breakfast cereals. Even with limited freezer space, fruit juice, berries and several vegetables can be kept on hand. And tuck in an extra loaf of bread and individually frozen fish fillets. It pays to be prepared.

Not only are our Shelf Solutions convenient, most are economical as well. So feature them regularly in your dinner selections with a fresh salad and one of the tasty side dishes suggested in other sections.

Salmon Bake   148

Salmon Cups with Parsley Sauce   149

Fettuccini with Salmon and Broccoli   150

Tuna Vegetable Patties   151

Tuna Rice Casserole   152

Tuna Over Noodles   153

Shrimp with Pasta and Greens   154

Creole Rice with Shrimp   155

Crab Cakes   156

Baby Clams with Linguine   157

Sardines on Toast with Mustard Sauce   158

Kipper Potato Bake   159

All-in-One Sun-Dried Tomato Quiche   160

Lentils and Rice Egyptian-Style   161

Salmon Bake

 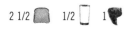
A can of salmon and the box of pasta waiting on your shelves combine with any kind of cheese to make a rewarding meal.

1 2/3 cups	**penne or small bow pasta, about 4 oz (120 g)**	400 mL
1/2 cup	**milk**	125 mL
1 tbsp	**all-purpose flour**	15 mL
1/4 cup	**shredded Cheddar cheese**	50 mL
3 tbsp	**salsa**	45 mL
1/2 tsp	**dried dill, or 1 tbsp (15 mL) chopped fresh**	2 mL
pinch	**salt and pepper**	pinch
1	**can (7.5 oz/213 g) salmon, drained**	1
1/4 cup	**fine dry bread crumbs**	50 mL
1 tbsp	**grated Parmesan cheese**	15 mL

1. In large pot of boiling salted water, cook pasta for 8 to 10 minutes or until tender yet firm. Drain and return to pot.

2. Meanwhile, in 2-cup (500 mL) glass measuring cup or microwave-safe bowl, whisk together milk and flour. Microwave on 100% power, stirring several times, for 1 1/2 min-utes or until thickened and bubbly. Stir in cheese, salsa, dill and salt and pepper.

3. Stir sauce into cooked pasta. Add salmon, breaking into pieces with a fork. Turn pasta into a small (1 qt/1 L) casserole dish.

4. In small bowl, combine bread crumbs and cheese; sprinkle over casserole. Bake in 350°F (180°C) oven for 25 minutes or until hot and bubbly.

Makes 2 servings.

Salmon Sense

Canned salmon is one of the most wholesome "natural" products. Nothing is added to the fish at the cannery except salt. Several types of salmon are commonly available in cans. Sockeye with its deep red colour, higher omega-3 fatty acid content and rich flavour is the most favoured. Coho has a lighter colour and contains less fat. Smaller and leaner Pink salmon has a more bland flavour and is generally the least expensive. Whichever one you use, be sure to crush the heat-softened bones with a fork and blend into the fish for a healthy dose of dietary calcium.

Salmon Cups with Parsley Sauce

This recipe ranks high on our list of favourite solutions from the pantry. Use green onion if you have it for a colourful presentation. The hollandaise-type sauce is easy to make but cooks very quickly so watch the time carefully.

1 tsp	**vegetable oil**	5 mL
2 tbsp	**finely chopped onion**	25 mL
1	**can (7.5 oz/213 g) salmon, undrained**	1
6	**saltine crackers, crushed**	6
1	**egg white, beaten**	1
1 tbsp	**milk**	15 mL

Sauce

1 tsp	**butter**	5 mL
1	**egg yolk**	1
1 tbsp	**lemon juice**	15 mL
pinch	**each: dry mustard and salt**	pinch
1 tbsp	**plain yogurt**	15 mL
1 tsp	**chopped fresh parsley, or 1/4 tsp (1 mL) dried**	5 mL

1. In small microwave-safe container, combine oil and onion; microwave on 100% power for 30 seconds.

2. Remove bones from salmon and crush with a fork. Stir bones, salmon and liquid into onion mixture. Mix in crackers, egg white and milk; pack into two 4-ounce (120 mL) custard cups. Microwave on 100% power for 2 minutes or until salmon mixture puffs slightly and is set. Let stand while making sauce.

3. Sauce: In small microwave-safe container, microwave butter on 100% power for 10 seconds or until melted. Whisk in egg yolk, lemon juice, mustard and salt; microwave on 70% power for 10 seconds and stir immediately. Mixture should be slightly thick; microwave on 70% power for 5 seconds longer if necessary. Stir in yogurt and parsley.

4. Invert salmon cups on serving plates; spoon sauce over top.

Makes 2 servings.

PER SERVING

Calories 300
Protein 23 g
Total Fat 19 g
  saturated 4.9 g
  monounsaturated 8.2 g
  polyunsaturated 4.3 g
Carbohydrate 10 g
  fibre 1 g
Calcium 279 mg
Folacin 26 mcg
Sodium 661 mg

FOOD GUIDE SERVINGS

 1/2   1 1/2

A Case for Weekly Fish

Among other things, a weekly intake of fish has been associated with a reduced risk of several types of cancer, especially those of the digestive tract.

Fettuccine with Salmon and Broccoli

PER SERVING

Calories 605
Protein 37 g
Total Fat 16 g
    saturated 4.7 g
    monounsaturated 5.8 g
    polyunsaturated 3.9 g
Carbohydrate 78 g
    fibre 4 g
Calcium 439 mg
Folacin 255 mcg
Sodium 863 mg

FOOD GUIDE SERVINGS

3  2 🍓 1/2 🥛 1 🍗

Calcium Feast

This dish is a calcium booster providing at least one-third of your daily requirements.

Pasta, a can of salmon and frozen broccoli florets combine to make a colourful and delicious supper from ingredients kept on hand.

6 oz	**fettuccine, linguine or spaghetti**	180 g
2/3 cup	**water**	150 mL
2 tsp	**chicken bouillon granules**	10 mL
1/4 tsp	**dried basil**	1 mL
2 cups	**frozen broccoli florets, about 6 oz (180 g)**	500 mL
1/2 cup	**milk**	125 mL
2 tbsp	**all-purpose flour**	25 mL
1	**can (7.5 oz/213 g) salmon including juice, flaked**	1
2 tbsp	**grated Parmesan cheese**	25 mL
	Freshly ground pepper	

1. In large pot of boiling salted water, cook fettuccine for 7 to 9 minutes or until tender yet firm. Drain.

2. In medium saucepan, bring water, bouillon and basil to a boil. Add broccoli, return to a boil, reduce heat and simmer for 5 minutes or until broccoli is tender crisp.

3. In small bowl, whisk together milk, flour and salmon liquid. Stir into broccoli mixture; cook, stirring constantly, for 1 to 2 minutes or until thickened and bubbly. Add salmon, cheese, pepper and drained fettuccine; toss to mix.

Makes 2 servings.

Variation:

Fettuccine with Turkey, Chicken or Ham

Replace salmon with 1 cup (250 mL) cut-up leftover turkey, chicken or ham. And replace broccoli with peas if desired.

Tuna Vegetable Patties

Sautéed vegetables give a nice flavour and pleasing texture to patties made with tuna, a pantry staple. Serve with a savoury chutney or in a toasted bun.

1/2 cup	**finely grated carrots**	125 mL
2 tbsp	**finely chopped onion**	25 mL
2 tbsp	**finely chopped celery**	25 mL
2 tsp	**vegetable oil, divided**	10 mL
1/4 tsp	**curry powder**	1 mL
1	**egg**	1
1/4 cup	**fresh bread crumbs**	50 mL
2 tbsp	**plain yogurt**	25 mL
1/4 tsp	**salt**	1 mL
1	**can (6 oz/170 g) water-packed tuna, drained and flaked**	1

1. In small microwave-safe container, combine carrots, onion, celery and 1 tsp (5 mL) oil. Microwave on 70% power, stirring once, for about 2 minutes or until vegetables are very soft. Sprinkle with curry powder.

2. In medium bowl, beat egg; mix in bread crumbs, yogurt, salt, tuna and cooked vegetables. Shape into 4 patties about 1/2 inch (2 cm) thick.

3. In nonstick skillet, heat 1 tsp (5 mL) oil over medium-high heat. Add patties; cook for 3 minutes per side or until slightly browned.

Makes 2 servings.

A Vitamin A Winner

With carrots, a little can go a long way in delivering a substantial amount of beta carotene, thus providing antioxidant power and fulfilling vitamin A needs. These tuna patties, for instance, contain nearly a full daily requirement of vitamin A. Moreover, the beta carotene in cooked carrots is more readily absorbed than in raw ones, especially in the presence of fat, both elements found here.

PER SERVING

Calories 230
Protein 22 g
Total Fat 9 g
 saturated 1.6 g
 monounsaturated 4.1 g
 polyunsaturated 2.1 g
Carbohydrate 16 g
 fibre 2 g
Calcium 90 mg
Folacin 33 mcg
Sodium 639 mg

FOOD GUIDE SERVINGS

 1/2 1/2 1

Tuna Rice Casserole

PER SERVING

Calories 430
Protein 26 g
Total Fat 11 g
  saturated 2.2 g
  monounsaturated 5.3 g
  polyunsaturated 2.6 g
Carbohydrate 56 g
  fibre 3 g
Calcium 127 mg
Folacin 13 mcg
Sodium 778 mg

FOOD GUIDE SERVINGS

1 1/2 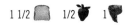 1/2 🍎 1 🐟

The flavours of basmati rice and curry give a new twist to the traditional tuna rice casserole. Another time replace the tuna with 1 cup (250 mL) cut-up turkey, chicken or ham.

1 tbsp	**vegetable oil**	15 mL
1	**small onion, chopped**	1
1/2 cup	**basmati rice**	125 mL
1 1/4 cups	**chicken broth**	300 mL
1/4 cup	**dried currants**	50 mL
1 tsp	**curry powder**	5 mL
pinch	**dry mustard**	pinch
1	**can (6 oz/170 g) water-packed tuna, drained and flaked**	1
2 tbsp	**grated Parmesan cheese**	25 mL

1. In medium saucepan, heat oil over medium heat. Add onion; cook for 5 minutes or until soft. Add rice; stir until well coated. Add broth, currants, curry powder and mustard. Bring to boil; reduce heat, cover and simmer for 20 minutes or until rice is soft and most of the liquid is absorbed.

2. Stir in tuna; spoon into a small greased casserole dish. Sprinkle top with Parmesan. Bake in 350°F (180°C) oven for 20 minutes or until heated through.

Makes 2 servings.

Queen Basmati

Literally named "queen of fragrance," basmati rice has been grown in the foothills of the Himalayas for thousands of years. A long-grained rice, it is valued for its aroma and nut-like flavour, which develops when the rice is aged to decrease its moisture content.

Tuna Over Noodles

Tuna and noodles are always a popular meal solution. Add some fresh herbs to the cream sauce if you have them on hand.

5 oz	**egg noodles**	150 g
1 tbsp	**butter or margarine**	15 mL
1	**small onion, chopped**	1
1 tbsp	**all-purpose flour**	15 mL
1/4 tsp	**dried thyme**	1 mL
1/4 tsp	**salt**	1 mL
3/4 cup	**milk**	175 mL
1 cup	**frozen peas, or peas and carrots**	250 mL
1	**can (6 oz/170 g) water-packed tuna, drained and flaked**	1
2 tbsp	**grated Parmesan cheese**	25 mL

PER SERVING

Calories 555
Protein 38 g
Total Fat 13 g
  saturated 6.7 g
  monounsaturated 3.7 g
  polyunsaturated 1.4 g
Carbohydrate 71 g
  fibre 6 g
Calcium 245 mg
Folacin 191 mcg
Sodium 858 mg

FOOD GUIDE SERVINGS

2 1/2  1 1/2 1

1. In a large pot of boiling salted water, cook noodles for 6 minutes or until tender yet firm; drain.

2. Meanwhile, in small nonstick skillet, heat butter over medium heat. Add onion; cook for 5 minutes or until softened. Stir in flour, thyme and salt until blended; stir in milk. Bring to a boil, stirring constantly; cook for 1 minute or until thickened and bubbly.

3. Place vegetables in small bowl. Pour boiling water over to thaw; drain. Add to sauce. Stir in tuna; cook for 2 minutes or until hot. Spoon over noodles and sprinkle with cheese.

Makes 2 servings.

Tuna Facts

In North America, five species of tuna are caught commercially. Albacore is the only one that carries the name "white tuna" on the label. It commands the highest price. "Light" on the label refers to the species of tuna; skipjack, yellowfin and bluefin are light in colour. It does not give an indication of its fat or calorie content. To cut down on calories, look for water-packed tuna. It offers a 30% calorie saving over tuna packed in oil.

Shrimp with Pasta and Greens

PER SERVING

Calories 485
Protein 29 g
Total Fat 10 g
    saturated 1.3 g
    monounsaturated 3.4 g
    polyunsaturated 3.7 g
Carbohydrate 72 g
    fibre 7 g
Calcium 240 mg
Folacin 303 mcg
Sodium 599 mg

FOOD GUIDE SERVINGS

3   1 1/2   1

The Enriched Difference

Most pasta on the market is enriched and contains added thiamine, riboflavin, niacin, folic acid and iron in significant amounts. In fact, enriched pasta is one of the best sources of folic acid available.

Sesame oil adds a delicious nutty flavour to this colourful pasta dish. If you have fresh spinach or Swiss chard available, use 4 cups (1 L) chopped in place of the frozen, cooking until wilted.

6 oz	**linguine or spaghetti**	180 g
1	**pkg (10 oz/280 g) frozen chopped spinach, defrosted**	1
1 tbsp	**soy sauce**	15 mL
1 tsp	**sesame oil**	5 mL
dash	**hot pepper sauce**	dash
pinch	**ginger**	pinch
1 tsp	**vegetable oil**	5 mL
1	**clove garlic, minced**	1
1	**can (3.75 oz/106 g) shrimp, drained**	1
1 tbsp	**sesame seeds, toasted (instructions below)**	15 mL

1. In large pot of boiling water, cook linguine for 8 to 10 minutes or until tender yet firm. Drain and rinse with hot water; drain and set aside.

2. Meanwhile, drain spinach in colander, pressing with back of spoon to remove moisture.

3. In small bowl, combine soy sauce, sesame oil, pepper sauce and ginger; set aside.

4. In medium nonstick skillet, heat oil over medium-high heat; add garlic and cook for 1 minute or until soft. Add spinach and soy sauce mixture; mix well and heat through. Carefully stir in shrimp. Toss with pasta. Sprinkle with sesame seeds.

Makes 2 servings.

To Toast Sesame Seeds

Microwave sesame seeds on 100% power, stirring frequently, for 2 minutes or until slightly browned, or toast in a dry skillet over medium heat.

Creole Rice with Shrimp

Creole cookery reflects New Orleans' Spanish heritage, and is generally characterized by tomatoes, green peppers and onions. Ready-to-eat salsa is a quick way to add Creole flavours to this traditional rice dish, which is made even better by the addition of some canned shrimp. Use brown rice if you prefer, but increase the cooking time.

1 tbsp	**olive oil**	15 mL
1	**clove garlic, minced**	1
1/2 cup	**coarsely chopped onion**	125 mL
2/3 cup	**salsa**	150 mL
2/3 cup	**water**	150 mL
1/8 tsp	**salt**	0.5 mL
1/2 cup	**long-grain white rice**	125 mL
1	**can (3.75 oz/106 g) shrimp, drained**	1
2 tbsp	**fresh chopped parsley, or 2 tsp (10 mL) dried**	25 mL

1. In medium saucepan, heat oil over medium heat. Add garlic and onions; cook for 5 minutes or until soft. Add salsa, water and salt. Bring to a boil; stir in rice. Reduce heat, cover and simmer for 20 minutes or until liquid is absorbed.

2. Stir in shrimp and parsley; heat through.

Makes 2 servings.

PER SERVING

Calories 330
Protein 17 g
Total Fat 9 g
  saturated 1.3 g
  monounsaturated 5.5 g
  polyunsaturated 1.2 g
Carbohydrate 46 g
  fibre 3 g
Calcium 95 mg
Folacin 23 mcg
Sodium 441 mg

FOOD GUIDE SERVINGS

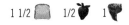

1 1/2   1/2   1

Shrimp Sense

The flavour and texture of canned shrimp cannot be compared to that of fresh, but when it comes to convenience the small canned shrimp blend wonderfully with other flavours to make a most satisfying dish. While shrimp are high in cholesterol compared to most seafood, let's not forget that the cholesterol in food has a limited impact on blood cholesterol. Moreover, the cholesterol in shellfish may not be absorbed as well as that in other foods.

Crab Cakes

PER SERVING

Calories 180
Protein 18 g
Total Fat 6 g
  saturated 1.3 g
  monounsaturated 2.7 g
  polyunsaturated 1.5 g
Carbohydrate 12 g
  fibre 1 g
Calcium 110 mg
Folacin 46 mcg
Sodium 433 mg

FOOD GUIDE SERVINGS

1/2   1

Crab, like most shellfish, brings few calories to the plate. Its delicate taste is enhanced by a touch of salsa and horseradish. If you have seafood sauce on hand, use it instead.

1	**can (6 oz/170 g) crabmeat, drained**	1
1	**egg**	1
1 tbsp	**finely chopped onion**	15 mL
1 tbsp	**thick salsa**	15 mL
2 tsp	**horseradish**	10 mL
1/4 cup	**dry bread crumbs**	50 mL
1/4 tsp	**dried parsley, or 1 tsp (5 mL) fresh**	1 mL
pinch	**salt**	pinch
1 tsp	**vegetable oil**	5 mL

1. In small bowl, combine crabmeat, egg, onion, salsa, horseradish, bread crumbs, parsley and salt. Shape into 2 patties, each about 1/2 inch (1 cm) thick.

2. In large nonstick skillet, heat oil over medium-high heat. Cook patties for 3 minutes per side or until well browned.

Makes 2 servings.

Not Crabby

Canned crab is the ultimate in convenience. All the shell has been removed, leaving only the succulent meat waiting for your pleasure. Like salmon, crab is canned in its natural juices and retains much of its unique flavour.

Baby Clams with Linguine

This dish tastes so good you'll be surprised at how quickly it's prepared. Evaporated milk adds a richness to the sauce without a lot of fat.

6 oz	**linguine**	180 g
1 tbsp	**olive oil**	15 mL
1	**onion, finely chopped**	1
1	**clove garlic, minced**	1
1	**can (5 oz/142 g) baby clams**	1
1/2 cup	**2% evaporated milk**	125 mL
1 tbsp	**all-purpose flour**	15 mL
1/2 tsp	**chicken bouillon granules**	2 mL
1 tbsp	**lemon juice**	15 mL
pinch	**ground black pepper**	pinch
	Chopped parsley (optional)	

PER SERVING

Calories 475
Protein 17 g
Total Fat 10 g
  saturated 2.0 g
  monounsaturated 5.8 g
  polyunsaturated 1.3 g
Carbohydrate 79 g
  fibre 3 g
Calcium 205 mg
Folacin 189 mcg
Sodium 690 mg

FOOD GUIDE SERVINGS

3 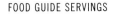 1/2 1/2 1

1. In large pot of boiling salted water, cook linguine for 10 minutes or until tender yet firm. Drain and rinse with hot water; drain thoroughly and set aside.

2. Meanwhile, in medium nonstick skillet, heat oil over medium heat. Add onion and garlic; cook for 5 minutes or until soft.

3. Drain juice from clams into skillet, setting clams aside. In small bowl, whisk together milk, flour and bouillon; add to skillet. Bring to a boil, stirring constantly; cook for 1 minute or until thickened and bubbly.

4. Stir in clams, lemon juice and pepper. Heat through and toss with pasta. Sprinkle with parsley (if using).

Makes 2 servings.

Clam Chowder

Clam chowder is the most well-known of the thick, chunky seafood soups. Canned clams retain much of the flavour of fresh ones and are delicious as well as convenient to use. Replace the fish fillets in the Maritime Fish and Vegetable Chowder (page 176) with a can or two of clams for a rewarding variation.

Sardines on Toast with Mustard Sauce

A dollop of sauce with a hint of mustard gives a new twist to the traditional sardines on toast.

Rare Finds

Sardines deliver two rare nutrition gems: omega-3 fatty acids and an alternative source of calcium.

1 tsp	**olive oil** 5 mL	
1	**small shallot, chopped or 2 tbsp /25 mL chopped onion**	1
1 tbsp	**all-purpose flour** 15 mL	
1/2 cup	**milk** 125 mL	
1 tbsp	**grainy mustard** 15 mL	
4	**slices whole wheat bread or English muffin halves, toasted**	4
1	**can (3.75 oz/106 g) sardines packed in water, drained**	1
1	**green onion, chopped (optional)**	1

1. Place oil and shallot in small microwave-safe container. Microwave on 100% power for 30 seconds or until shallot is soft. Blend in flour; add milk. Microwave on 100% power, stirring twice, for 1 1/2 minutes or until thickened and bubbly. Stir in mustard.

2. Place toast on baking sheet. Place a quarter of the sardines on each piece of toast, flattening slightly or mashing. Spoon sauce over top. Broil until bubbly and heated through. Scatter green onions over top (if using).

Makes 2 servings.

Shallots

Members of the onion family, shallots look like a cross between a small onion and a head of garlic. The flavour of a shallot is milder than that of other onions and gives a subtle aromatic note to a dish. The flesh can vary from white to purple. Underneath the dry papery skin are often several smaller bulbs that can be pulled apart; use only one for a small amount. Fresh green shallots are sometimes confused with the more general category of green onions. Choose dry-skinned shallots that are firm and plump with no sign of wrinkling or sprouting. They can be kept in a dry cool place for up to a month.

Kipper Potato Bake

A popular Swedish dish called Jansson's Temptation, which uses either kippers, sardines or anchovies, was the inspiration for this dish. Although the dish is traditionally made with heavy cream, the evaporated milk in our version is a calorie saver as well as a calcium booster.

1 tsp	**vegetable oil**	5 mL
1	**onion, thinly sliced**	1
2	**potatoes, peeled and thinly sliced**	2
1	**can (3.5 oz/100 g) kippered herring, drained and sliced**	1
	Salt and ground black pepper	
1 cup	**2% evaporated milk**	250 mL
1/4 cup	**dry bread crumbs**	50 mL

1. In small nonstick skillet, heat oil over medium heat; add onion; cook for 5 minutes or until soft.

2. Lightly grease a 2 L (2 qt) casserole dish. Arrange potatoes, herring and onions in layers, seasoning each layer with salt and pepper to taste. Pour milk over top and sprinkle with bread crumbs.

3. Bake in 350°F (180°C) oven for 45 minutes or until bubbly and potatoes are soft.

Makes 2 servings.

Herring History

Herring, with over a hundred different species, is a popular saltwater fish, especially in the Scandinavian countries. High in omega-3 fatty acids, herring are an excellent choice for a heart-healthy diet. Kippered herring, also known as kippers, are first split and then cured by salting, drying or cold-smoking, which makes the flesh more firm. Young herring are sometimes sold as sardines.

PER SERVING

Calories 375
Protein 23 g
Total Fat 10 g
  saturated 3.0 g
  monounsaturated 4.3 g
  polyunsaturated 2.1 g
Carbohydrate 48 g
  fibre 3 g
Calcium 408 mg
Folacin 43 mcg
Sodium 574 mg

FOOD GUIDE SERVINGS

 1/2 1 1/2 1 1

All-in-One Sun-Dried Tomato Quiche

PER SERVING

Calories 380
Protein 25 g
Total Fat 21 g
  saturated 11.5 g
  monounsaturated 6.4 g
  polyunsaturated 1.3 g
Carbohydrate 23 g
  fibre 1 g
Calcium 518 mg
Folacin 45 mcg
Sodium 806 mg

FOOD GUIDE SERVINGS

1/2   1/2   1 1/2   1

Calcium Power

Milk and cheese combine
here to provide well over
40% of the calcium
intake goal and other
bone-building nutrients
such as vitamin D,
magnesium and protein.

This easy quiche forms its own crust. Sun-dried tomatoes give a lively flavour. Keep this dish in mind when you are looking to add interest to leftover turkey, ham or chicken. If you have frozen broccoli, scatter some on top of the tomatoes for extra nutrition and colour.

1/4 cup	**sun-dried tomatoes**	50 mL
1 tbsp	**fine dry bread crumbs**	15 mL
1/2 cup	**shredded old Cheddar cheese**	125 mL
1/4 cup	**finely chopped onion**	50 mL
2	**eggs**	2
3/4 cup	**milk**	175 mL
3 tbsp	**all-purpose flour**	45 mL
1/8 tsp	**salt**	0.5 mL
	Freshly ground black pepper	
1/4 cup	**grated Parmesan cheese**	50 mL

1. In small bowl, cover tomatoes with hot water and let stand 10 minutes. Drain and chop coarsely.

2. Spread bread crumbs over bottom of lightly greased 8 x 4-inch (1.5 L) loaf pan or 6-inch (15 cm) pie plate or quiche dish. Sprinkle Cheddar cheese over bread crumbs; scatter onion and tomatoes over top.

3. In small bowl, whisk together eggs, milk, flour, salt and pepper to taste. Pour over tomatoes. Sprinkle evenly with Parmesan cheese. Bake in 400°F (200°C) oven for 30 minutes or until top is puffed and centre is set. Let stand 5 minutes.

Makes 2 servings.

Variations:

Ham, Turkey or Chicken Quiche

Replace the tomatoes and cheese with 1 cup (250 mL) diced cold ham, turkey or chicken or 1 can (6 oz/170 g) ham or turkey flakes. Omit salt if using ham.

Broccoli Cheese Quiche

Replace the tomatoes with 1 cup (250 mL) chopped broccoli.

Lentils and Rice Egyptian-Style

Kushari is an Egyptian dish featuring the high-protein combination of lentils and rice topped with a spicy tomato sauce and a garnish of browned onions. This simplified version makes a tasty vegetarian main dish. In Egypt it is usually accompanied by plain yogurt. Add a dash of hot pepper sauce if you like more heat.

1 1/3 cups	**water**	325 mL
1/3 cup	**long-grain white rice**	75 mL
1/3 cup	**green or brown lentils**	75 mL
1/4 tsp	**salt**	1 mL
1 tbsp	**vegetable oil**	15 mL
1	**large onion, sliced thinly**	1
1	**clove garlic, minced**	1
1 cup	**salsa**	250 mL
1/2 tsp	**cumin**	2 mL

1. In medium saucepan, bring water to a boil. Stir in rice, lentils and salt. Return to a boil; reduce heat, cover and simmer for 20 minutes or until water is absorbed and lentils are tender.

2. Meanwhile, in small saucepan, heat oil over medium heat. Add onions and garlic; cook for 10 minutes or until very soft and slightly browned. Remove onions and garlic and set aside.

3. Add salsa and cumin to the pan. Bring to a boil, reduce heat to low and let stand until rice finishes cooking. Add a bit of water if mixture becomes too thick.

4. To serve, divide rice and lentils onto 2 serving plates, spoon sauce over rice-lentil mixture and top with browned onions.

Makes 2 servings.

Meatless Meal

A healthy diet relies both on plant and animal protein. Combining different plant sources enhances the protein quality of a meatless meal. Pairing a legume with a grain, as is done in this recipe, delivers all the essential amino acids as well as a bundle of fibre and other nutrients.

PER SERVING

Calories 340
Protein 14 g
Total Fat 8 g
  saturated 0.7 g
  monounsaturated 4.3 g
  polyunsaturated 2.5 g
Carbohydrate 56 g
  fibre 7 g
Calcium 100 mg
Folacin 128 mcg
Sodium 600 mg

FOOD GUIDE SERVINGS

1   1 1/2   1

Satisfying Soups

*O*ur soups come in many moods. Some, such as the Chilled Leek and Zucchini Soup, can be a delicate prelude to an elaborate meal. Others, like Curried Carrot Parsnip Soup, are perfect luncheon companions to sandwiches or crackers and cheese. The hearty Lentil Soup with Vegetables yearns for some wholesome bread and a fruit yogurt to turn itself into a satisfying feast.

These soup selections were designed as avenues to gain greater access to a wider variety of vegetables and to become better acquainted with the world of legumes. In some recipes we have married a few of the more robust flavours with the smooth taste of milk; in others we have highlighted distinctive ingredients. The result is a mix of stimulating flavour and a healthy dose of nutrients. Twelve of the soups are an excellent source of vitamins A or C, and eight can be said to make a significant contribution to your calcium or fibre intake.

How much you fill that bowl depends on how you choose to feature soup as part of your meal. Our serving size suggestions are just that – suggestions; if you are looking for a taste-teaser, then go for only a three-quarter cup. But if you intend to anchor your meal with the soup, a double serving may well be in order. The nutrition analysis and the food guide profile give guidance on how to complete the meal. Keep in mind that 500 calories and three food groups are a good aim for a lunch or supper.

In keeping with the principles of Savoury Wisdom, these soups appeal to a range of tastes — from the traditional Scotch Barley to the more exotic flavour of a Hot and Sour Soup. Search for the ones that suit your mood — then sit down and enjoy!

Chilled Leek and Zucchini Soup   166

Gazpacho   167

Two-Melon Swirl Soup   168

Hot and Sour Soup   169

Onion Soup with Emmenthal   170

Quick Vegetable Soup Chinese-Style   171

Curried Carrot Parsnip Soup   172

Sherried Cream of Broccoli Soup   173

Fresh Tomato Soup   175

Maritime Fish and Vegetable Chowder   176

Corn Tomato Chowder   177

Chili with Beans and Squash   178

Lentil Soup with Vegetables   179

Scotch Barley Soup   180

Chilled Leek and Zucchini Soup

PER SERVING
(1 CUP/250 mL)

Calories 75
Protein 4 g
Total Fat 4 g
  saturated 2.0 g
  monounsaturated 1.1 g
  polyunsaturated 0.3 g
Carbohydrate 7 g
  fibre 3 g
Calcium 38 mg
Folacin 30 mcg
Sodium 404 mg

FOOD GUIDE SERVINGS

1/2

The subtle flavour of zucchini enhanced by a sprig of tarragon makes a delightful soup to enjoy on a hot summer day.

1 tbsp	**butter or margarine**	15 mL
1	**small leek, thinly sliced**	1
2	**zucchini, sliced, about 1 lb (500 g)**	2
2 cups	**chicken broth**	500 mL
1	**sprig fresh tarragon, chopped, or 1 tsp (5 mL) dried**	1
	Salt and ground black pepper	
	Salsa or fresh tarragon sprig for garnish (optional)	

1. In large saucepan, melt butter over medium heat. Add leek; cook for 10 minutes or until softened.

2. Add zucchini, broth and tarragon. Bring to a boil; reduce heat, cover and simmer for about 10 minutes or until zucchini is very soft. Let cool. Place in blender or food processor and process until smooth. Season with salt and pepper to taste.

3. Chill until serving time. Garnish each bowl with a dollop of salsa or sprig of fresh tarragon (if using).

Makes 4 servings, about 1 cup (250 mL) each.

Leeks

Members of the onion family, leeks look like overgrown green onions. But their sweeter and more complex flavour makes them an esteemed partner with other mild vegetables such as zucchini. The broad overlapping leaves often trap soil so careful cleaning is in order. Discard the tough green top and roots. Then make a lengthwise slice in the outer white layers. Spread the layers apart and wash under running water.

Gazpacho

Originating in southern Spain, this cold vegetable soup is wonderfully refreshing on a hot summer day. The name derives from the Arabic word for "soaked bread." Traditionally, the vegetables and bread were rubbed through a sieve, removing some of the seeds and pulp. Commercial tomato juice and the use of a blender make the job a lot easier. Although not traditional, beef broth adds a nice depth of flavour; for a spicier version, add a few drops of hot pepper sauce.

1	**clove garlic, crushed**	1
1/4 tsp	**salt**	1 mL
1 tbsp	**olive oil**	15 mL
1/4 cup	**red wine vinegar**	50 mL
1/2 tsp	**Worcestershire sauce**	2 mL
2 cups	**crumbled French or Italian bread with crusts removed**	500 mL
2 cups	**tomato vegetable cocktail or tomato juice**	500 mL
1 cup	**beef broth**	250 mL
1	**large tomato, diced**	1
1	**sweet green pepper, chopped**	1
1 cup	**chopped cucumber**	250 mL
1/2 cup	**chopped onion**	125 mL
	Garnish: croutons, chopped tomatoes, cucumbers, green pepper and onions	

1. In small bowl, mash garlic and salt together with the back of a spoon to form a paste. Whisk in oil, vinegar and Worcestershire sauce.

2. Transfer oil mixture to blender container; add bread, juice, broth, tomato, pepper, cucumber and onion. Process until smooth. Chill several hours before serving.

3. Serve gazpacho with the croutons and chopped vegetables presented in separate serving bowls to be added to the soup as desired.

Makes 6 servings, about 1 cup (250 mL) each.

PER SERVING
(1 CUP/250 mL)

Calories 100
Protein 3 g
Total Fat 3 g
   saturated 0.5 g
   monounsaturated 1.9 g
   polyunsaturated 0.5 g
Carbohydrate 16 g
   fibre 2 g
Calcium 34 mg
Folacin 47 mcg
Sodium 607 mg

FOOD GUIDE SERVINGS

1/2   1 1/2

Terrific Tomatoes

Evidence is mounting that tomato consumption reduces the risk of various cancers. The red pigment, lycopene, found mostly in tomato products such as juice, sauce or paste, is thought to be responsible for this effect. The body takes up the lycopene more easily from tomato products following their transformation under heat. Tomato juice tops the list of best sources of lycopene.

Two-Melon Swirl Soup

PER SERVING
(1 CUP/250 mL)

Calories 130
Protein 2 g
Total Fat 1 g
  saturated 0 g
  monounsaturated 0 g
  polyunsaturated 0 g
Carbohydrate 33 g
  fibre 3 g
Calcium 31 mg
Folacin 80 mcg
Sodium 32 mg

FOOD GUIDE SERVINGS

2

Honeydew and cantaloupe blend for a delightfully refreshing cold soup. Process each melon separately, then swirl together for an attractive presentation that requires very little effort.

Honeydew

1	small honeydew melon, seeded and diced, about 6 cups (1.5 L)	1
1/4 cup	fresh lime juice	50 mL
2 tsp	granulated sugar	10 mL
1/4 tsp	ground cinnamon	1 mL

Cantaloupe

1	large cantaloupe, seeded and diced, about 6 cups (1.5 L)	1
1/4 cup	apple juice	50 mL
1 tbsp	fresh lemon juice	15 mL
	Garnish: mint leaves and strawberry slices	

1. Honeydew: In food processor or blender container, place honeydew, lime juice, sugar and cinnamon; process until smooth. Pour into bowl, cover and chill several hours.

2. Cantaloupe: In food processor or blender container, place cantaloupe, apple juice and lemon juice; process until smooth. Pour into bowl, cover and chill several hours.

3. To serve, fill each of two cups with about 1/2 cup (125 mL) of each soup and pour into soup bowl at the same time allowing colours to meet in the middle. Draw the tip of a knife through surface to create a swirl pattern. Garnish with mint leaves.

Makes 6 servings, about 1 cup (250 mL) each.

Pretty Plus

More than just pretty to look at, this melon swirl puts over 100 mg of vitamin C on your plate and 20% of the desirable folate intake. As you would expect from its orange colour, cantaloupe brings a sizeable amount of vitamin A, winning the title of the most nutritious melon.

Hot and Sour Soup

This soup has a lively, robust flavour that will arouse the appetite for the course to follow. Don't let the number of ingredients deter you; they cook together in only a few minutes.

1	boneless butterfly pork chop, about 4 oz (125 g)	1
1	large portobello mushroom, cut into thin slices	1
1	carrot, grated	1
1/2 cup	thinly sliced bamboo shoots	125 mL
1/4 cup	thinly sliced water chestnuts	50 mL
1 tbsp	grated fresh gingerroot	15 mL
6 cups	chicken broth	1.5 L
3 tbsp	rice vinegar	45 mL
1 tbsp	soy sauce	15 mL
1 tbsp	hot chili paste or 1 tsp (5 mL) hot pepper sauce	15 mL
1/4 cup	snow peas	50 mL
2 tbsp	cornstarch	25 mL
2 tbsp	water	25 mL
1/4 cup	finely chopped green onions	50 mL
1 tsp	sesame oil	5 mL

1. Trim all visible fat from pork and cut into thin slices across grain. Stack slices and cut into thin strips.

2. Place pork in large saucepan. Add mushroom, carrot, bamboo shoots, water chestnuts, gingerroot, broth, vinegar, soy sauce and chili paste. Bring to a boil; reduce heat, cover and simmer for 5 minutes.

3. In small bowl, mix together cornstarch and water; stir into soup. Add snow peas; cook, stirring constantly, for 1 to 2 minutes or until thickened and bubbly. Stir in green onions and sesame oil. Adjust seasoning if necessary.

Makes 6 servings, about 1 1/3 cups (325 mL) each.

PER SERVING
(1 1/3 CUPS/325 mL)

Calories 105
Protein 10 g
Total Fat 3 g
  saturated 0.8 g
  monounsaturated 1.2 g
  polyunsaturated 0.7 g
Carbohydrate 9 g
  fibre 1 g
Calcium 24 mg
Folacin 13 mcg
Sodium 891 mg

FOOD GUIDE SERVINGS

1/2

Sesame Oil

Extracted from sesame seeds, sesame oil has a delicious nutty flavour. Roasting the seeds before pressing gives a darker oil with a stronger flavour. Just a small amount of the darker oil is all that is needed to bring a hint of Asia.

Onion Soup with Emmenthal

PER SERVING
(3/4 CUP/175 mL)

Calories 130
Protein 5 g
Total Fat 7 g
  saturated 4.1 g
  monounsaturated 2.2 g
  polyunsaturated 0.4 g
Carbohydrate 8 g
  fibre 1 g
Calcium 127 mg
Folacin 11 mcg
Sodium 314 mg

FOOD GUIDE SERVINGS

1/2 🍓

Onion soup makes a savoury starter to sharpen the appetite. Cheese cubes hiding in the bottom add interest and flavour.

1 tbsp	**butter or margarine**	15 mL
2	**large onions, thinly sliced, about 8 oz (250 g)**	2
1	**can (10 oz/284 mL) condensed beef broth**	1
1 cup	**water**	250 mL
3 tbsp	**sherry or Madeira**	45 mL
1/3 cup	**diced Emmenthal cheese, about 1.5 oz (45 g)**	75 mL
1/2 cup	**plain croutons**	125 mL

1. In medium saucepan, heat butter over medium heat. Add onions, mixing well to coat. Reduce heat, cover and cook for 15 minutes or until very tender.

2. Add broth and water. Bring to a boil; reduce heat, cover and simmer for 20 minutes. Remove from heat and add sherry. Strain soup if desired.

3. To serve, divide cheese among 4 soup bowls. Pour soup over cheese and garnish with croutons.

Makes 4 servings, about 3/4 cup (175 mL) each.

The Flavourful Onion

Thanks to their unique seasoning properties and versatility, onions are among the leading vegetable crops grown around the world. Their nutrient value is rather modest but they have been traditionally associated with healing. Like other members of the allium family of vegetables, including leeks and garlic, onions contain allyl sulfides, phytochemicals that may protect against cancer.

Quick Vegetable Soup Chinese-Style

Frozen vegetables add colour and flavour to traditional Chinese egg-drop soup, ready in just ten minutes.

1	**can (10 oz/284 mL) condensed chicken broth**	1
1 1/2 cups	**water**	375 mL
1 tsp	**soy sauce**	5 mL
1 cup	**frozen peas and carrots or mixed vegetables**	250 mL
1/3 cup	**fine egg or rice noodles**	75 mL
1	**egg**	1
1	**green onion, sliced (optional)**	1

1. In medium saucepan, bring broth, water and soy sauce to a boil. Add vegetables and noodles. Return to a boil; reduce heat, cover and simmer, stirring frequently, for 5 minutes.

2. In small bowl, beat egg lightly. Slowly pour egg into simmering soup. Ladle into bowls and garnish with green onion (if using).

Makes 4 servings, about 3/4 cup (175 mL) each.

Soy Sauce

Widely used in Asian cooking, soy sauce is a dark, salty condiment made by fermenting soybeans, salt and roasted wheat or barley. It has many forms in China and Japan ranging from thin light sauces to thicker, richer-flavoured dark ones. Japanese soy sauces tend to be sweeter than those used in China. Tamari is a similar sauce made from soybeans; sodium-reduced soy sauce is also available. Soy sauce will keep for many months if stored in a cool, dark place.

PER SERVING
(3/4 CUP/175 mL)

Calories 105
Protein 6 g
Total Fat 2 g
  saturated 0.7 g
  monounsaturated 0.8 g
  polyunsaturated 0.4 g
Carbohydrate 15 g
  fibre 1 g
Calcium 23 mg
Folacin 17 mcg
Sodium 555 mg

FOOD GUIDE SERVINGS

1/2   1/2

Curried Carrot Parsnip Soup

PER SERVING
(1 CUP/250 mL)

Calories 135
Protein 7 g
Total Fat 5 g
  saturated 2.5 g
  monounsaturated 1.5 g
  polyunsaturated 0.4 g
Carbohydrate 17 g
  fibre 3 g
Calcium 119 mg
Folacin 29 mcg
Sodium 633 mg

FOOD GUIDE SERVINGS

1 1/2

The blend of flavours in this simple soup is delectable. Serve it as a meal starter or add a half sandwich for a light lunch or supper.

1 tbsp	**butter or margarine**	15 mL
1/3 cup	**chopped onions**	75 mL
1 1/2 cups	**chopped carrots, about 3 medium carrots**	375 mL
1 cup	**chopped parsnips, about 2 medium parsnips**	250 mL
3 cups	**chicken broth**	750 mL
1/2 tsp	**medium curry powder**	2 mL
1/2 cup	**2% evaporated milk**	125 mL
	Salt and ground black or white pepper	

1. In large saucepan, melt butter over medium heat. Add onions; cook for 3 minutes or until soft. Add carrots and parsnips; cook for 4 minutes.

2. Add chicken broth and curry powder. Bring to a boil; reduce heat, cover and simmer for 20 minutes or until vegetables are tender. Transfer to blender and purée until very smooth. Return to saucepan; stir in milk. Heat to serving temperature. Add salt and pepper to taste.

Makes 4 servings, about 1 1/4 cups (300 mL) each.

Variation:
Rutabaga Apple Soup

Replace carrots and parsnips with 4 cups (1 L) diced rutabaga. Add 1 peeled cubed apple in step 2 and replace curry powder with 2 tbsp (25 mL) maple syrup.

Broth Benefits

Homemade broth, often called stock, has less salt than commercial varieties as well as superior flavour. Either cooked or uncooked bones can be used. If you debone your own chicken breasts, store the bones in the freezer until you have enough to make a batch. And don't forget the turkey carcass. The bones left after the bird has been carved, along with the neck, tail and wing tips, make a superb full-flavoured broth.

Sherried Cream of Broccoli Soup

There are two essentials to a good broccoli soup. First, the broth needs to be rich and full-bodied, and second, the broccoli must not be overcooked, allowing it to develop a strong flavour. Homemade broth is the best way to achieve the first (see page 174), and cooking the broccoli separately in a microwave accomplishes the second. This recipe provides a guide to delicious variations using different garden vegetables.

2 tbsp	**butter or margarine**	25 mL
1	**large onion, chopped**	1
1/4 cup	**all-purpose flour**	50 mL
3 cups	**chicken broth**	750 mL
4 cups	**fresh or frozen broccoli pieces**	1 L
1 cup	**milk**	250 mL
2 tbsp	**sherry**	25 mL
1/2 tsp	**salt**	2 mL
	Ground black pepper	

1. In large saucepan, heat butter over medium heat. Add onion; cook for 10 minutes or until very soft.

2. In small bowl, whisk flour and broth together; add to saucepan. Bring to a boil, stirring constantly; cook for 1 minute or until thickened and bubbly.

3. Meanwhile, rinse broccoli in water, drain and place in a large microwave-safe container. Microwave on 100% power for 5 minutes or just until tender.

4. Place broccoli including cooking liquid in blender. Add broth; process until smooth. Return to saucepan; stir in milk, sherry and salt. Heat until hot but not boiling. Season with more salt and pepper to taste.

Makes 4 servings, about 1 1/4 cups (300 mL) each.

PER SERVING
(1 1/4 CUPS/300 mL)

Calories 185
Protein 10 g
Total Fat 8 g
   saturated 4.6 g
   monounsaturated 2.5 g
   polyunsaturated 0.7 g
Carbohydrate 17 g
   fibre 3 g
Calcium 127 mg
Folate 67 mcg
Sodium 935 mg

FOOD GUIDE SERVINGS

1/2   1

Processing Pointers

Most food processors do not have liquid-tight lids, so a blender works best for puréeing soups. To use a food processor, strain the solids from the liquid and process the solids until smooth, then add them back to the liquid. Another method for puréeing a soup is to put both liquid and solids through a food mill.

Variations:

Sherried Cream of Cauliflower Soup

Replace broccoli with small cauliflower florets.

Sherried Cream of Asparagus Soup

Replace broccoli with 3 cups (750 mL) asparagus pieces. Reduce cooking time to 3 minutes or just until tender.

Sherried Cream of Mushroom Soup

Replace broccoli with 8 oz (250 g) sliced fresh mushrooms, increase the butter to 3 tbsp (45 mL) and cook the mushrooms at the same time as the onion. Omit step 3.

Sherried Cream of Carrot Soup

Replace broccoli with 3 cups (750 mL) sliced carrots. Place carrots in medium saucepan; add 1/2 cup (125 mL) orange juice. Bring to a boil; reduce heat, cover and simmer 15 minutes or until tender. Omit step 3.

Homemade Chicken Broth

For the most flavourful soups, make your own chicken broth.

In large saucepan, place bones from 3 to 4 whole chicken breasts, the backs and wings from 3 or 4 chickens or a roast chicken or turkey carcass. Add enough cold water to cover bones by 1 inch (2.5 cm). Add 1 whole onion, 1 stalk celery, 1 carrot, 2 sprigs parsley, 3 peppercorns and 1/2 tsp (2 mL) salt for every 6 cups (1.5 L) water. Bring to a boil; reduce heat, cover and simmer for 2 to 3 hours. Strain, discarding bones, and chill. When stock is cold, remove fat congealed on surface. For longer storage, pour broth with fat removed into plastic containers and freeze.

Fresh Tomato Soup

Take advantage of fresh vine-ripened tomatoes to make this superb cream soup. Thickening the milk before adding the tomatoes is the secret to preventing the soup from curdling. If fresh tomatoes aren't available, use either diced canned tomatoes or tomato juice. And add any leftover cooked rice to make a hearty variation.

1 tbsp	**vegetable oil**	15 mL
2 tbsp	**finely chopped onion**	25 mL
2 tbsp	**finely chopped celery**	25 mL
1 tbsp	**all-purpose flour**	15 mL
1 tsp	**granulated sugar**	5 mL
1/2 tsp	**salt**	2 mL
pinch	**ground black pepper**	pinch
1 cup	**milk**	250 mL
3 cups	**finely diced, seeded, peeled ripe tomatoes**	750 mL

1. In large saucepan, heat oil over medium-low heat; add onion and celery; cook for 10 minutes or until very soft.

2. Stir in flour, sugar, salt and pepper; gradually stir in milk. Bring to a boil, stirring constantly; cook for 1 minute or until thickened and bubbly.

3. Stir in tomatoes. Return to boil, stirring frequently; reduce heat and simmer for 5 minutes. If a smooth texture is desired, put soup through a food mill to remove seeds.

Makes 4 servings, about 1 cup (250 mL) each.

TLC for Tomatoes

For peak flavour and to enhance the ripening process, store tomatoes at room temperature. To avoid the need for refrigeration, buy tomatoes at different stages of ripeness, remembering that fully ripe tomatoes will keep a day or two at room temperature.

PER SERVING
(1 CUP/250 mL)

Calories 105
Protein 4 g
Total Fat 5 g
  saturated 1.1 g
  monounsaturated 2.5 g
  polyunsaturated 1.3 g
Carbohydrate 13 g
  fibre 2 g
Calcium 81 mg
Folate 22 mcg
Sodium 321 mg

FOOD GUIDE SERVINGS

1

Maritime Fish and Vegetable Chowder

PER SERVING
(1 1/4 CUPS/300 mL)

Calories 280
Protein 26 g
Total Fat 6 g
  saturated 3.4 g
  monounsaturated 1.7 g
  polyunsaturated 0.7 g
Carbohydrate 31 g
  fibre 3 g
Calcium 326 mg
Folacin 38 mcg
Sodium 405 mg

FOOD GUIDE SERVINGS

1 1/2   1   1

Bone Up

Bone up on calcium with
this Maritime delight,
which brings you nearly
30% of your requirement
in one bowl.

This is a warming soup for a cold night. Some fresh baked bread is all that is needed for a satisfying meal with servings from all four food groups. For a "shelf solution," use any combination of canned or frozen fish you have on hand.

1 tbsp	**butter or margarine**	15 mL
1/2	**onion, chopped**	1/2
1/2 cup	**chopped celery**	125 mL
1/2 cup	**chopped carrots**	125 mL
1 cup	**water**	250 mL
1 1/2 cups	**diced potato**	375 mL
1/4 tsp	**dried thyme**	1 mL
8 oz	**fish fillets (sole, cod, haddock or whitefish), cut in pieces**	250 g
1 cup	**frozen peas**	250 mL
1	**can (14 oz/385 mL) 2% evaporated milk**	1
1/2 tsp	**Worcestershire sauce**	2 mL
1/4 tsp	**salt**	1 mL
	Ground black pepper	

1. In large saucepan, melt butter over medium heat; add onion, celery and carrots; cook for 5 minutes or until soft. Add water, potato and thyme. Bring to a boil; reduce heat, cover and simmer for 15 minutes or until potato is almost tender.

2. Add fish. Return to boil and simmer for 5 minutes or until fish flakes easily.

3. Add peas. Return to boil. Stir in milk, Worcestershire sauce and salt. Heat thoroughly, but do not allow to boil. Add pepper to taste.

Makes 4 servings, about 1 1/4 cups (300 mL) each.

Corn Tomato Chowder

This rich-tasting chowder is quick to prepare for a lunch or light supper. If you don't have bacon on hand, cook the onion in a bit of vegetable oil with a dash of chili powder to heighten the flavour.

4	**slices bacon, diced**	4
1	**small onion, chopped**	1
1	**can (19 oz/540 mL) diced tomatoes**	1
1	**can (12 oz/341 mL) kernel corn, or 1 1/3 cups (325 mL) frozen corn and 1/4 cup (50 mL) water**	1
2 cups	**diced raw potatoes**	500 mL
1 cup	**water**	250 mL
1 tsp	**granulated sugar**	5 mL
1 tsp	**salt**	5 mL
pinch	**ground black pepper**	pinch
3 cups	**milk**	750 mL

PER SERVING
(1 3/4 CUPS/425 mL)

Calories 275
Protein 13 g
Total Fat 8 g
  saturated 3.4 g
  monounsaturated 2.7 g
  polyunsaturated 0.9 g
Carbohydrate 43 g
  fibre 3 g
Calcium 258 mg
Folacin 41 mcg
Sodium 958 mg

FOOD GUIDE SERVINGS

 2   1/2

1. In large saucepan, fry bacon over medium heat until well browned; drain off and discard accumulated fat. Add onion; cook slowly for 5 minutes or until soft.

2. Add tomatoes, corn including liquid, potatoes, water, sugar, salt and pepper. Bring to a boil; reduce heat, cover and simmer for 25 minutes or until potatoes are tender. Slowly stir in milk. Heat to serving temperature, but do not allow to boil.

Makes 4 servings, about 1 3/4 cups (425 mL) each.

To Peel or Not to Peel

Eat potatoes with their skins for a rich source of fibre and a higher nutrient concentration than you would get from peeled potatoes. But do remove the skin if it has turned a green colour. The green is chlorophyll, and while not harmful in itself, it may indicate the presence of a toxic alkaloid called solanine, which can cause digestive discomfort and fatigue.

Chili with Beans and Squash

PER SERVING
(2 1/4 CUPS/540 mL)

Calories 255
Protein 11 g
Total Fat 5 g
  saturated 0.4 g
  monounsaturated 2.2 g
  polyunsaturated 1.6 g
Carbohydrate 47 g
  fibre 10 g
Calcium 163 mg
Folacin 116 mcg
Sodium 394 mg

FOOD GUIDE SERVINGS

3 1/2   1

Chili has become such a popular dish that there are about as many versions as there are cooks. The big debate is whether or not it should contain beans. Here we've kept the beans but not the meat. However, the flavour from the vegetables and spices is so dynamic you won't miss it.

1 tbsp	**vegetable oil**	15 mL
3	**stalks celery, chopped**	3
3	**cloves garlic, minced**	3
1	**sweet green pepper, chopped**	1
1	**large onion, chopped**	1
2 tbsp	**chili powder**	25 mL
1 tsp	**oregano**	5 mL
1 tsp	**ground cumin**	5 mL
2 cups	**water**	500 mL
1	**can (28 oz/796 mL) diced tomatoes**	1
3 cups	**cubed butternut squash**	750 mL
1	**can (19 oz/540 mL) kidney beans, drained and rinsed**	1
	Salt and ground black pepper	

1. In large saucepan, heat oil over medium heat; add celery, garlic, pepper and onion; cook for 5 minutes or until soft. Stir in chili powder, oregano and cumin; cook for 1 minute.

2. Add water, tomatoes and squash. Bring to a boil; reduce heat, cover and simmer for 20 minutes or until squash is soft. Add beans. Return to a boil; reduce heat and simmer 10 minutes. Season with salt and pepper to taste.

Makes 4 servings, about 2 1/4 cups (550 mL) each.

Chili Powder Power

Chili powder sold in North America usually has extra seasonings such as cumin, oregano, coriander and garlic as well as dried chiles. Mexican chili powder is made only from crushed ancho or other dried red chiles and so contains far more heat. The two are not interchangeable!

Lentil Soup with Vegetables

This hearty soup has an impressive nutritional scorecard as well as exceptional taste. Just a moderate serving offers an excellent amount of fibre and folate as well as plenty of iron, vitamin A and vitamin C.

6 oz	**fat-reduced sausage meat**	180 g
1 cup	**chopped onion**	250 mL
1 cup	**chopped celery**	250 mL
1 cup	**chopped carrot**	250 mL
2	**cloves garlic, minced**	2
4 cups	**chicken broth**	1 L
1 cup	**dried lentils**	250 mL
1	**can (19 oz/540 mL) diced tomatoes**	1
3 tbsp	**chopped fresh parsley, or 1 tbsp (15 mL) dried**	45 mL
1 tbsp	**red wine vinegar**	15 mL
1/2 tsp	**salt**	2 mL
1/2 tsp	**dried oregano**	2 mL
1/4 tsp	**ground pepper**	1 mL

1. In large saucepan, brown sausage over medium-high heat, breaking up meat, until no longer pink. Add onion, celery, carrot and garlic; cook over medium heat for 5 minutes or until vegetables are beginning to get soft.

2. Add broth, lentils, tomatoes, parsley, vinegar, salt, oregano and pepper. Bring to a boil; reduce heat, cover and simmer for 1 hour.

Makes 6 servings, about 1 1/3 cups (325 mL) each.

Lentil Advantage

A staple throughout much of the Middle East and India, the tiny, disk-shaped lentil is a major source of protein. A big advantage for the cook is that these legumes need no soaking and cook quickly compared to some of their dried bean and pea relatives. Green and brown lentils retain their shape after cooking, whereas the red variety cooks to a purée making it very suitable for sauces (see Red Lentils Pasta Topping, page 114).

PER SERVING
(1 1/3 CUPS/325 mL)

Calories 240
Protein 18 g
Total Fat 5 g
 saturated 1.3 g
 monounsaturated 0.5 g
 polyunsaturated 2.7 g
Carbohydrate 33 g
 fibre 6 g
Calcium 70 mg
Folacin 124 mcg
Sodium 1009 mg

FOOD GUIDE SERVINGS

 1 1

Scotch Barley Soup

PER SERVING
(1 2/3 CUPS/400 mL)

Calories 220
Protein 10 g
Total Fat 9 g
  saturated 3.7 g
  monounsaturated 3.5 g
  polyunsaturated 0.9 g
Carbohydrate 26 g
  fibre 4 g
Calcium 48 mg
Folacin 24 mcg
Sodium 464 mg

FOOD GUIDE SERVINGS

1  1 1/2

A hearty soup with the rich taste of lamb, it is even better the next day when the barley thickens and the flavours develop more fully. If you have some left over, it freezes well to keep on hand for another time.

2	**lamb shoulder chops, about 12 oz (350 g)**	2
8 cups	**water**	2 L
2/3 cup	**pearl or pot barley**	150 mL
3	**beef bouillon cubes or packets**	3
2	**bay leaves**	2
2 cups	**diced carrot**	500 mL
1 cup	**diced celery**	250 mL
1 cup	**diced rutabaga**	250 mL
1/2 cup	**diced onion**	125 mL
1/2 tsp	**dried parsley**	2 mL
1/8 tsp	**dried thyme**	0.5 mL

1. Trim away as much visible fat from chops as possible. In large saucepan, brown chops on each side over medium heat. To prevent sticking, allow meat to brown fully before turning.

2. Add water, barley, bouillon and bay leaves. Bring to a boil; reduce heat, cover and simmer for 1 hour.

3. Remove chops from broth; trim away bone and any remaining fat. Cut remaining meat into cubes and return to saucepan. Add carrot, celery, rutabaga, onion, parsley and thyme. Return to a boil; reduce heat, cover and simmer for 30 minutes or until barley and vegetables are tender.

Makes 6 servings, about 1 2/3 cups (400 mL) each.

The Barley Cholesterol Link

An excellent source of soluble fibre, barley can be effective in lowering blood cholesterol. True Scotch barley still retains much of the outer husk and many of the nutrients. See page 111 for the difference between pearl and pot barley.

Happy Endings

A happy ending to a meal brings joy to both the eye and the palate and adds a positive note in the total nutrition harmony. Fruits score high on all of these accounts; so, not surprisingly, they are featured prominently in our sweet suggestions.

Plentiful all year long and convenient to buy in small quantities, fresh fruit fits perfectly into a meal plan for two. A bowl filled with the pick of the season is the simplest of happy endings. Dried fruits and frozen berries give variety. Be sure to try our Simple Desserts for Two for fruits with an added touch.

Other champion performers for happy endings are dairy products. By dessert time, if you have not had your full measure of calcium, it's smart to opt for yogurt, milk pudding and occasionally cheese or ice cream. These pair perfectly with fruit, giving double goodness.

With guests at the table, something special is in order. From Crème Brûlée to Apple Berry Clafouti, we offer a number of enticing solutions to the dessert challenge guaranteed to suit all occasions and meet the golden rule of great taste, great looks and wise choice.

Dessert often spells sweetness and creaminess, two wonderful attributes bound to carry with them a bundle of calories. Wise choice of ingredients and attention to portion sizes will go a long way in containing the calorie count. Consequently, we have opted for lower fat evaporated milk in our Crème Brûlée and stretched our mouth-watering Raspberry Ricotta Tart to ten portions. We invite you to follow our lead.

Simple Desserts for Two

Ricotta Cream Topping for Fruit   185

Raspberries in Chambord with Ice Cream   185

Caribbean Bananas   185

Warm Peach Gratin   186

Maple Bananas   186

Amaretti Apples or Pears   186

Strawberries in Red Wine   186

Orange Ambrosia   186

Pears in Port   187

Apple Bake   187

Desserts for 4

Pineapple and Strawberries with Maple Syrup   188

Lemon Lime Mousse   189

Double Chocolate Meringues   190

Microwave Butterscotch Pudding   191

Desserts for 6

Apple Berry Clafouti   192

Fruit Crumble   193

Maple Crème Brûlée   195

Dried Fruit Compotes with Custard Sauce   196

Desserts for 8 and 10

Yogurt Cake with Berries and Lemon Yogurt Cream   298

Spiced Fruit Flan with Streusel Topping   200

No-Roll Oil Pastry and Two Fillings   201

Raspberry Ricotta Tart   204

Simple Desserts for Two

For a no-fuss ending to a meal, simply bring a fruit bowl to the table at dessert time along with small knives for cutting. For a more elegant occasion, accompany the fruit with one or two kinds of cheese and plain crackers such as oat cakes or water crackers.

Select fruit that is free from bruises and with different degrees of ripeness to meet your needs. Wash thoroughly in water to remove dirt and any pesticide residues. There is no need to use any special product or to be especially concerned with the wax finish that may have been applied to protect the fruit.

To add interesting taste to fruit, try these suggestions. Each brings one serving from the Vegetables and Fruit food group.

Ricotta Cream Topping for Fruit

In small bowl, combine 1/4 cup (50 mL) ricotta cheese with 2 tsp (10 mL) icing sugar or to taste. Add a bit of grated lemon zest, crystallized ginger and vanilla if desired. Spoon over fresh fruit such as a sliced peach or over blueberries, strawberries and raspberries.

PER SERVING
Calories 105
Fat 4 g

Raspberries in Chambord with Ice Cream

In small bowl, combine 1 cup (250 mL) fresh or defrosted frozen raspberries and 1 tbsp superfine (fruit) sugar; let stand for 20 minutes. Stir in 1 tbsp Chambord or kirsch liqueur. Spoon over half-cup (125 mL) servings of ice cream or frozen yogurt.

PER SERVING
Calories 215
Fat 9 g

Caribbean Bananas

Slice half a banana and half a peeled orange into each of 2 small microwave-safe custard cups. Sprinkle each with 2 tsp (10 mL) brown sugar and 1 tsp (5 mL) rum. Microwave on 100% power for 1 1/2 to 2 minutes or until banana is slightly soft. Top with ice cream or frozen yogurt if desired.

PER SERVING
Calories 130
Fat 0 g

Warm Peach Gratin

PER SERVING

Calories 85

Fat 1 g

Slice 1 peach or nectarine into each of 2 small microwave-safe custard cups. Spread each with 1/4 cup (50 mL) vanilla yogurt and sprinkle with 1/2 tsp (2 mL) brown sugar. Broil for 2 minutes or until sugar is bubbly. Serve immediately.

Maple Bananas

PER SERVING

Calories 155

Fat 1 g

Slice 1 banana into each of 2 small serving dishes. Pour 1 tbsp (15 mL) maple syrup over each. If desired microwave on 100% power for 40 seconds or just until banana is hot.

Amaretti Apples or Pears

PER SERVING

Calories 205

Fat 4 g

Peel and slice 1 apple or pear into each of 2 microwave-safe custard cups. Sprinkle each with 1/2 tsp (2 mL) granulated sugar. Crush 10 Amaretti cookies (available in most Italian super-markets) and sprinkle over apples. Microwave on 100% power for 2 to 2 1/2 minutes or until apples are soft. Serve with a dollop (2 tbsp/25 mL) vanilla yogurt or ice cream.

Strawberries in Red Wine

PER SERVING

Calories 135

Fat 2 g

In a medium bowl, combine 1 1/2 cups (375 mL) sliced strawberries and 2 tbsp (25 mL) gran-ulated sugar. Let berries stand for 4 to 10 hours. Drain liquid into a small microwave-safe con-tainer. Add 2 tbsp (25 mL) dry red wine; microwave on 100% power for 40 seconds or until boiling. Pour sauce over berries; top with a dollop (2 tbsp/25 mL) frozen yogurt or ice cream.

Orange Ambrosia

PER SERVING

Calories 145

Fat 7 g

Combine grated zest from 1 large seedless orange with 1/4 cup (50 mL) shredded unsweetened coconut and 1 tsp (5 mL) fruit sugar. Peel 2 oranges and slice into circles. Layer oranges and coconut mixture in small serving dishes ending with a layer of coconut. Chill several hours.

Pears in Port

In small saucepan, bring 1/2 cup (125 mL) port wine and 1/4 cup (50 mL) granulated sugar to a boil. Add 2 peeled and halved pears. Cover and boil gently for 30 to 40 minutes or until pears are soft and translucent. Remove pears. Continue boiling syrup until about 2 tbsp (25 mL) remains. Pour over pears and chill until serving time.

PER SERVING
Calories 290
Fat 1 g

Apple Bake

Peel, core and slice 1 apple into each of 2 small serving dishes. Mix each with 1 tsp (5 mL) brown sugar and a dash of cinnamon. Dot each with 1 tsp (5 mL) red currant jelly. Microwave on 100% power for 2 to 2 1/2 minutes or until apples are soft. Serve with a dollop (2 tbsp/ 25 mL) vanilla yogurt.

PER SERVING
Calories 125
Fat 1 g

Desserts for 4   *Pineapple and Strawberries with Maple Syrup*

PER SERVING

Calories 110
Protein 1 g
Total Fat 1 g
  saturated 0.1 g
  monounsaturated 0.1 g
  polyunsaturated 0.3 g
Carbohydrate 28 g
  fibre 2 g
Calcium 24 mg
Folacin 20 mcg
Sodium 3 mg

FOOD GUIDE SERVINGS

1 1/2 🍓

The new golden varieties of pineapples are generally very sweet, thus eliminating the worry about picking an unripe one. The refreshing flavour is nicely complemented by maple syrup and the berries add a colourful note.

1	**small fresh pineapple, about 2 lb (1 kg)**	1
3 tbsp	**pure maple syrup**	45 mL
1 tbsp	**lemon juice**	15 mL
1 tsp	**kirsch (optional)**	5 mL
8-12	**strawberries**	8-12

1. Remove skin and top from pineapple and cut in half lengthwise; with a small knife remove core. Cut crosswise into slices about 3/4 inch (1.5 cm) thick. Arrange slices in a flat serving dish with sides.

2. Combine maple syrup, lemon juice and kirsch (if using). Pour over pineapple; cover and refrigerate for 1 to 6 hours.

3. Just before serving, slice strawberries and scatter over pineapple. Serve each person 2 to 3 slices of pineapple, several strawberries and a bit of the syrup.

Maple Syrup

Pure maple syrup with its unique taste is incomparable. Famed as a topping for pancakes and French toast, it also gives ambrosial flavour to fruit, rice pudding and ice cream; so use your imagination. Canada #1 syrup is sold in three grades reflecting colour and taste. Extra Light or Light is mild and subtle in flavour; Medium has a stronger flavour. For cooking, use Canada #2 Amber to impart a stronger flavour that will hold its own with other ingredients.

Lemon Lime Mousse

Desserts for 4

Fresh lemon and lime combine for a refreshing, light dessert that is a perfect ending for a heavy meal.

1/3 cup	**granulated sugar**	75 mL
2	**eggs, separated**	2
	Grated zest of 1 lemon	
3 tbsp	**fresh lemon juice**	45 mL
1 tbsp	**fresh lime juice**	15 mL
1/2 cup	**water**	125 mL
1 tsp	**unflavoured gelatin**	5 mL
2 tbsp	**granulated sugar**	25 mL

1. In small microwave-safe container, combine 1/3 cup (75 mL) sugar, egg yolks, zest, lemon juice, lime juice and water. Sprinkle gelatin over top; let stand for 1 minute to soften. Microwave at 50% power, stirring several times, for 4 minutes or until mixture is slightly thickened and gelatin is dissolved; be careful not to overcook.

2. Transfer to metal bowl; freeze for 30 minutes or until mixture becomes thickened; stir several times.

3. In small bowl, beat egg whites until frothy. Gradually beat in 2 tbsp (25 mL) sugar until stiff peaks form. Fold into lemon mixture and pour into serving dishes. Chill at least 2 hours before serving.

Egg Safety

When using eggs in a recipe in which they will not be cooked, be sure to use fresh Grade A eggs and check that they have no cracks. Keep them in the refrigerator until just before using, and keep the finished dish well chilled until it is served.

PER SERVING

Calories 135
Protein 3 g
Total Fat 3 g
 saturated 0.8 g
 monounsaturated 1.0 g
 polyunsaturated 0.3 g
Carbohydrate 26 g
 fibre 0 g
Calcium 14 mg
Folacin 14 mcg
Sodium 34 mg

FOOD GUIDE SERVINGS

1/2

Double Chocolate Meringues

PER SERVING

Calories 260

Protein 3 g

Total Fat 12 g

  saturated 7 g

  monounsaturated 3.6 g

  polyunsaturated 0.4 g

Carbohydrate 39 g

  fibre 1 g

Calcium 20 mg

Folacin 2 mcg

Sodium 35 mg

FOOD GUIDE SERVINGS

None

Sugar Savvy

The secret to tender, crisp meringues is to add the sugar very gradually and to use very fine sugar which dissolves more easily in the egg whites. It also helps to choose a dry day, since meringues tend to pick up drops of moisture when the humidity is very high. Superfine sugar is sometimes sold as fruit or berry sugar.

A rich chocolate filling with a hint of mocha nestled on melt-in-your-mouth meringues. What could be a better choice for chocolate-lovers?

Meringue

2	**egg whites**	2
1/8 tsp	**cream of tartar**	0.5 mL
1/2 cup	**superfine sugar, divided**	125 mL
2 tbsp	**unsweetened cocoa powder**	25 mL

Filling

2	**squares (1 oz/28 g each) semi-sweet chocolate**	2
2 tbsp	**strong espresso coffee**	25 mL
2 tsp	**coffee liqueur**	10 mL
1/3 cup	**whipping cream**	75 mL
2 tsp	**icing sugar**	10 mL

1. Meringue: Line a baking sheet with parchment or heavy brown paper. Draw four 3 1/2-inch (9 cm) circles at least 1 inch (2.5 cm) apart.

2. In large bowl, beat egg whites and cream of tartar until foamy. Very gradually beat in about two-thirds of the sugar, beating until thick and glossy. Combine remaining sugar with cocoa; gradually beat into meringue, beating until very stiff.

3. Using the back of a spoon, spread meringue inside circles, making edges a bit thicker to form a rim. Bake in 275°F (140°C) oven for 1 hour or until crisp. Turn oven off and leave in oven with door ajar for 30 minutes longer. Let cool completely and carefully peel meringues from paper.

4. Filling: In small saucepan or microwave-safe container, melt chocolate over low heat or microwave at 30% power, stirring frequently. Add coffee and liqueur; cool to room temperature.

5. In small deep bowl, beat cream until it forms soft peaks. Add icing sugar; beat until mixture forms stiff peaks. Stir about one-third of cream into chocolate. Then pour chocolate into remaining cream and carefully fold in. Spoon filling into centre of meringue shells.

Microwave Butterscotch Pudding

Homemade butterscotch pudding is the ultimate comfort food. And this lighter version delivers full flavour from butter and dark brown sugar.

2 cups	**milk**	500 mL
1/2 cup	**packed brown sugar**	125 mL
2 tbsp	**cornstarch**	25 mL
pinch	**salt**	pinch
1	**egg**	1
2 tbsp	**butter**	25 mL
1/2 tsp	**vanilla extract**	2 mL

PER SERVING

Calories 250
Protein 6 g
Total Fat 9 g
  saturated 5.4 g
  monounsaturated 2.8 g
  polyunsaturated 0.5 g
Carbohydrate 37 g
  fibre 0 g
Calcium 171 mg
Folacin 9 mcg
Sodium 173 mg

FOOD GUIDE SERVINGS

1/2

1. In 4-cup (1 L) glass measuring cup or microwave-safe container, microwave milk on 100% power for 4 minutes or until hot but not boiling.

2. In small bowl, combine sugar, cornstarch and salt. Gradually blend in about half of the milk, then stir cornstarch mixture back into remaining milk. Microwave on 100% power for 1 to 2 minutes, stirring every 30 seconds, until mixture is thickened and has come to a boil.

3. In small bowl, beat egg. Blend in a small amount of hot pudding, then stir egg mixture back into remaining pudding. Microwave on 70% power for 1 minute, stirring after 30 seconds, or until thickened. Stir in butter and vanilla. Pour into serving cups or bowl; chill until serving time.

Variation:

Microwave Ginger Pudding

Replace brown sugar with granulated sugar and add 3 tbsp (45 mL) finely chopped candied ginger with the butter and vanilla.

Comfort Food Indeed

The reputation of milk as a comfort food could very well be linked to its lactalbumin content. There is an indication that this milk protein can improve coping ability and mood in individuals vulnerable to stress.

Desserts for 6 — *Apple Berry Clafouti*

PER SERVING

Calories 280
Protein 6 g
Total Fat 6 g
  saturated 2.4 g
  monounsaturated 1.7 g
  polyunsaturated 0.7 g
Carbohydrate 53 g
  fibre 2 g
Calcium 60 mg
Folacin 24 mcg
Sodium 111 mg

FOOD GUIDE SERVINGS

1/2 🍞   1 🍓   1/2 🥛

Clafouti is classic dessert from France resembling an oven-baked pancake. Traditionally made with cherries, it is equally delicious in this apple version. Try it another time with peaches or plums and, of course, sweet pitted cherries.

1 tbsp	**butter or margarine**	15 mL
6 cups	**peeled sliced tart apples, about 2 lb (1 kg)**	1.5 L
1/4 cup	**dried cranberries, blueberries or cherries**	50 mL
3/4 cup	**milk**	175 mL
1/2 cup	**all-purpose flour**	125 mL
1/2 cup	**granulated sugar**	125 mL
1/8 tsp	**salt**	0.5 mL
3	**large eggs**	3
1 tbsp	**brandy or rum or 1 tsp (5 mL) vanilla extract**	15 mL
1 tbsp	**granulated sugar**	15 mL
1/2 tsp	**ground cinnamon**	2 mL

1. In large microwave-safe container, microwave butter on 100% power for 20 seconds or until melted. Add apples; toss to coat evenly. Microwave at 100% power for 4 minutes or until apples are barely tender, stirring once.

2. Turn apples into a 10-inch (25 cm) quiche dish. Sprinkle with dried berries.

3. In medium bowl, whisk together milk, flour, sugar, salt, eggs and brandy until smooth. Pour over apples.

4. In small bowl, combine sugar and cinnamon; sprinkle over top of clafouti. Bake in 350°F (180°C) oven for 45 minutes or until top is puffed and a toothpick inserted into the centre comes out clean. Cool about 20 minutes. Cut into wedges and serve warm.

All-round Apples

Thanks to modern storage systems, apples are available year-round. At home, store them in their original plastic bag in the refrigerator, where they will keep for up to one month. A number of varieties are grown in Canada, each differing in taste and cooking quality. McIntosh leads in popularity for eating but when cooked its smooth texture may not always be desirable. For a firmer texture, choose Northern Spy, Idared or Cortland.

Fruit Crumble

Your choice – rhubarb, plums, blueberries, peaches – all blend together to create this ambrosial fruit dessert with a crumbly oatmeal topping. Stretching this generous dessert to 8 servings will give at least a 70 calorie saving.

Fruit Base

5 cups	**fruit (see combinations)**	1.25 L
3/4 cup	**packed brown sugar**	175 mL
3 tbsp	**cornstarch**	45 mL

Topping

1 1/4 cups	**quick-cooking rolled oats**	300 mL
1/3 cup	**packed brown sugar**	75 mL
2 tbsp	**whole wheat flour**	25 mL
1 tsp	**cinnamon**	5 mL
2 tbsp	**melted butter or margarine**	15 mL

1. Combine fruits in 8-cup (2 L) square baking dish.

2. In small bowl, combine sugar and cornstarch. Add to fruit; toss to mix.

3. In small bowl, combine oats, brown sugar, flour and cinnamon. Stir in butter; mix well. Sprinkle over fruit.

4. Bake in 375°F (190°C) oven for 40 minutes or until topping is browned and edges start to bubble. Or microwave at 100% power for 10 to 15 minutes or until bubbly.

Fruit Combinations

Rhubarb

5 cups	**diced rhubarb**	1.25 L

Rhubarb and Pineapple

4 cups	**diced rhubarb**	1 L
1 cup	**drained crushed pineapple**	250 mL

PER SERVING

Calories 310
Protein 4 g
Total Fat 6 g
    saturated 2.6 g
    monounsaturated 1.5 g
    polyunsaturated 0.7 g
Carbohydrate 63 g
    fibre 3 g
Calcium 129 mg
Folacin 15 mcg
Sodium 57 mg

FOOD GUIDE SERVINGS

1   1

Rhubarb and Berry

| 4 cups | **diced rhubarb** 1 L |
| 1 cup | **fresh or frozen raspberries or sliced strawberries** 250 mL |

Plum and Blueberry

| 4 cups | **sliced red or purple pitted plums** 1 L |
| 1 cup | **fresh or frozen blueberries** 250 mL |

Peach and Blueberry

Reduce brown sugar in fruit base to 1/3 cup (75 mL) and cornstarch to 1 tbsp (15 mL).

| 4 cups | **sliced pitted peaches or nectarines** 1 L |
| 1 cup | **fresh or frozen blueberries** 250 mL |

Apple

Reduce brown sugar in fruit base to 1/3 cup (75 mL) and omit cornstarch.

| 5 cups | **sliced cored apples** 1.25 L |
| 2 tbsp | **dried currants or raisins** 25 mL |

Apple and Cranberry

Omit cornstarch in fruit base.

| 3 cups | **sliced cored apples** 750 mL |
| 2 cups | **chopped fresh or frozen cranberries** 500 mL |

Pear

Reduce brown sugar in fruit base to 1/3 cup (75 mL) and cornstarch to 2 tbsp (25 mL).

| 5 cups | **sliced cored pears** 1.25 L |
| 2 tbsp | **chopped crystalline ginger or dried currants** 25 mL |

Fruit Crumble Singles

Make a quick fruit dessert for one or two with a topping mix kept ready to use in the fridge.

Combine the topping ingredients for Fruit Crumble in a bowl; store in a covered container in the refrigerator. To make individual servings, place your choice of fruit in a small microwave-safe cup. Mix with a bit of brown sugar and sprinkle 1/4 cup (50 mL) of the topping mix over top. Microwave on 100% power for 40 to 60 seconds for one serving and 1 1/2 to 2 minutes for two servings or until fruit is soft.

Maple Crème Brûlée

This classic dessert derives its velvety smoothness from rich cream and eggs. Evaporated milk gives a lighter version and you won't miss the fat. The appeal of this dessert is the delicate caramel glaze on top. Professional cooks use a kitchen tool called a salamander to get the candy-like crust, but putting the custards under the broiler is an easy option.

1	**can (14 oz/385 mL) 2% evaporated milk**	1
1/2 cup	**pure maple syrup**	125 mL
3	**large eggs**	3
2 tbsp	**packed light brown sugar**	25 mL

1. In 4-cup (1 L) glass measuring cup or microwave-safe bowl, combine milk and maple syrup. Microwave on 100% power for 3 to 4 minutes or until hot.

2. Meanwhile, in medium bowl, whisk eggs until well blended. Gradually whisk in milk. Strain mixture through a fine-mesh sieve.

3. Place six 4-ounce (120 mL) custard cups in a 9 x 13-inch (3.5 L) baking pan. Pour custard into cups. Fill pan with hot water to a depth of 1 inch (2.5 cm). Bake in 275°F (140°C) oven for 1 to 1 1/2 hours or until almost set but surface still quivers when shaken gently.

4. Remove cups from pan; let cool to room temperature. Cover each custard tightly with plastic wrap and refrigerate until serving time.

5. Just before serving, adjust broiler rack so that the top of the custards will be about 2 inches (5 cm) from the broiler. Preheat broiler. Carefully sprinkle brown sugar evenly over top of custards and place under broiler. Broil just until sugar melts and starts to bubble. Do not allow to burn.

Variation:
Coffee Crème Brûlée

Replace maple syrup with 2/3 cup (175 mL) granulated sugar and add 1/2 cup (125 mL) strong brewed coffee.

PER SERVING
WITH CUSTARD

Calories 185
Protein 8 g
Total Fat 4 g
  saturated 1.6 g
  monounsaturated 1.4 g
  polyunsaturated 0.4 g
Carbohydrate 30 g
  fibre 0 g
Calcium 212 mg
Folacin 13 mcg
Sodium 106 mg

FOOD GUIDE SERVINGS

1/2   1/2

Dual Personality

This creamy delight can be featured on your light "happy endings" list or, with its generous protein content, can boost an otherwise light meal.

Desserts for 6 # Dried Fruit Compotes with Custard Sauce

A mixture of dried fruits cooked slowly in a sweetened syrup makes a happy ending to a meal. Any mixture of dried fruits may be used to give different flavours. Serve warm or chilled and garnish with a custard sauce or vanilla yogurt.

Winter Fruit Compote

1/2 cup	**dried apricots**	125 mL
1/2 cup	**pitted prunes**	125 mL
1/2 cup	**cut dried apples**	125 mL
1/4 cup	**dried cherries or blueberries**	50 mL
1 cup	**orange juice**	250 mL
1/3 cup	**packed brown sugar**	75 mL
3 tbsp	**fresh lemon juice**	45 mL
2 tbsp	**chopped crystallized ginger**	25 mL
2	**navel oranges, peeled and sliced**	2

1. In medium saucepan, combine apricots, prunes, apples and cherries. Add orange juice, sugar, lemon juice and ginger. Cover and let stand for 1 hour.

2. Bring to a boil; reduce heat, cover and simmer for 10 minutes or until fruit is tender. Cool and serve slightly warm, or refrigerate and serve cold.

3. At serving time, add oranges.

Breakfast Fare

Turn a breakfast into a feast by serving Winter Fruit Compote with yogurt and a Lemon Flax Muffin (page 35).

Figs in Anise Rum Sauce

There is much mythology connected to figs. Considered to be sacred by some ancient peoples, they have also been esteemed as a symbol of peace and posterity. We prize them as well, but mainly for their ambrosial flavour, enhanced here with a touch of rum.

16 oz	**dried figs**	500 g
2 cups	**water**	500 mL
1/2 tsp	**anise seed**	2 mL
1/4 cup	**granulated sugar**	50 mL
1/4 cup	**dark rum**	50 mL

1. Wash figs and remove stems. Place figs and water in small saucepan. Cover and let stand for 1 hour.

2. Add anise seed. Bring to a boil; reduce heat, cover and simmer for 15 minutes or until figs are tender. Stir in sugar; heat until sugar is dissolved. Remove from heat and let cool. Stir in rum. Chill until serving time.

Microwave Custard Sauce

The secret to making a very quick custard sauce in your microwave is to stir it frequently and not allow it to boil.

3/4 cup	**milk**	175 mL
2	**large eggs**	2
1/4 cup	**granulated sugar**	50 mL
1/2 tsp	**vanilla**	2 mL

1. In 2-cup (500 mL) glass measuring cup or microwave-safe container, microwave milk on 100% power for 1 minute or until hot but not boiling.

2. In small bowl, beat eggs and sugar until well blended. Stir in about a quarter of the milk, blending well. Then stir egg mixture back into remaining milk. Microwave custard on 70% power for 1 minute, stirring every 20 seconds, until just thickened. Do not allow to boil. Stir in vanilla.

PER SERVING
WITH CUSTARD

Calories 225
Protein 2 g
Total Fat 1 g
  saturated 0.2 g
  monounsaturated 0.2 g
  polyunsaturated 0.4 g
Carbohydrate 52 g
  fibre 6 g
Calcium 93 mg
Folacin 4 mcg
Sodium 7 mg

FOOD GUIDE SERVINGS

1

Focus on Figs

Among dried fruits, figs take the lead for their fibre content, bringing along a sizeable amount of calcium in addition to iron and other nutrients.

Desserts for 8

Yogurt Cake with Berries and Lemon Yogurt Cream

When berries are in season, make this simple great-tasting cake to serve at the end of a special meal. It is also delicious with other fruits and vanilla yogurt, or topped with a fudge sauce.

1/2 cup	**granulated sugar**	125 mL
1/4 cup	**milk**	50 mL
1/4 cup	**plain yogurt**	50 mL
3 tbsp	**vegetable oil**	45 mL
1 tsp	**vanilla extract**	5 mL
1	**egg, separated**	1
3/4 cup	**all-purpose flour**	175 mL
1/2 tsp	**baking soda**	2 mL
2 2/3 cups	**sweetened fresh raspberries or strawberries or defrosted frozen berries**	650 mL
	Lemon Yogurt Cream (recipe below)	

1. In large bowl, whisk together sugar, milk, yogurt, oil, vanilla and egg yolk.

2. In small bowl, combine flour and soda. Blend into yogurt mixture.

3. In same small bowl, beat egg white until it holds soft peaks; gently fold into flour mixture. Pour into lightly greased 8-inch (1.2 L) round cake pan lined with parchment or wax paper. Bake in 350°F (180°C) oven for 25 minutes or until centre is firm to touch. Cool on rack for 10 minutes. Invert onto rack and peel off paper; let cool completely.

4. To serve, cut cake into 8 wedges and top each wedge with 1/3 cup (75 mL) berries and 2 tbsp (25 mL) Lemon Yogurt Cream.

Makes 8 servings.

Lemon Yogurt Cream

Fresh lemon makes a refreshing topping for cake and fresh fruit. If extra-thick yogurt is not available, see below for instructions to make your own.

In bowl, combine 1 cup (250 mL) extra-thick plain yogurt, 1/3 cup (75 mL) superfine or fruit sugar, 1 tbsp (15 mL) fresh lemon juice and grated zest of 1 lemon. Cover and refrigerate until serving time. Makes about 1 cup (250 mL) or eight 2 tbsp (25 mL) servings.

Variation:
Yogurt Cake with Fudge Sauce

When you have a craving for chocolate, try this sauce over ice cream or plain cake. It has an incredibly rich flavour with only a trace of fat.

Make cake as above and serve with 2 tbsp (25 mL) fudge sauce instead of Lemon Yogurt Cream.

Fudge Sauce: In 2-cup (500 mL) glass measuring cup, combine 1/2 cup (125 mL) granulated sugar, 1/2 cup (125 mL) cocoa, 1/3 cup (75 mL) corn syrup and 1/3 cup (75 mL) hot water. Microwave on 70% power about 2 minutes or until boiling. Makes 1 cup (250 mL) or eight 2 tbsp (25 mL) servings.

Extra-thick Yogurt

You can make your own extra-thick yogurt from plain yogurt with no added gelatin (check the ingredient list to be sure the yogurt does not include gelatin). Simply line a strainer with one or two layers of cheese-cloth. Place the strainer over a bowl, and spoon the yogurt into the strainer. Let drain in the refrigerator for several hours or until yogurt has lost about half its liquid. Thick yogurt can be used in many recipes to replace sour cream or whipping cream.

Spiced Fruit Flan with Streusel Topping

PER SERVING

Calories 275
Protein 5 g
Total Fat 8 g
  saturated 4.1 g
  monounsaturated 2.2 g
  polyunsaturated 0.5 g
Carbohydrate 49 g
  fibre 2 g
Calcium 84 mg
Folacin 27 mcg
Sodium 135 mg

FOOD GUIDE SERVINGS

1   1/2

Blueberries

Big or small? Both the larger high-bush cultivated berries and the smaller wild ones are powerhouses of anti-oxidants which have the ability to counteract the damaging effects of free radicals. It is thought these antioxidants could possibly slow down some aspects of the aging process.

A fruit-topped dessert is a favourite at any time of year. Use fresh fruits in season. At other times use well-drained fruit from a 14 oz (398 mL) can.

1 1/3 cups	**all-purpose flour**	325 mL
1 1/4 tsp	**baking powder**	6 mL
1/2 tsp	**ground cardamom**	2 mL
1/4 tsp	**ground ginger**	1 mL
2/3 cup	**granulated sugar**	150 mL
1/4 cup	**butter or margarine, softened**	50 mL
2	**eggs**	2
1/3 cup	**milk**	75 mL
1 cup	**fresh or frozen blueberries**	250 mL
1 cup	**sliced fruit such as peaches, mangoes, plums or pears**	250 mL
1/3 cup	**packed brown sugar**	75 mL
1 tbsp	**all-purpose flour**	15 mL

1. In small bowl, mix together flour, baking powder, cardamom and ginger.

2. In large bowl, beat sugar and butter until well blended; add eggs 1 at a time, beating well after each addition. Add flour mixture and milk; beat just until blended, about 1 minute on medium speed with an electric mixer.

3. Pour into lightly greased 10-inch (3 L) springform pan. Arrange blueberries and sliced fruit over cake.

4. In small bowl, combine brown sugar and 1 tbsp (15 mL) flour; sprinkle over fruit. Bake in 350°F (180°C) oven for 50 minutes or until toothpick inserted in centre of cake comes out clean. Cool on rack. Remove sides of pan.

Makes 8 servings.

No-Roll Oil Pastry and Two Fillings

Making this very tender and crisp pastry is a snap as no rolling is required. And best of all, it uses heart-friendly canola oil. Use it as you would any pastry but feature it only occasionally. Keeping the caloric balance on target is as important for your heart as choosing the right kind of fat.

1 1/2 cups	**all-purpose flour**	375 mL
1 tsp	**granulated sugar**	5 mL
1/2 tsp	**salt**	2 mL
1/3 cup	**canola oil**	75 mL
3 tbsp	**milk**	45 mL
1/4 cup	**packed light brown sugar**	50 mL

1. In 9-inch (23 cm) pie plate, combine flour, granulated sugar and salt.

2. In 1-cup (250 mL) glass measuring cup, measure oil. Whisk in milk until well blended. Pour into flour mixture; toss with a fork to mix. Add more milk or flour if needed to form crumbs that will stick together when pressed. Remove 1/2 cup (125 mL) of the crumb mixture and place in a small bowl. Using a fork and your fingers, pat remaining crumbs into pie plate, forming a shell.

3. Pour in your choice of filling.

4. Add brown sugar to reserved crumbs and sprinkle over top of filling.

5. Bake as specified in recipe.

Pastry Perfection

The role of making a tender pastry falls to the fat and different fats produce different results. Solid fat is left in coarse pieces that create thin layers in the flour-water dough, giving a flaky texture. Pastry made from oil is more crumbly. Blending milk with the oil in this pastry helps disperse it evenly, resulting in a very tender crust.

Rhubarb Blueberry Pie Filling

PER SERVING

Calories 315
Protein 4 g
Total Fat 10 g
  saturated 0.8 g
  monounsaturated 5.4 g
  polyunsaturated 2.8 g
Carbohydrate 55 g
  fibre 3 g
Calcium 50 mg
Folacin 35 mcg
Sodium 147 mg

FOOD GUIDE SERVINGS

1   1 🍓

3/4 cup	**granulated sugar**	175 mL
1/3 cup	**all-purpose flour**	75 mL
2 1/2 cups	**finely chopped rhubarb**	625 mL
2 cups	**fresh or frozen blueberries**	500 mL

1. In large bowl, combine sugar and flour. Add rhubarb and blueberries; toss gently to mix. Pour into pie shell; continue with Step 4 in Pastry recipe.

2. Bake in 425°F (220°C) oven for 40 to 50 minutes or until juice begins to bubble through topping.

Makes 8 servings.

Lemon Tart in a Baked Shell

The ambrosial flavour of fresh lemon makes this simple dessert a real winner.

3	**eggs**	3
2/3 cup	**granulated sugar**	150 mL
	Grated zest of 2 lemons	
1/2 cup	**fresh lemon juice**	125 mL
1 tbsp	**icing sugar**	15 mL

1. Prepare a 9-inch (23 cm) pie shell as in Pastry recipe, using all crumbs in the base and omitting the brown sugar. Prick shell with fork. Bake in 475°F (240°C) oven for 8 to 10 minutes or until lightly browned. Cool slightly before adding filling.

2. In large bowl, beat eggs and sugar until very thick, about 5 minutes with an electric beater. Gradually on slow speed, beat in zest and juice. Pour into pie shell. Bake in 350°F (180°C) oven for about 20 minutes or until outside is slightly puffed and centre is slightly jiggly. Cool on rack. Sift icing sugar over top just before serving.

Makes 8 servings.

PER SERVING

Calories 270
Protein 5 g
Total Fat 11 g
 saturated 1.3 g
 monounsaturated 6.1 g
 polyunsaturated 3.1 g
Carbohydrate 38 g
 fibre 1 g
Calcium 21 mg
Folacin 38 mcg
Sodium 163 mg

FOOD GUIDE SERVINGS

1

Desserts for 10 *Raspberry Ricotta Tart*

Raspberries and ricotta cheese combine to make an exceptional dessert. Toasted ground almonds added to the base heighten the flavour.

2 tbsp	**ground almonds**	25 mL
1 cup	**all-purpose flour**	250 mL
1/3 cup	**butter or margarine**	75 mL
1/3 cup	**granulated sugar**	75 mL
1/2 tsp	**baking powder**	2 mL
1	**egg, separated**	1
3 cups	**fresh or frozen raspberries**	750 mL
2 cups	**ricotta cheese, about 1 lb (450 g)**	500 mL
1/2 cup	**granulated sugar**	125 mL
1	**egg**	1
	Grated zest of 1 orange	

1. In small microwave-safe cup, microwave almonds, stirring every 15 seconds, for 1 minute or until slightly browned.

2. In food processor, place almonds, flour, butter, sugar and baking powder. Process until crumbly. Add egg white; process until just mixed. Press into bottom of 10-inch (3 L) springform pan. Spread raspberries evenly over top.

3. In food processor, place cheese, sugar, egg, egg yolk and zest; process until very smooth. Pour over raspberries. Bake in 350°F (180°) oven for 1 hour or until puffed around the edges and almost set in the centre. Cool on rack. Remove sides of pan.

Makes 10 servings.

Calorie Wise

Portion size is all important when it comes to watching calories and fat. By cutting this fruit ricotta tart into 10 portions instead of 8, we managed a 20% caloric reduction. Still, this is not everyday fare. Having treats in smaller servings and at greater intervals adds to the pleasure.

Index

Antioxidants, 7
Appetizers. *See* Hors d'oeuvres
Apple(s)
    about, 192
    Amaretti, 186
    bake, 187
    berry calfouti, 192
    carrot parsnip medley, 143
    chicken in cider, 70
    cranberry crumble, 194
    crumble, 194
    French toast with, 38
    rutabaga soup, 172
    tuna melt, 56
    winter fruit compote, 196
Apricots
    oat bran pancakes, 37
    winter fruit compote, 196
Asparagus
    sherried cream soup, 174
    with orange butter, 133
Avocados
    about, 4, 12, 69
    grapefruit salad, 144
    guacamole, 68
    Mexican cauliflower
        ensalada, 137

Bagel, egg-topped bruschetta,
    58
Banana(s)
    breakfast blends, 30

Caribbean, 185
    maple, 186
Barley
    about, 111
    and wild rice salad, 60
    lentil bake, 110
    Scotch soup, 180
Beans
    about, 13, 180
    Caribbean and rice, 104
    chili with squash, 178
    Mexican lasagne, 136
    soy beans with snow peas
        and pineapple, 106
    to cook, 105
    vegetarian paella, 139
Beef
    hot taco with rice, 90
    Mexican lasagne, 136
    orange stir-fry, 84
    outback flank steak, 126
    roast vin rouge, 140
    steak with mushroom
        wine sauce, 88
    two-pepper stew with
        farfalle, 86
    warm steak salad with
        fruit, 64
Beets, romaine salad with blue
    cheese dressing, 107
Beta carotene, 7, 151
Beverages, breakfast blends, 30

Blood pressure, controlling, 7,
    15
    role of potassium, 52
Blueberry(ies)
    about, 200
    breakfast blends, 30
    peach crumble, 194
    plum crumble, 194
    rhubarb pie, 202
    spiced fruit flan with
        streusel topping, 200
    wheat germ muffins, 34
Bread, two-oat, 44
Breakfast
    about, 26
    blends, 30
    recipe list, 27
Broccoli
    about, 113
    and ham pasta topping,
        113
    cauliflower gratin, 122
    cheese quiche, 160
    ground turkey with
        vegetables and rice, 76
    sherried cream soup, 173
    topped potatoes, 52
    two-cheese pizza with
        sun-dried tomatoes, 134
    vegetable sauté, 131
    with broccoli and pine
        nuts, 129

with peppers, 111
with peppers and pine
    nuts, 129
with salmon and
    fettuccine, 150
with sun-dried tomatoes,
    93
Broth, chicken, 174
Brussels sprouts
    and carrots, 141
    orange-glazed, 81
Bulgur
    about, 61
    Australian salad, 127
    for two, 109
    tabbouleh, 61

Cabbage
    about Chinese, 131
    mixed vegetable salad, 103
    quick coleslaw, 99
    toss, 73
    vegetable sauté, 131
    with greens and Roquefort
    dressing, 75
Cake, yogurt with berries and
    lemon yogurt cream, 198
Calcium
    about, 15, 54, 109
    and vitamin D, 15
    selecting foods, 17
Canada's Food Guide to
    Healthy Eating, vii
    food guide serving
      symbols, vii
    Grain Products, 10
    Meat & Alternatives, 5,
      12, 18, 20
    Milk Products, 15
    Vegetables & Fruit, 6
Cancer, and healthy eating, 3,

6, 7, 9, 14, 15, 35, 113, 131,
    135, 141, 149, 167, 170
Cantaloupe
    about, 168
    Australian bulgur salad,
      127
    breakfast blends, 30
    two-melon soup, 168
Carrots
    about, 151
    and Brussels sprouts, 141
    apple parsnip medley, 143
    curried parsnip soup, 172
    pineapple salad with
      creamy dressing, 105
    Provençales, 73
    Scotch barley soup, 180
    sherried cream soup, 174
    tuna vegetable patties, 151
    vegetable sauté, 131
    warm quinoa salad, 59
    with fennel, 127
Cauliflower
    and green beans with red
      onion, 71
    broccoli gratin, 122
    Mexican ensalada, 137
    sherried cream soup, 174
Cereal
    hot oat with flax, 28
    microwave granola, 29
Cheese
    about, 54
    about ricotta, 103
    and lactose, 16
    breakfast sandwich, 36
    broccoli cauliflower gratin,
      122
    broccoli quiche, 160
    cream with chutney, 119
    fillets Parmesan, 101

hot Brie with chutney, 118
Mediterranean chicken
    salad, 62
Mexican lasagne, 136
microwave omelet, 42
on toast, 43
onion soup with
    Emmental, 170
pasta layers with spinach
    and ricotta, 102
polenta with peppers, 50
presto pizzas, 53
quesadillas, 54
ricotta cream topping for
    fruit, 185
raspberry ricotta tart, 204
salmon bake, 148
seafood with fennel in
    vermouth sauce, 132
sun-dried tomato quiche,
    160
tabbouleh salad, 61
tuna melt, 56
two-cheese pizza with
    broccoli and sun-dried
    tomatoes, 134
Chick-peas
    hummus-stuffed pita, 55
    vegetarian paella, 139
Chicken
    bake with wild rice and
      mushrooms, 128
    baked with herbed glaze,
      120
    fajitas, 68
    food safety, 71
    homemade broth, 174
    in cider, 70
    Mediterranean salad, 62
    premier paella, 138
    quiche, 160

roasted with vegetables, 74
sesame baked, 72
with fettuccine, 150
Chocolate
double meringues, 190
fudge sauce, 199
Cholesterol
blood , 4, 7, 10, 13, 20
in food, 20, 155
Citrus. *See also* Grapefruit;
Lemon; Lime; Orange
grapefruit salad with
currant glaze, 91
greens with citrus dressing,
131
shrimp with Asian
noodles, 98
zest, 98
Clams
chowder, 157
with linguine, 157
Coffee Crème Brûlée, 195
Company meals
about, 116
recipe list, 117
Conjugated linoleic acid
(CLA), 3
Corn
polenta with peppers and
feta, 50
tomato chowder, 177
warm quinoa salad, 59
wild rice and barley salad,
60
Cornish hens, with herbed
glaze, 120
Couscous
about, 61, 97
with lemon and herbs, 97
Crab
about, 156

cakes, 156
seafood with fennel in
vermouth sauce, 132
Cranberry(ies)
apple berry clafouti, 192
apple crumble, 194
bulgur for two, 109
Cucumber
and yogurt topping, 85
gazpacho, 167
Custard sauce, microwave, 197

Desserts
about, 182
recipe list, 183
Diabetes, 10, 13
Dinners
about, 66
recipe list, 67
Dips and spreads
crudites with fresh herb,
118
hummus, 118

Eggplant, baked vegetable
Provençe-style, 124
Eggs
about, 20, 58
and cholesterol, 20
bruschetta bagel, 58
maple poached on waffles,
40
microwave in a cup, 40
microwave omelet, 42
omega-3 enriched, 4, 21
quick vegetable soup
Chinese-style, 171
safety, 189
salsa bake, 41
western wrap, 57
zucchini frittata, 39

Fajitas, chicken, 68
Fat
about, 2
and healthy weights, 5
animal, 3
conjugated linoleic acid, 3
hydrogenated, 4
in fish, 5
monounsaturated, 4
omega-3, 4, 5, 21, 92
polyunsaturated, 4
role in pastry, 201
saturated, 3, 15, 18
trans fatty acids, 4
vegetable, 4
Fennel
about, 133
seafood in vermouth
sauce, 132
seafood with fennel in
vermouth sauce, 132
with carrots, 127
Fibre
about, 10
and healthy weights, 11
insoluble, 10
selecting foods, 11
soluble, 7, 10
Figs
about, 197
in anise rum sauce, 197
Fish. *See also* Salmon; Tuna
about fat in, 5
baked with vegetables *en
papillote*, 96
halibut with roasted red
peppers, 94
kipper potato bake, 159
Maritime vegetable
chowder, 176
quick ways with, 100

sardines on toast with
mustard sauce, 158
Flan, spiced fruit with streusel
topping, 200
Flax seeds
about, 4, 28, 35
hot oat cereal, 28
lemon muffins, 35
turkey stuffed peppers, 78
Folate, 7–9, 13
Food safety
and chicken, 71
and eggs, 189
and meat, 19
French toast with apples, 38
Fruit. *See also specific fruits*
and health, 7
breakfast blends, 30
crumble, 193
dried compotes with
custard sauce, 196
grapefruit salad with
currant glaze, 91
raspberry ricotta tart, 204
spiced flan with streusel
topping, 200
warm steak salad with, 64
with ricotta cream
topping, 185
Fudge sauce, 199

Garbanzo beans. *See* Chick-
peas
Gazpacho, 167
Grains. *See also* Barley; Bread;
Bulgur; Cereal; Corn;
Couscous; Pasta; Quinoa;
Rice; Wheat
about, 10
Grapefruit
about, 91

avocado salad, 144
salad with currant glaze,
91
spinach and mushroom
salad, 135
Green beans
and cauliflower with red
onion, 71
Mediterranean, 120
orange beef stir-fry, 84
Oriental, 99
warm quinoa salad, 59
Guacamole, 68

Ham
about, 36
and broccoli pasta
topping, 113
breakfast sandwich, 36
microwave omelet, 42
premier paella, 138
quiche, 160
topped potatoes, 52
western wrap, 57
with fettuccine, 150
Heart health, and healthy
eating, 2–5, 7, 9, 10, 12–15,
20, 35, 37, 92, 159
Honeydew
Australian bulgur salad,
127
two-melon soup, 168
Hors d'oeuvres, 118–119
Hummus
stuffed pita, 55
with dippers, 118
Hydrogenated oils, 4

Iron
in meat, 18
Isoflavones, 14

Jalapeño peppers
Mexican ensalada, 137
Mexican lasagne, 136
Jam, apricot pineapple, 45
Julienne, how to cut, 144

Kippered herring
about, 43, 159
on toast, 43
potato bake, 159
Kiwifruit
outback flank steak, 126

Lactose intolerance, 16
Lamb
grilled chops Dijon, 124
Scotch barley soup, 180
Lasagne, Mexican, 136
Leeks
about, 166
and ham topped potatoes,
52
and zucchini soup, 166
ham and broccoli pasta
topping, 113
two-rice pilaf bake, 143
Legumes. *See also* Beans;
Lentils; Soybeans
about, 12
and digestive discomfort,
12, 14
and fibre, 12, 13
Lemon
couscous with herbs, 97
flax muffins, 35
lime mousse, 189
rice, 93
tart, 203
yogurt cream, 199
Lentils
about, 179

and rice, 105
and rice Egyptian-style, 161
barley bake, 110
curried pasta salad with
    wild rice, 121
pasta topping, 114
soup with vegetables, 179
Lettuce
    about romaine, 125
    greens with pear and
        poppy seed citrus
        dressing, 131
    Mandarin orange salad,
        93
    Mexican cauliflower
        ensalada, 137
    Mexican salad toss, 79
    mixed greens with
        favourite vinaigrette, 81
    mixed vegetable salad, 103
    orange and sweet onion
        salad, 125
    orange date salad with
        honey mustard dressing,
        111
    pineapple salad with
        creamy dressing, 105
    romaine salad with blue
        cheese dressing, 107
    romaine with watercress
        and Dijon yogurt
        dressing, 89
    salad with herb dressing,
        77
    watercress salad with
        Asian pear, 141
    with cabbage and
        Roquefort dressing, 75
    with chutney dressing, 83
    with green goddess
        dressing, 139

with Parmesan dressing, 87
with Ranch dressing, 71
Lime
    lemon mousse, 189
    Mexican ensalada, 137
    outback flank steak, 126
    two-melon soup, 168
Lunch
    about, 48
    recipe list, 49
Lutein, about, 135
Lycopene
    and cancer protection, 7,
        167

Mango(es)
    cilantro salsa, 79
    salad with mint and honey
        dressing, 129
    spiced fruit flan with
        streusel topping, 200
Maple syrup
    about, 188
    crème brûlée, 195
    pineapple and strawberries
        with, 188
    poached eggs on waffles,
        40
Marinade
    about, 126
    outback flank steak, 126
Meat
    and healthy eating, 18
Melon, two-melon soup, 168
Microwave
    Amaretti apples, 186
    apple bake, 187
    butterscotch pudding, 191
    Caribbean bananas, 185
    custard sauce, 197
    eggs in a cup, 40

fruit crumble singles, 194
ginger pudding, 191
granola, 29
hot oat cereal with flax, 28
lemon lime mousse, 189
maple bananas, 186
omelet, 42
quick ways with, 100
salsa egg bake, 41
strawberries in red wine,
    186
turkey stuffed peppers, 78
Milk
    breakfast blends, 30
    evaporated, 89, 113, 141,
        157, 159, 172, 176, 195
    lactose intolerance, 16
    products and healthy
        eating, 15
    ways with, 17
Molasses
    about, 38
    French toast with syrup, 38
Muffins
    blueberry wheat germ, 34
    lemon flax, 35
    molasses prune, 33
Mushroom(s)
    about, 89
    baked vegetables
        Provence-style, 124
    barley lentil bake, 110
    chicken bake with wild
        rice, 128
    fish baked en papillote, 96
    ham and broccoli pasta
        topping, 113
    hot and sour soup, 169
    seafood with fennel in
        vermouth sauce, 132
    sherried cream soup, 174

spinach salad with
grapefruit, 135
steak with wine sauce, 88

Nutrient analysis, about, vi

Oat bran
about, 10, 37
apricot pancakes, 37
bread machine oat bread,
44
breakfast blends, 30
hot oat cereal with flax, 28
Oats
about, 44
bread machine oat bread,
44
hot cereal with flax, 28
microwave granola, 29
Oils
canola, vi, 4
hydrogenated, 4
no-roll pastry, 201
olive, 4, 60
Onions
about, 170
soup with Emmental, 170
Orange(s)
ambrosia, 186
and sweet onion salad, 125
asparagus with butter, 133
beef stir-fry, 84
citrus shrimp with Asian
noodles, 98
date salad with honey
mustard dressing, 111
Mandarin salad, 93
salad with vinaigrette, 93
warm steak salad, 64
winter fruit compote, 196
Osteoporosis, 15

Paella, premier, 138
Pancakes, apricot oat bran, 37
Papaya, salsa, 120
Parsnip
apple carrot medley, 143
curried carrot soup, 172
mashed with potatoes, 81
Pasta
about, 154
about Asian noodles, 99
citrus shrimp with Asian
noodles, 98
clams with linguine, 157
creamed noodles, 89
curried salad with wild
rice and lentils, 121
layers with spinach and
ricotta, 102
measures, 114
Mediterranean chicken
salad, 62
quick vegetable soup
Chinese-style, 171
salmon bake, 148
seafood with fennel in
vermouth sauce, 132
spinach with orzo, 79
toppings, 112
tuna and, 153
two-pepper beef stew with
farfalle, 86
two-pepper stew, 86
with salmon and broccoli,
150
with shrimp and greens,
154
Pastry, no-roll oil, 201
Peach(es)
blueberry crumble, 194
spiced fruit flan with
streusel topping, 200

warm gratin, 186
warm steak salad, 64
Pear(s)
crumble, 194
greens with poppy seed
citrus dressing, 131
in port, 187
pork chops with ginger, 82
spiced fruit flan with
streusel topping, 200
warm steak salad, 64
watercress salad, 141
Peas
Maritime fish and
vegetable chowder, 176
premier paella, 138
tuna over noodles, 153
vegetable soup Chinese
style, 171
with mint and lemon, 89
Peppers
about, 51, 79
and broccoli, 111
baked vegetables
Provençe-style, 124
beef stew with farfalle, 86
Caribbean beans and rice,
104
chicken fajitas, 68
chili with beans and
squash, 178
reole fillets, 101
gazpacho, 167
ground turkey stuffed, 78
halibut with roasted red,
94
Mediterranean chicken
salad, 62
Mexican ensalada, 137
papaya salsa, 120
polenta with, 50

premier paella, 138
presto pizzas, 53
snow pea salad, 123
soybeans with snow peas
    and pineapple, 106
to roast, 94
tofu stir-fry, 108
turkey Italian pasta
    topping, 112
two-rice pilaf bake, 143
wild rice and barley salad,
    60
with broccoli and pine
    nuts, 129
Pesto, presto pizza, 53
Pilaf
    rice, 71
    rice quinoa, 95
    two-rice bake, 143
Pineapple
    and strawberries with
        maple syrup, 188
    breakfast blends, 30
    carrot salad with creamy
        dressing, 105
    Polynesian roasted turkey
        breast, 142
    rhubarb crumble, 193
    soy beans with snow peas,
        106
Pita, hummus-stuffed wraps, 55
Pizza
    about, 53
    dough, 134
    presto, 53
    two-cheese with broccoli
        and sun-dried tomatoes,
        134
Plum(s)
    blueberry crumble, 194
    spiced fruit flan with

streusel topping, 200
Polenta, with peppers and feta,
    50
Pork
    chops with pears and
        ginger, 82
    glazed tenderloins with
        roasted sweet potatoes,
        122
    herbed loin with roasted
        potatoes, 130
    hot and sour soup, 169
    schnitzel with salsa, 80
Potassium, 7, 52
Potatoes
    about, 52, 63, 177
    baked mashed, 141
    baked vegetables
        Provençe-style, 124
    corn tomato chowder, 177
    glazed pork tenderloins
        with roasted sweet
        potatoes, 122
    herbed loin of pork with
        roasted, 130
    kipper potato bake, 159
    Maritime fish and
        vegetable chowder, 176
    mashed with parsnip, 81
    roasted, 73
    roasted chicken with, 74
    salad with smoked oysters,
        63
    two-potato bake, 83
    with ham and leeks, 52
Probiotics, 17
Protein, about, 53, 161
Prunes
    about, 33
    molasses muffins, 33
    winter fruit compote, 196

Pudding
    microwave butterscotch,
        191
    microwave ginger, 191

Quesadillas, 54
Quiche, sun-dried tomato, 160
Quinoa
    about, 59
    and rice pilaf, 95
    warm vegetable salad, 59

Raspberry(ies)
    breakfast blends, 30
    in Chambord with ice
        cream, 185
    rhubarb crumble, 194
    ricotta tart, 204
    vinaigrette, 135
    yogurt cake with lemon
        yogurt cream, 198
Rhubarb
    berry crumble, 194
    blueberry pie, 202
    crumble, 193
    pineapple crumble, 193
Rice
    about, 91
    about Basmati, 152
    and lentils Egyptian-style,
        161
    and quinoa pilaf, 95
    Caribbean beans and, 104
    creole with shrimp, 155
    ground turkey with
        vegetables and, 76
    hot taco beef with, 90
    lemon, 93
    lentils and, 105
    pilaf, 71
    pilaf bake, 143

premier paella, 138
soybeans with snow peas
 and pineapple, 106
tuna casserole, 152
Rutabaga
  about, 77
  apple soup, 172
  ground turkey with
   vegetables and rice, 76
  Scotch barley soup, 180

Salad dressings
  balsamic, 95
  blue cheese, 107
  chutney, 83
  creamy, 105
  curried, 121
  Dijon yogurt, 89
  favourite vinaigrette, 81
  green goddess, 139
  herb, 77
  honey, 129
  honey mustard, 111
  Mexican, 79
  orange, 125
  orange vinaigrette, 93
  Parmesan, 87
  poppy seed citrus, 131
  ranch, 71
  raspberry vinaigrette, 135
  Roquefort, 75
  salsa, 103
  sesame, 97
  yogurt, 73
Salads
  Australian bulgur, 127
  avocado grapefruit, 144
  cabbage toss, 73
  cherry tomatoes with
   basil, 95
  cucumbers and yogurt

topping, 85
curried pasta with wild
 rice and lentils, 121
grapefruit with currant
 glaze, 91
greens with chutney
 dressing, 83
greens with favourite
 vinaigrette, 81
greens with pear and
 poppy seed citrus
 dressing, 131
greens with red cabbage
 and Roquefort dressing,
 75
lettuces with green
 goddess dressing, 139
lettuces with ranch
 dressing, 71
Mandarin orange, 93
mango with mint and
 honey dressing, 129
Mediterranean chicken, 62
Mexican toss, 79
mixed vegetable, 103
oak leaf with herb
 dressing, 77
orange and sweet onion,
 125
orange date with honey
 mustard dressing, 111
pineapple carrot with
 creamy dressing, 105
potato with smoked
 oysters, 63
quick coleslaw, 99
romaine with beets and
 blue cheese dressing, 107
romaine with watercress
 and Dijon yogurt
 dressing, 89

snow pea with red
 peppers, 123
spinach sprout, 97
tabbouleh with feta, 61
warm quinoa vegetable, 59
warm steak with fruit, 64
wild rice and barley, 60
with Parmesan dressing, 87
Salmon
  about, 5, 92, 148
  bake, 148
  cups with parsley sauce,
   149
  whirls, 119
  wine-poached with capers,
   92
  with fettuccine and
   broccoli, 150
Salsa
  egg bake, 41
  lentils and rice Egyptian-
   style, 161
  mango cilantro, 79
  papaya, 120
  quesadillas, 54
  schnitzel with, 80
Salt
  about, 22
  in nutrient analysis, vi
Sandwiches
  breakfast French-style, 36
  classic western, 57
  quesadillas, 54
  tuna melt, 56
  western wrap, 57
Sardines, on toast with
 mustard sauce, 158
Sausage
  lentil soup with vegetables,
   179
  premier paella, 138

Scallops, with fennel in vermouth sauce, 132
Seafood. *See also* Fish; Salmon; Smoked Oysters; Shrimp; Tuna
    clams with linguine, 157
    crab cakes, 156
    kipper potato bake, 159
    sardines on toast with mustard sauce, 158
    with fennel in vermouth sauce, 132
Sesame oil, about, 169
Sesame seeds
    about, 72
    to toast, 123
Shallots, about, 158
Shelf Solutions
    about, 146
    recipe list, 147
Shrimp
    about, 155
    citrus with Asian noodles, 98
    premier paella, 138
    seafood with fennel in vermouth sauce, 132
    with creole rice, 155
    with pasta and greens, 154
Smoked oysters, potato salad with, 63
Snow peas
    hot and sour soup, 169
    salad with red peppers, 123
    soybeans with pineapple, 106
    tofu vegetable stir-fry, 108
Sodium. *See* Salt
Soups
    about, 164
    recipe list, 165

Soy sauce, about, 171
Soybeans
    about, 13
    soy nuts, 107
    with snow peas and pineapple, 106
Spinach
    about, 135
    butternut and greens, 95
    Florentine fillet cups, 100
    grapefruit and mushroom salad, 135
    Mexican lasagne, 136
    pasta layers with ricotta, 102
    sprout salad, 97
    with orzo, 79
    with shrimp and pasta, 154
Squash
    butternut and greens, 95
    chili with beans, 178
    ground turkey with vegetables and rice, 76
Strawberry(ies)
    and pineapple with maple syrup, 188
    breakfast blends, 30
    in red wine, 186
    rhubarb crumble, 194
    warm steak salad, 64
    yogurt cake with lemon yogurt cream, 198
Surimi, about, 133
Sweet potato(es)
    about, 83
    glazed pork tenderloins with, 122
    ground turkey with vegetables and rice, 76
    roasted chicken and, 74
    two-potato bake, 83

Swiss chard
    and Balsamic vinegar, 105
    butternut and greens, 95
    sauté, 83
Tabbouleh, 61
Tart, raspberry ricotta, 204
Toast toppings, 43
Tofu
    about, 109
    vegetable stir-fry, 108
Tomato(es)
    about, 7, 13, 167
    baked vegetables Provençe-style, 124
    broccoli with sun-dried, 93
    chili with beans and squash, 178
    corn chowder, 177
    egg-topped bruschetta bagel, 58
    gazpacho, 167
    guacamole, 68
    hot taco beef with rice, 90
    lentil soup with vegetables, 179
    Mediterranean chicken salad, 62
    Mediterranean slices, 109
    Mexican cauliflower ensalada, 137
    Mexican lasagne, 136
    pasta layers with spinach and ricotta, 102
    quick baked, 97
    salad with basil, 95
    soup, 175
    sun-dried tomato quiche, 160
    tabbouleh salad with feta, 61

turkey Italian pasta
topping, 112
two-cheese pizza with
broccoli and sun-dried
tomatoes, 134
two-pepper beef stew with
farfalle, 86
warm quinoa vegetable
salad, 59
wild rice and barley salad,
60
Tortilla
chicken fajitas, 68
dippers, 118
Mexican lasagne, 136
quesadillas, 54
salmon whirls, 119
wedges, 119
western wrap, 57
Trans-fats, 4
Tuna
about, 153
melt, 56
over noodles, 153
rice casserole, 152
topped potatoes, 52
vegetable patties, 151
Turkey
ground in peppers, 78
ground with vegetables
and rice, 76
Italian pasta topping, 112
Polynesian roasted breast,
142
quiche, 160
with fettuccine, 150

Vegetable(s)
and health, 7
baked *en papillote*, 96

baked Provençe-style, 124
crudites with fresh herb
dip, 118
ground turkey with rice
and, 76
lentil soup, 179
Maritime fish chowder,
176
roasted chicken with, 74
soup Chinese style, 171
tofu stir-fry, 108
tuna patties, 151
vegetable-topped fillets,
100
warm quinoa salad, 59
Vitamins
vitamin A, 2, 7, 75, 151
vitamin B$_{12}$, 9, 18
vitamin B$_6$, 9, 18
vitamin C, 7, 13, 79, 91
vitamin D, 2, 15
vitamin E, 2, 4

Watercress
lettuce salad with Asian
pear, 141
romaine salad with Dijon
yogurt dressing, 89
Weight, maintaining healthy, 5,
11
Wheat germ
about, 34
blueberry muffins, 34
microwave granola, 29
Wheat, about, 61
Wild rice
about, 129
and barley salad, 60
chicken bake with
mushrooms, 128

curried pasta salad with
lentils, 121
two-rice pilaf bake, 143
Wine
onion soup with
Emmental, 170
pears in, 187
poached salmon with
capers, 92
roast vin rouge, 140
seafood with fennel in
vermouth sauce, 132
sherried cream of broccoli
soup, 173
strawberries in, 186
Yogurt
about, 17
breakfast blends, 30
cake with berries and
lemon yogurt cream,
198
extra-thick, 199
lemon cream, 199

Zest, about, 98
Zinc, and beef, 18, 85
Zucchini
and leek soup, 166
baked vegetables
Provençe-style, 124
chicken fajitas, 68
fish baked *en papillote*, 96
frittata, 39
Mediterranean chicken
salad, 62
roasted chicken with, 74
turkey Italian pasta
topping, 112